CHAUCER

AND THE

MEDIAEVAL SCIENCES

BY
WALTER CLYDE CURRY, 1887 –
Professor of English, Vanderbilt University

And out of olde bokes, in good feith,
Cometh al this newe science that men lere.

REVISED AND ENLARGED
EDITION, 1960
BARNES & NOBLE, INC.   •   NEW YORK

To

KATHRYN AND JOSEPHINE

CONTENTS

PROLOGUE TO THE SECOND EDITION

A BOOK with life in it has an individual personality of its own. Even the author dare not attempt to violate its integrity. In such fashion, *Chaucer and the Mediaeval Sciences* has, since its publication in 1926, manifested and maintained a persistent identity peculiar to itself. Therefore, as its author, I have not presumed to infringe upon the original text with more than minor revision.

But the addition of some organic materials, by way of supplementing and supporting the initial concept and design of the book, appears to be appropriate. For instance, the rich astrological and dream-lore elements in *Troilus and Criseyde* deserve fuller treatment than was accorded them in the 1926 text. After further study, therefore, I published in 1930 an essay called, "Destiny in Chaucer's *Troilus*" which expands the concept of astrological influence to include power of the fixed stars as well as of the wandering planets and emphasizes how astrology and the science of dreams are integrated in the Providence of God with other destinal forces for the government of the world and man. Again in 1930 I published an article called "Arcite's Intellect" designed to supplement the original treatment of the science of mediaeval faculty psychology in the *Knight's Tale*. In the first edition I was primarily concerned with the purely scientific aspects and functions of the vegetative and sensitive faculties of the human soul, barely mentioning the rational soul under which these lower faculties are subsumed. The later study, therefore, explains the dual functions of the rational soul, one of which Chaucer identifies with intellect, and shows that it is this intellect or spirit which "changes house" and achieves immortality with its Source. Thus in these two essays the pure sciences are, in accordance with mediaeval natural philosophy, made to assume their proper places in subjection to the divine Force or Mind which creates and controls them. I am greatly indebted to the editors of *Publications of the Modern Language Association* and the *Journal of English and Germanic Philology* for permission to use, respectively, these studies, with alterations and corrections, in the new edition.

Examination of Chaucer scholarship and criticism during the past two or three decades discloses some gratifying changes in emphasis and direction. For example, it is noteworthy that the bibliographer sometimes finds it expedient to reserve one section of his work for scientific backgrounds. Alchemy appears to be attracting curiosity. Catalogues of alchemical manuscripts in England, Ireland, and America are made available to the scholar, and alchemical manuscripts of works with which Chaucer may have been acquainted are in process of being edited for publication. The lecturer occasionally feels it necessary to devote a large part of his lecture to a detailed analysis of Chaucer's macrocosm and its functioning. And Chaucer scholarship and modern criticism seem significantly to be approaching each other. Recently a review of Chaucer scholarship in England and America emphasizes this new direction. The appended Selected Bibliography is designed to illustrate these and other trends in Chaucer scholarship and criticism.

Late as this, my earnest tribute is paid to the amazingly fertile mind of the late J. S. P. Tatlock whose "Astrology and Magic in the *Franklin's Tale*" provided the initial stimulus for my studies in the mediaeval sciences.

I shall always treasure the warm companionship offered me by my former graduate students who, during my forty years of teaching in Vanderbilt University, joined me in studying Chaucer's wide knowledge of books and men, his artistry however uneven in quality, and especially his profound magnanimity. To future students who may elect "to goon on pilgrimages" with me in these pages to Chaucer's Canterbury, I bid welcome to our fellowship,

> And syn that ye han herd al myn entente,
> I prey yow to my wyl ye wole assente.

W. C. C.

Vanderbilt University
May 12, 1959

INTRODUCTION

THIS volume is the result of an attempt to follow Geoffrey Chaucer in his studies of the mediaeval sciences and to indicate with what degree of success he has employed scientific materials in the creation of his poetical works. My researches have been in the nature of delightful but perplexing adventures. When, some eight years ago, I began an investigation of natural and celestial physiognomy, metoposcopy, geomancy, alchemy, mediaeval medicine, and the science of dreams, together with astrology, upon which all these are based, it was with the general purpose of reproducing, if possible, a sort of fourteenth century scientific background, against which certain stories and characters created by the poet might with advantage be thrown into strong relief. The execution of this aim has necessitated a consideration of Chaucer's personal attitude toward these branches of learning, his more or less accurate knowledge of the philosophy underlying them, and his relation of scientific principles to artistic production. Since poetry and science are now supposed to be antithetical and mutually exclusive, it has been difficult to conceive that one of the major English poets ever exercised his mind to any remarkable extent in the realm of scientific theory and abstraction; and that he should have been impressed to the point of taking seriously — at least for artistic purposes — these monstrosities of error, now seems almost unbelievable. Yet such appears to have been the case. The problems

arising in these studies may be simplified, however, by
the establishing of a convenient perspective from which
fourteenth century thought and life may be viewed and
by the observation of a proper subordination of elements.

It must be remembered that Chaucer was in his poetical works first an artist and secondarily a philosopher or
a scientist. Though he no doubt thought philosophically
and satisfied an intense curiosity regarding the sciences of
his time, he, like every other great poet, was concerned
with the concrete rather than with the abstract. Apparently caring but little for the spirit of beauty and knowing next to nothing about any theory of esthetics, he was
nevertheless passionately aroused in the presence of beautiful objects — fresh May flowers, busy larks singing
salutations to the rising sun, stars following their prescribed courses, or dew-drops sparkling upon the grass.
He was not greatly affected by the joys or sorrows of
humanity in general, but he seems to have been pro-
foundly touched by the experiences of particular persons
whom he created — the death of Arcite, the despair of
Troilus, the wanderings of Constance, the advancing age
of the Wife of Bath. His poetical world was a world
of concrete perceptions filled with a variety of individual
human beings, whose characters and personalities, observed as acting or reacting in specific environments,
constituted the materials with which he worked. And
all the elements which he employed in his creations were
carefully subordinated to one outstanding purpose, the
concrete representation of life.

But not even Chaucer could conceive his characters
and body them forth in a vacuum. Though most of his

people are in one sense universal, still they are products
of a certain age; their modes of thought, their faiths,
superstitions, ambitions, prejudices, and emotional reactions are human but definitely mediaeval. Troilus and
Criseyde are among the world's great lovers, but their
code of morals was that embodied in the laws of Courtly
Love; the Knight is a man of truth and honor, but his
ideals belonged to the age of chivalry; Theseus is a wise
man, but his philosophy was that of Boethius. Chaucer's
poetical and dramatic conceptions were inevitably determined in some measure by the mediaeval outlook upon
life, and his artistic execution of them was consum-
mated with a fourteenth century audience in mind.
Consequently, if the modern reader would understand
Chaucer's work at its best, he must learn to think in
terms of mediaeval customs and manners, mediaeval philosophy, religion, and science; these are the outward
trappings of an inward reality. Although *what* men
in any age believe or hold to be true is *per se* of no great
consequence ultimately — customs and manners change
from year to year, moral standards alter with every generation, philosophical ideals and religious beliefs are continually discarded to be replaced by others, and truth
seems to masquerade in a multitude of often fantastic
shapes — still the earnest student of human nature must
recognize that only through a study of these manifestations can he approach the soul of an age or understand
the heroic human spirit in its search after truth. One
may hold no brief now for either the truth or falsity of
mediaeval alchemy or geomancy or chiromancy, or for
the philosophy of Boethius, but the implications inherent

xiv   *Chaucer and the Mediaeval Sciences.*

in these activities regarding the mediaeval mind are start-ling and significant. For often the reason *why* men be-lieve so-and-so and the effects of a particular manner of thinking upon their characters may be of supreme im-portance.

Curiously enough your literary artist in any age, standing in the midst of contemporary influences and participating in the flux and flow of social, political, moral, and religious ideals, seems to possess a sort of dual personality. On the one hand, as a human being he is inescapably a part of the society in which he lives, and as such he may be touched by the heat of controversy or the joy of scientific discovery, be subject to the demoral-izing or happy effects of his own actions, or be com-forted in a perhaps disorganized life by philosophy or in-spired by a religious zeal. In all things he reacts, like other men, to the multifarious stimuli of his environ-ment. On the other hand, as artist — particularly if he be endowed with a dramatic instinct — he seems to withdraw himself from life and to view it objectively and from a distance as a kind of marvellous spectacle, highly colored or drab, complex or simple, joyous or tragic as the case may be. In a sense he appears to mirror nature and to reflect men and women as he observes them acting their respective rôles in familiar situations. But in reality he accomplishes more than that. He does not merely represent by description actual historical persons with whom he may have been acquainted; his world is not merely a facsimile or photograph of the phenomenal world of his experience. Your sincere artist — some-thing like the Boethian God — conceives a completely new universe of his own, a poetical world peopled with men and women — distinct personalities in their own right — who seem to act after the manner of human beings in real life. But in order to realize his conceptions and accomplish his designs, he is compelled to employ those actual life-materials with which his observation and experience have made him most familiar. In passing from the phenomenal world into the realm of art, however, these materials suffer an inexplicable sea-change; though they may seem still to be informed with the appearance and vitality of life, they are nevertheless transformed and fused by the creative imagination and absorbed into the original conception of the artist. But he stands completely outside his creation, permitting his world to proceed without intruding his own personal beliefs or doubts or hopes or fears. Chaucer was, presumably, such an artist.

It is, therefore, probably both a futile and a useless procedure — except for the biographer — to attempt to reconstruct, from a study of his poetical works, Chaucer's personal attitude toward the mediaeval sciences. Did he believe in astrology, or in alchemy, or in astrological medicine? The answers to all such questions as this affect only indirectly our main problem, which is to determine how and to what extent he made use of scientific material in the creation of his works of art. His primary purpose was evidently to create characters acting in stories before a specific audience whose beliefs and prejudices were known; and as artist, with his personal attitudes carefully concealed, he permitted his people to discuss whatever subjects they liked and to express whatever conclusions they pleased. The Franklin's strictures upon natural magic cannot be said to reflect Chaucer's opinion; the Canon's Yeoman's complete disgust with the practices of alchemists need not necessarily indicate Chaucer's attitude toward that science. If he chose to employ physiognomical principles in the presentation of some of his characters, the main question is not whether he himself believed in physiognomy but whether his use of it gave greater verisimilitude to the characters in the eyes of his audience; if he motivated two narratives by referring the action to planetary influences, the principal inquiry concerns itself not with the poet's faith in astrology but with the results of his innovations upon the technique of the stories. No one need expect to find that Chaucer has gone about elaborating his own scientific — or, for that matter, his philosophical or religious — creed in his later poetry; it is no part of a mature artist's prerogative to raise or to settle disputes in the realm of science. He probably looked upon astrology and metoposcopy and all the other sciences as just so much crude material, parts of which might be employed to advantage in furthering his creative designs.

To the twentieth century reader and critic, therefore, Chaucer's use of the mediaeval sciences presents an exceedingly difficult problem of complicated aspect. Unwary students of his work are likely to conclude at first — or indeed after long investigation — that an erudite and somewhat pedantic poet, fond of digression and display of learning for their own sake, has at times marred an otherwise artistic poem by the introduction of unassimilated fragments of scientific lore. Editors of definitive editions — and following them the critics — interested principally in determining his indebtedness to this or that primary source and in locating the origin of certain interpolations, sometimes leave the impression that the finished work is little more than a mosaic of jarring elements. Compilers of selections from Chaucer, unable to reconcile these independent additions with their preconceived ideas of unity or unwilling to grant him the privilege of exercising an enlightened judgment in matters of artistic import, frequently take the unwarranted liberty of omitting such passages altogether. In both cases violence is done to Chaucer's work. If in the prosecution of his larger purpose he merely indicated to his fourteenth century audience that the Reeve was a choleric man, it was neither more reasonable nor more necessary for him to enter upon a full discussion of the four humours — their origin in the four elements, their natures, mixtures and action in the human body, their relation to complexions and dispositions, and his estimate of their validity as an explanation of observed phenomena — than it is for a present-day poet, who may wish to employ the term *Paleozoic Epoch*, to stop the progress of his poem and explain the whole system of modern geology and attach his " attitude " toward it. If he indicated that the Wife of Bath's character was in part determined by the conjunction of Mars and Venus in Taurus and that her " marks " were significant, it was no more expedient for him to present the horoscope with full interpretation and to explain in detail the principles of metoposcopy — together with his personal approval or disapproval — than it is now for the literary artist, who may chance to refer to the Missing Link, to launch forth upon a résumé of the theory of evolution and to intrude a personal faith. He has permitted Chauntecleer and Pertelote to reveal their characters in a short controversy over two types of dreams; but it would have been as unseemly, and as unnecessary then, for him to classify all dreams according to their origin and with respect to their validity as harbingers of coming events as it would be now for a poet who may speak of " suppressed complexes " to load his poem with a full discussion of Freudian psychology. Certain passages in Chaucer's work, which may seem to be more or less disconnected fragments torn at random from some ancient scientific treatise and thrust into the smooth flow of a story, often represent in reality the most careful selection of pertinent details from a well-known body of universally accepted scientific principles. These details, when transferred back to their proper setting and viewed as integral parts of a system, are usually found to be in strict accord with the best scientific thought of the time; and when correctly correlated with the literary *milieu* in which the poet has placed them, they are observed to be fully assimilated and, therefore, absolutely essential to the finished work of art. The remarkable thing is that a mediaeval writer should have exercised such admirable restraint and such discriminating judgment in the employment of these materials.

Consequently, if the modern reader — with his mind centered upon " truths " about molecules, and electrons, and leucocytes, and relativity, and bacteria — is to secure the full flavor of Chaucer's work, he must reconstruct, or at least have sketched for him, whole systems of these despised pseudo-sciences. While literary critics have been profitably busy for centuries reproducing fourteenth century religious and philosophical thought, attempting to revivify fourteenth century social customs and literary manners, they have, for the most part, passed over the sciences of the Middle Ages as being outworn or perhaps as being couched in a meaningless jargon, assuming presumably — being touched by the arrogance of the modern scientific spirit — that a revival of erroneous beliefs of a dark age could be of no service in the interpretation of a literary artist of that time. The omission has been particularly unfortunate, it seems to me. The mediaeval sciences, however ludicrously inadequate they now seem to have been, were doubtless as significant to the people of the fourteenth century as accepted principles of to-day are to us — and as powerful in helping to shape and mould character. Hence they must have exerted no little influence upon the formation of Chaucer's artistic ideas. He has merely indicated, for example, that the fortunes of Palamon and Arcite were subject in large measure to the conflicting influences of Mars and Saturn, that the tragic suffering of Constance was brought upon her by the conjunction of Mars and Luna in Scorpio, and that the character of Hypermnestra was determined by the planets Venus and Jupiter; but because the mystery of astral influences has been long forgotten, it now becomes necessary to set forth, more or less completely, the philosophical principles underlying the whole system of mediaeval astrology and to discuss in detail the natures of specific planets, their hours and positions of greatest strength and weakness, and their destinal power in the affairs of men. He has suggested that the Doctor of Physic was a good practical and theoretical physician who understood the origin of diseases in combinations of hot, cold, moist, and dry and who knew the supreme science of image-making; but since these curious ideas have become completely obsolete, it now seems necessary to revive the whole " occult philosophy of medicine," which deals with the ultimate causes and cures of diseases emanating from the stars, the immediate relation of the four elements to the planets, on the one hand, and to the humours and complexions of the human body, on the other, and the crowning marvel of the entire system, astrological amulets and charms. Regarding Arcite's illness we are informed that the virtue expulsive, or animal, could not expel the poison from that virtue which was called natural; but since nobody remembers how in olden times the Reasonable Human Soul was supposed to get its work done in the human body, it now seems imperative that the Soul's activities, as it expresses itself through the mediate functioning of the *virtus naturalis,* the *virtus animalis,* and the *virtus spiritualis,* should be described and that the interrelations and interactions of these forces should be explained in some detail. Pertelote says that dreams are caused by the presence of too much cholera in the blood and Chauntecleer insists that *his* dream of last night was a vision; but because ancient dream-lore has been entirely superseded, one is compelled now to review mediaeval psychology and to analyze dreams into three classes, the *somnium naturale,*

somnium animale, and the *somnium coeleste.* And a
passing reference to " tertian fever " necessitates a classification of fever as *aegritudinis* or *putredinis,* the latter
being further divided into *tertiana, quartana, quotidiana,*
and *causon,* all of which are the result of corrupted humours in the body. Thus, for a just understanding of
the poet's ultimate purpose in his use of scientific fragments, a more or less complete view of the systems from
which he took his materials is essential.

But the outlining of scientific systems of the Middle
Ages, with the idea of establishing Chaucer's sources,
raises a problem of unusual complexion. The critic must
always find it comparatively easy to determine the extent to which the poet may have drawn upon any given
literary productions, because these have the distinguishing
stamp of authorship and personality upon them; by comparing the *Knight's Tale,* for example, with Boccaccio's
Teseide one may come to fairly definite conclusions regarding Chaucer's borrowing from the Italian's work.
But the accepted principles of mediaeval science are not
found exclusively in the treatises of any single writer;
they are generally discovered to have been held by many
men in various countries through centuries. Bernard
of Gordon, for example, had little to add to Galen's
theory of the four humours in the body, which was accepted, restated, and elaborated by all reputable physicians down at least to 1400. When Chaucer, therefore,
found it convenient to base a medical diagnosis upon
the theory, it is manifestly impossible to determine
whether he read Galen or Constantinus Africanus or
Gilbertus Anglicus, or a host of others. If he chose to

present on various occasions questions involving the classification and validity of dreams, one cannot be sure whether he obtained his information from contemporary medical men or from the natural philosophers or from the theologians, all of whom were in agreement on fundamentals. He undoubtedly delved extensively in astrology and elaborated astrological ideas in his poems, but it would be extremely precarious to maintain conclusively that he drew upon the Arabians or the Spanish translators or upon any particular copier of his own time, all of whom were practically at one upon the essential laws. Consequently I have made no effort whatever to establish definite sources for the allusions to science found in Chaucer's poetical works. It has seemed to me rather a more reasonable and a more profitable procedure to review the generally accepted conclusions of the wise ones through sometimes ten or twelve centuries, and to demonstrate that the highly educated English poet was, as artist handling crude materials, in accord usually with the best scientific opinion of his age.

Any correct estimate of Chaucer's knowledge of the mediaeval sciences, therefore, must be arrived at largely by inference. To note merely that he probably read Galen or Ptolemy or Constantinus Africanus, because some of his allusions may be traced to the works of these writers, is entirely misleading; quite frequently his employment of a single and apparently casual reference to one of the sciences presupposes a thorough acquaintance with a complete scientific system, the full influence of which he has brought to bear upon a given situation. Furnishing the Wife of Bath with a horoscope, for example, may seem a simple and indeed a more or less unimportant thing for him to have done; but when her constellation is fully interpreted and we come to understand that her complexities of character and vicissitudes of fortune seem to have been determined largely by astral influences, it appears that the poet must have had deep insight into the mysteries of genethliac astrology and metoposcopy. The astrological references in the *Knight's Tale* compass less than one hundred and twenty-five lines, but through them he has fashioned an occult story of conflicting planetary influences and has thus spread back of a human narrative the destinal power of the stars. Such admirable economy of details implies an accurate knowledge of the whole structure of judicial and horary astrology. From his diagnosis of the Summoner's malady and his suggestions regarding the Doctor's erudition the inference may be drawn that he understood perfectly the philosophy of mediaeval medicine and was familiar with the theory and practice of it. Moreover, the exact correspondence between the characters and physical appearances of certain Canterbury Pilgrims indicates that he had the principles of natural and celestial physiognomy at his finger-tips. And his constant preoccupation with visions that come to men waking or asleep and his enumeration of all the types mentioned by wise men of the time suggests that he knew all there was to be known about dreams and their ways.

But regarding his knowledge of alchemical principles I have been able to form no opinion whatever. It may be, as some critics have held, that the *Canon's Yeoman's*

Tale is a violent satire inspired by personal irritation and directed against alchemy and alchemists. Or, knowing the famous " secret " himself and sympathizing with the true science, he perhaps wrote the *Tale* as a warning to the public against false practitioners and added the correct formula for multiplying in order that honest and serious searchers after truth might be encouraged.* Both of these conjectures, however, are probably beside the mark; at least positive evidence in support of them is wanting. Chaucer was no more a pamphleteer than an exponent of pure science; he was a literary artist, creating characters and setting them forth by means of whatever materials his age afforded. His interest was evidently centered in the personality of the Canon's Yeoman, one of the most dramatically conceived and delightfully presented ignoramuses in the course of English literature. Chaucer stands aside while the stupid fellow, sweating profusely and greatly flustered, vents his spleen upon his former master and inducts the Canterbury Pilgrims into the mysteries of alchemical practices. He has a fly-paper mind which collects everything and understands nothing — except that an explosion usually marks the end of the experiment. But enjoying for once the center of the stage and finding his hearers attentive, he pours forth a flood of marvellous alchemical terms —· names of substances, processes, and implements mixed in a fine confusion without rime or reason — which he has heard during his late apprenticeship. He suspects that his former master is a fraud, like

* S. F. Damon, "Chaucer and Alchemy," *PMLA.*, XXXIX, 782 ff.

the alchemist in the *Tale*, but he is never quite certain; being entirely ignorant of the significance of processes and terms with which he is superficially familiar, he clings almost involuntarily to the belief that there may be something in the practice after all.   Consequently, near the end of the story, he repeats from memory a formula from Arnold of the New Town and garbles phrases from a man called Senior, to the effect that no philosopher ever writes the great secret in a book and that, indeed, God does not reveal it at all except to a few chosen ones.   In that case, being but an educated, superstitious man and never having had any success at making gold anyway, he resolves to give up multiplying forever.   So Chaucer has created the Canon's Yeoman, but there is no indication whatever that he himself either approved or contemned alchemy or alchemists.   One may suspect, however, that his reading in alchemical literature must have been wide — the variety and range of terms occurring in the Yeoman's list are remarkable — but whether he read intelligently or was an initiate in the great secret must remain a mystery. He may or may not have been a good alchemist; he was certainly the conscious artist when using alchemical material.

In conclusion, it must be observed that in this book the emphasis placed upon Chaucer's relation to the mediaeval sciences should not be taken to indicate in any way the comparative importance of scientific influences upon the poet.   Among all the other powerful influences which must have thronged upon him — social, literary, philosophical, religious — that of the mediaeval sciences was probably least effective in helping to produce the finished writer. But that they contributed in some measure to the moulding of his artistic ideas cannot be doubted. If my revival of these fourteenth century scientific principles makes it possible for a twentieth century audience to read Chaucer's poetical works with clearer understanding and with greater appreciation, in ever so small a degree, I shall be satisfied.

CHAUCER AND THE MEDIAEVAL
SCIENCES

CHAPTER ONE

THE DOCTOR OF PHYSIC AND MEDIAEVAL MEDICINE

COMMENTATORS are happily agreed, it would seem, that the Doctor of Physic is possessed of sufficient erudition and experience to rank him among the foremost theoretical and practising physicians of his time. Indeed, he has no peer when it comes to *speaking* of physic and even of surgery. He has " dronkyn of that swete drynke of Astronomye " so deeply that he is enabled to diagnose without fault any malady with respect to both the ultimate or primary causes emanating from the stars and the immediate causes residing in the various compoundings of hot, cold, moist, and dry humours in the blood. And having located the seat of trouble in the human system, he skilfully employs the principles of natural magic in the creation of appropriate astrological images and in the compounding of medicines for the purpose of effecting cures. He is favored with an extraordinarily wide acquaintance with the works of ancient and mediaeval authors upon medicine, having the distinction of being, perhaps, the only physician who has ever perused the writings of that mythical founder of medicine, Esculapius. For years he and his apothecaries have worked together in brotherly fashion — to their mutual benefit — against the ravages of the Black Death and other diseases; and such have been his thrift and temperance that he is blessed with superior physical comforts in the way of good health and distinctive wearing apparel. His thinking is but little on the Bible.[1] It has seemed to me that possibly Skeat, Morris, and others [2] have not done justice quite to his learning and to the subtlety with which his character is drawn. Perhaps it might be well to reconsider, in the light of mediaeval medical lore and contemporary opinion upon physicians in general, the evidence which Chaucer presents in support of this particular Doctor's claim to fame and to estimate the art with which the poet has created his character.

As to education, no one must discredit the Doctor of Physic if he seems to fail in measuring up to the high standard set by Isidore Hispalensis (600 A.D.). "It is sometimes asked," says Isidore, "why the art of medicine is not included among the other liberal arts. It is because they deal with single causes, but medicine with all. For a medical man should know the *ars grammatica,* that he may be able to understand and expound that which he reads; and the *ars rhetorica,* that he may be able to support with sound arguments the matters with which he deals; and also the *ars dialectica,* so that by the exercise of reason he may investigate the causes of sickness for the purpose of cure. So too he should know the *ars arithmetica,* so as to calculate the times (of fever) and its periods; and he should be acquainted with the *ars geometrica,* so that he may teach what every man ought to consider with regard to different districts and the lie of different places. Moreover, he must know something of music, for many things may be done for the sick by means of this art . . . Asclepiades restored a madman to

his former health by means of a concord of sounds.
Lastly let him have a knowledge of astronomy, by means
of which he may understand the calculation of the stars
and the changes of the seasons. For a physician says,
our bodies are affected by their qualities, and therefore
medicine is called a second philosophy; for either art
arrogates to itself the whole man, since by the one the
soul and by the other the body is cured." [3] But the
good Doctor's success indicates that he employs at least
the principles of all these arts — with the possible exception of music — whether he has studied them formally
or not; he reads with intelligence, he has great facility
in expression, he is an excellent diagnostician, his *Tale*
embodies his evident studies in the *ars rhetorica* and he
knows astronomy (astrology). He is proficient in both
theory and practice, the two main branches into which
mediaeval medicine is usually divided.

John of Salisbury might have considered him of no
more importance professionally than some other bragging, mediaeval physicians. "The theoretical physicians
do what concerns them," says the author of *Polycraticus*,
"and for love of you will go even further. You can
get from them information as to the nature and causes
of particular phenomena, they are judges of health, of
sickness, and of the mean estate. Health, so far as words
go, they provide and preserve, and as for the mean estate
they bid one incline in the direction of health. Of sickness they foresee and declare the causes, and lay down
its beginning, its continuance, and its decline. What
more shall we say? When I hear them talk, I fancy
that they can raise the dead and are in no way inferior

to either Esculapius or Mercury. . . . Again, what shall I say about the practising physicians? God forbid that I should say anything bad about them! since for my sins I fall only too often into their hands. They should rather be soothed by politeness than angered by words, and I do not wish that they should treat me hardly, nor could I endure all the evils about which they constantly talk. I would rather say with blessed Solomon: All medicine is from the Lord, and he that is wise will not despise it." [4]   But undoubtedly John of Burgundy would have applauded the union of theory and practice in Chaucer's Doctor, against whom his strictures upon certain improperly equipped practitioners in the time of the pestilences could not have been leveled. " Ther have bene many grete maistirs," complains John of Burgundy, "and ferre lernyd in theoric or speculation and groundly in sight of medecyne, but they bene litill proued in practik and therto allefully ignorant in the sience of Astronomy, the which science is in phisik wonder nedefull . . . for why astronomye and phisik rectifien yche other in effect and also that one science sheweth forthe many thynges hidde in the other. . . . And I 40 yere and more have oftyn tymes proued in practise that a medecyn gyven contrary to the constellacion all thogh hit were both wele compownyd or medled and ordynatly wroght after the science of phisik yet it wroght nowther aftur the purpose of the worcher nor to the profite of the pacient. . . . Wherfore they that have not dronkyn of that swete drynke of Astronomye mowe putte to thise pestilentiall sores no perfite remedie, for bicause that they knowe not the cause and the qualitie of the siknesse they may not hele it. . . . He that knowith not the cause hit is onpossible that he hele the sikenes. The comentour also *super secundum phisicorum* seith thus: A man knowith not a thing but if he knowe the cause both ferre and nygh. Sithen therfor the hevenly or firmamentall bodies bene of the first and primytif causes, it is behovefull to have knowlechyng of hem; for yf the first and primytif causes be onknowen, we may not come to know the causes secondary. Sithen therfor the first cause bryngeth in more plentevously his effecte than doth the cause secondary . . . therfor it shewith wele that without Astronomy litill vayleth phisik, for many man is perisshed in defawte of his councelour." [5] Indeed, a knowledge of astronomy is so absolutely essential in medical practice that Hippocrates is credited with having said, "The medical man, whatever else he may be, cannot be considered a perfect physician if he is ignorant of astronomy; no man ought to commit himself into his hands." [6]

Since mediaeval medicine is grounded firmly upon the principles of astrology, it might be well to sketch briefly the rationale of celestial influences as they affect the healthy or diseased human body. For as Rhazes says, "Wise physicians are agreed that all things here below, air, water, the complexions, sickness, and so on, suffer change in accordance with the motions of the planets." [7] First, it must be observed, in astro-medical lore the Zodiacal signs have certain " qualities " or " virtues " assigned to them: Aries, Leo, and Sagittarius are fiery; Taurus, Virgo, and Capricorn are earthy; Gemini, Libra, and Aquarius are airy; Cancer, Scorpio, and Pisces are watery. Again, for example, Aries, Cancer, Libra, and Capricorn are called "movable" or "tortuous" signs, because in them are renewed the four principal complexions of all things, that is to say, hot and dry in Cancer, cold and dry in Libra, cold and moist in Capricorn; Taurus and the likewise following are called "fixed" signs, because in them the complexions are constant; Gemini and following are "common" signs, because in them the complexions decline. The planets, moreover, are diverse in their qualities or complexions, Saturn being cold and dry, Mars hot and dry, Jupiter and Venus hot and moist, Luna cold and moist, and so on. But so far as their "virtues" or influences are concerned the ultimate natures of planets depend largely upon their configuration in the various signs through which they revolve.[8]

From Aristotle on down, we must observe, wise men are agreed that the stars, incorruptible and voluntary in their movements — whether guided by celestial intelligences or not — are the "causes of generation and corruption in all inferior things," the artificers who use as tools the four terrestrial elements, earth, air, fire, and water. "Per coelum ergo," says Roger Bacon, "complexiones omnium rerum habentur et non solum regiones diversificantur per coelum, sed res ejusdem regionis partes eiusdem rei, et non solum in generatione recta sed monstruosa, et peccatis ac erroribus naturae."[9] From the sky, therefore, come the influences which determine the fundamental "complexion" or physical constitution of the human body at conception and at birth; the configuration of certain stars is all powerful in controlling the various proportions of elements which are compounded in its creation. Not only that, but the parts of the body are distributed severally among the signs of the Zodiac; [10] and every passing hour, which brings a change in the positions of stars in the signs, sees the human " complexion " governed by a new celestial influence. In the diagnosis of a malady, therefore, it is manifestly of prime importance that the physician should know something of the patient's nativity, i.e., the influence responsible for the given complexion, and that by observation of the present configuration of stars he should be able to determine how, why, and to what extent the proportions of original element-compounds have been upset or disordered. This, in brief, furnishes the basis of the " occult philosophy of medicine " so popular in the Middle Ages. To quote John of Burgundy again, " Since, therefore, the heavenly or firmamental bodies are the first and primitive causes (of disease), it is necessary to have knowledge of them; for if the first or primitive causes be unknown, we may not come to know the causes secondary." Chaucer's Doctor of Physic, well grounded in astronomy, is first of all a theoretical physician and accordingly an excellent diagnostician; he knows the cause of every malady, whether it be of a hot, cold, moist, or dry humour. This knowledge he doubtless gains from observation of the stars.

What of the causes secondary or immediate? And what of the qualifications of the practising physician? Skeat has already explained that the whole system of mediaeval medicine rests upon the teaching of Galen in respect to the relation of the bodily humours to sickness and health. Galen and other physicians assume that there are four elements or simple bodies in creation, earth, fire, air, and water, which are thought to possess certain " qualities "; earth is cold and dry; fire, hot and dry; air, hot and moist; and water, cold and moist. Corresponding with these four elementary qualities are the four bodily humours, namely, melancholia, cholera, phlegm, and blood, generated in the brain, heart, liver, and stomach. And arising from the compounding of these humours in the body come the four complexions or temperaments of men, viz., the melancholic, the choleric, the phlegmatic, and the sanguine. The *melancholic man* is cold and dry, after the nature of earth; the *choleric man* is hot and dry, after the nature of fire; the *phlegmatic man* is cold and moist, after the nature of water; and the *sanguine man* is hot and moist, after the nature of air. In health there is a just proportion of qualities or humours mingled together in the human body; in sickness there is an excess of one or more qualities, according as the distemper is simple or compound.[11] It is, therefore, evidently impossible for the theoretical physician, however much of astrology he may know, to arrive at the complete diagnosis of a given disturbance in the body unless he is fully acquainted with the character and inter-actions of the four humours. In other words, he must recognise both the primitive and the immediate causes. Accordingly, Chaucer says that his Doctor of Physic knows not only the cause of every malady, whether it is from a compounding of hot, or cold, or moist, or dry, but also where it is generated and of what humour. Having determined this much, your practising physician may find his way comparatively easy; he has only to prescribe remedies laid down in great detail in every medical treatise.   As Chaucer says further of the Doctor:

> He was a verrey parfit practisour:
> The cause y-knowe, and his harm the rote,
> Anon he yaf the seke man his bote.
> (*C. T.*, A, 422 ff.) [12]

Let us see in some detail how a mediaeval physician, by observing the course of the moon through the signs of the Zodiac, might prognosticate what diseases a man is likely to be subject to, what treatment to apply, how long the malady may be expected to continue, and whether the patient will recover or not.   First, according to Galen,[13] by observing the position of Luna he may determine precisely from what humour or combination of humours the malady proceeds.   For example, if Luna is in Cancer when the sickness begins and in conjunction with Saturn and Mars, the infirmity comes from a superabundance of black cholera; if Luna in quartile or sextile aspect with Saturn is discovered in Leo, the malady is caused by too much phlegm, but if in the same aspect with Mars, by too much blood; if Luna is in Gemini and crescent, the disease is from red cholera; if in Pisces and in quartile or septile aspect with Mars, from too much blood and cholera — and so on.   Your wise physician may determine, moreover, the nature, location in the body, and duration of all diseases, and may apply specified remedies to each with confidence of success.

For example, if the patient should be taken sick when Luna is in Aries, conjoined with Mars and Sol, his affliction will be in the head or lungs on account of the sun's heat; he will suffer with raging fevers and will have a strong pulse.   It is necessary in such a case to diminish blood in the veins (by cupping) and to administer cooling drinks and foods.   If Luna is conjoined with Mars and Saturn in Aries, the patient will die in seven days when the moon comes into quartile aspect with Sol — that is, if Luna is crescent.   (Si non ab Astronomia nescis non poteris scire eius infirmitatem.)   When Luna in Aries is in oppositional or quartile aspect with Mars, the infirmity is *ex sanguine;* the patient then experiences heat and drought; he is unable to sleep at night and has a desire to drink wine or anything that is cooling.   It is, therefore, necessary to diminish blood and to give medicines whose property is to produce cold and moisture.   And if in this position Saturn aspects Luna and if no fortunate planet exerts its influence to the contrary, then the patient will die in about nine days after the malady began — that is, if Luna is progressive and crescent.   When Luna in Leo is in quartile or sextile aspect with Saturn, the infirmity is *ex fleumate* and affects the head; but the patient will recover after Luna has passed through four signs.   If, however, Luna in Leo is aspected by Mars *ex quarto vel sexto,* the disease comes from a superabundance of blood, which produces fevers; the patient must be given cool and dry drinks.   He will escape after great depletion of energies if a fortunate planet can be found in good aspect; but if no good influence is felt, he will die when Luna arrives opposite the position she was in when the illness began. Thus your mediaeval physician is provided with a definite system upon which he may base his prognosis, diagnosis, and practice in the treatment of diseases. He observes carefully the position of Luna at the hour when the sickness begins; he understands thoroughly the development of the disease by calculating hourly the changes in the influences from constellations; he knows precisely, therefore, at what hour the crisis will come; he administers hour by hour — or may change at any hour — the medicine or medicines which he feels would alleviate the sufferings of his patient or work a cure. In certain cases he may even prognosticate the death of the sick man. Such an uncanny knowledge and ability Chaucer ascribes to his Doctor of Physic:

> For he was grounded in astronomye;
> He kepte his pacient a ful greet del
> In houres, by his magik naturel
>   (*C. T.*, A, 414 ff.).

This business of keeping a patient " a ful greet del in houres " becomes further immensely complicated when it comes to administering medicines and performing surgical operations. Your mediaeval physician must understand that the four humours of the body fluctuate in volume and power according to the waxing and waning of the moon; when Luna is full, they are most strong and abundant; when she declines, they decrease. In the first and third quarter, the humours " withdraw from the interior to the exterior, just as a stream flows in its channel "; in the second and fourth quarters, " they recede from the exterior to the interior." (Hoc est magna transmutatio et mirabilis).[14]   Generally speaking, consequently, the wise physician may upon occasion employ exterior evacuants such as phlebotomy in the first and third quarters of the moon, but in the second and fourth quarters he will use interior purgatives and laxatives.[15] He must observe, moreover, that humours have dominion variously in respective hours of the day: the first six hours of the natural day, i.e., after midnight, are hot and moist, and during that time blood is said to have dominion; the second six hours are hot and dry, and cholera is in power; the next six are cold and dry, and melancholia rules; the last six are cold and moist, and phlegm is supreme.[16] And finally, the practising physician will do well to remember that in each hour of the twenty-four in a day some particular planet is most powerful.   The planet of the day, e.g., Sol on Sunday, is assigned the first (after sunrise), the eighth, fifteenth, and twenty-second hours, and to the other planets are given respective hours in the following order: Sol, Venus, Mercury, Luna, Saturn, Jupiter, Mars.[17]   Understanding these mysteries, however, and recognising how and why each planet is responsible for a varied assortment of particular diseases,[18] the practitioner may proceed to elect propitious hours for the administering of medicines and the surgeon for his operations.

For example, let us postulate the simplest case imaginable.   Suppose the physician is called to the bedside of his patient in the early morning hours of Sunday, and finds the poor man burning up with a fever of some description.   Upon inquiry he finds, say, that the malady was

first felt nine days ago. If he is properly prepared for
his business, his astrological calculations may show (see
Plate I) that, when the illness began, Luna was near the
end of her first quarter and situated in the third " face "

PLATE I

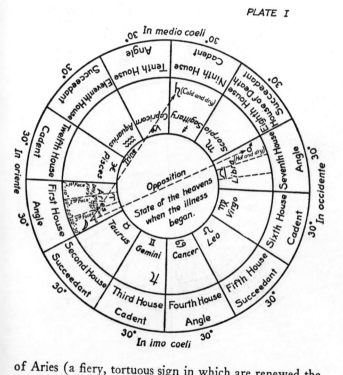

of Aries (a fiery, tortuous sign in which are renewed the
qualities, cold and moist), in oppositional aspect with
Mars (hot and dry), and in, say, trine aspect with Saturn
(cold and dry). He will conclude from the observation

and from the symptoms that his patient suffers from that type of fever called " continuous," which is caused from the corruption of blood in the veins.[19] He is doubtless horrified to discover upon present observation — nine days

PLATE II

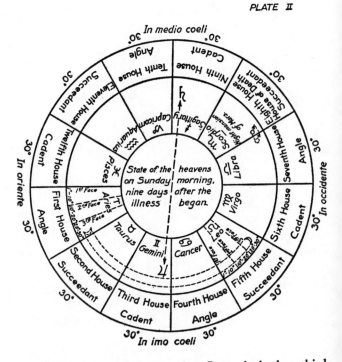

after the sickness began — that Luna is in her third quarter (indicating that humours are abundant and strong), that the hour comes within the first six of the natural day (in which blood has dominion), that Aries (one of the " mansions " of Mars) is in the ascendency and therefore powerful, and that Mars (lord of the ascendent) has progressed a single day's journey in the eighth "house" of the astrological figure (the house of death). This is one of the most malignant of planetary configurations; [20] not even the beneficent Jupiter situated in Gemini can make himself felt (see Plate II). The doctor may try letting blood, since the corrupted humours are now " exterior " and the root of the malady may be reached most directly in that manner, but he will find the accumulated influences of the stars too strong to be overcome. The patient surely dies — in all likelihood precisely one hour before sunrise (the astrological " hour " of Mars, lord of the ascendent),[21] on this Sunday (the first " hour " of which is attributed to Sol), nine days after the illness began.[22]

Let us suppose, however, that the physician is called in two days earlier, in the early morning hours of Friday, just *seven* days after the malady's beginning (see Plate III). In that event the patient stands a good chance of recovery. For Luna (the moist and cold planet, ruler of phlegm) is found to have progressed (during the seven days) through exactly three signs and to be now situated in the third face of Cancer (a watery sign), her only " mansion," in which she is most powerful in producing comforting cold and moist humours. Her kindly influence is further increased by virtue of her position in an " angle," the most favorable of the three locations, angle, succeedant, and cadent.[23] On Friday, moreover, Mars is found to be situated in the seventh house (where he is weakened) and falling from the sign

Libra, one of his positions of least influence (being situated, as it is, opposite his mansion, Aries).[24]   And on Friday, finally, the most beneficent of all planets, Jupiter, situated in Gemini and in strong oppositional aspect with

PLATE III

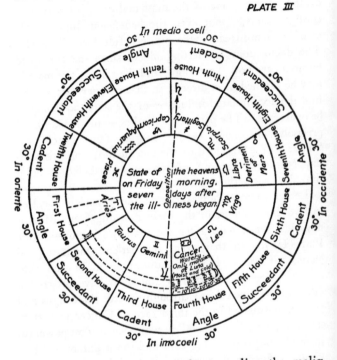

Saturn in Sagittarius effectively neutralises the malignancy of this greater infortune.[25]   Thus on Friday Saturn is rendered helpless, Mars is weakened by reason of his position in an unfavorable sign and of his being cadent from an angle, and Luna, not strongly aspected by

any wicked planet and rejoicing in her place of greatest dignity, is left free to exert all her beneficent influence upon the feverish patient. But this happy configuration of stars can continue for only one day or less; it behooves the physician to bestir himself. During the first six hours of the natural day (when blood is in the ascendency) he must bleed the patient; but during the remainder of the day, since Luna is in her second quarter and the humours are " interior," he must have recourse to purgatives and digesters of hot and dry humours and to cold and moist drinks. The most dangerous hours of Friday are the fourth and eleventh after sunrise (the " hours " of Saturn) and the sixth and thirteenth (" hours " of Mars); at these hours he should give digesters of melancholia (ruled by Saturn) and of cholera (ruled by Mars).[26] The most favorable hours are the fifth and twelfth (" hours " of Jupiter) and the third, tenth, and seventeenth (" hours " of Luna); during these hours the accomplished physician may give cold and moist drinks in abundance and apply " comforters " of phlegm. The patient's continuous fever should be completely broken by the afternoon of Friday, some time during the last six hours of the natural day (when phlegm is in the ascendency), probably at the tenth " unequal hour " or perhaps at the seventeenth (the hours when Luna is most powerful). And his recovery is assured if, upon inquiry concerning his nativity, it is found that his complexion is phlegmatic. And if your practising physician is exceptionally wise, he will concentrate and perpetuate the beneficent influences of the above constellation in an astrological image.

Chaucer's Doctor of Physic at least, knowing that the science of images is the very cream of all the other sciences and of philosophy, has prepared himself to "fortunen the ascendent of his images for his pacient." The making of images is so important that Aristotle is reported to have said: "He who reads philosophy, geometry, and all the other sciences and knows nothing of astronomy occupies himself in vain, for more worthy than geometry and higher than philosophy is the science of images." [27] Precisely what does it mean to "fortunen" (or to "infortunen") the ascendent of an image? [28] Skeat's description of the Doctor's activities in this respect is perhaps not well advised: "He knew well how to choose a fortunate ascendent for treating images." [29] The science of image-making is the ultimate step in the sciences of nativities and elections. We have seen already how the influence of a constellation — the aggregate of certain planetary and sign qualities — so impresses itself upon the elements compounded in the body of a man at birth that there is produced a just equilibrium of qualities (or humours) which determines the fundamental complexion of the native. We have observed also how the constantly changing face of the heavens sometimes disturbs the right proportion of the bodily qualities (causing a superabundance of one or more humours), and how diseases, produced by such planetary influences, must be treated at specified hours when the stars are propitious. And, now, we must note especially that *all things* of a material nature which are made or created by the hands of men receive the impress of the constellation which reigns at the instant when they are formed, and that the impress of this celestial energy is never lost so long as the objects are not corrupted or destroyed.[30] This is particularly true of astrological images, formed with or without characters, figures, or incantations; they receive and store up the tremendous energy of either beneficent or malignant constellations, which the clever practitioner of natural magic may use at will to work health or sickness or death here below. "Because it is difficult to comprehend the truth about celestial things," says Roger Bacon, "there is found among many men great error in the practice of this science; and they are few who know how to employ it usefully and with justice." [31]

In the making of images, however, any natural philosopher must give especial attention to the ascendent (its favorable or unfavorable qualities in the given instance), to the good or bad position of Luna in relation to other planets, to the location of the lord of the ascendent, and to the favorable or unfavorable position of the lord of the house of death. Thebit ibn Corat, probably the most celebrated of all the image-makers (" inter omnes Christianos summus philosophus," [32] Bacon), gives explicit directions for the making of seven useful and marvellous images.[33] For example, if you want to drive out scorpions from a place, says he in effect, begin your operations when Scorpio is in the ascendent. Make an image of a scorpion out of copper or tin or silver, and engrave above the image the names of the ascendent, of the lord of the ascendent, of the lord of the day-hour, and of the moon (Luna should be in Scorpio). And you shall place in a fortunate position (*fortunabis*) the lord of the house of death or join him in quartile or sextile aspect with one of the infortunes, Saturn or Mars. Then bury the image with the head downwards and say these words, *Haec est sepultura illius, vel speciei illius, vt non intret illum, vel illum locum.* And the scorpions will disappear! Similarly, if you wish to work the destruction of a whole region, make an image under the ascendent of this region. Then you shall place in a fortunate position (*fortunabis*) the lord of the house of death and in an unfortunate position (*infortunabis*) the lord of the ascendent, and Luna, and the lord of the mansion of Luna, and the lord of the house of the ascendent. Bury the image so engraved in the midst of the region, and you will see wonderful results.

Arnoldus de Villa Nova, moreover, relying apparently more upon incantation than upon astrology, gives directions for the creation of twelve medical seals of standard quality, so to speak, which correspond to the signs of the Zodiac [34] and which the physician may have ready prepared in cases of emergency. They are not made with special reference to any individual case; but if the physician is supplied with these images in the twelve signs, he is certain to have something in stock to meet the instant demand. For example, let us consider the Libra-image. Take the purest gold and melt it, says he in effect, and form it into a round seal; while you are making it, say these words: *Exurge Domine in statere, & exaudi vocem meam, qua clamaui ad te; miserere mei, & exaudi me,* and repeat the Psalm beginning, *Dominus illuminatio mea, &c.* Having made the seal so, you must put it away for awhile; afterwards when the Sun enters Libra,

Luna being situated in Capricorn or Aquarius, engrave on one side the figure of a man holding in his hands a balance and in the circumference, *Heli, Heli lama Sabatani, consummatum est;* on the other side engrave in the circumference, *Iesus Nazarenus Rex Iudeorum,* and in the middle, *Michael, Mattheus.* This most sacred image is powerful against insidious demons on land and sea, against wind-storms and the inundations of water, and against all maladies which are produced *ex sanguine.* It is evident, therefore, that to " fortunen " the ascendent of an image signifies much more than " choosing a fortunate ascendent for the treatment of images "; it means also that the dealer in natural magic must fortune (i.e., place in a favorable position) both Luna and the lord of the ascendent, and infortune (place in unfavorable positions) the lord of the house of death and the malefic planets. And contrariwise, to infortune the ascendent of an image is to infortune Luna, and the lord of the ascendent, and the lords of the day and hour, and to fortune the lord of the house of death and the wicked planets. "And this is the supreme wisdom which the most high God wishes to disclose to His servants," concludes Thebit ibn Corat, " in order that His name may be honored, praised, and forever exalted world without end." [35]

No one must imagine, therefore, that Arnoldus de Villa Nova and Thebit ibn Corat are to be classed with necromancers and other exponents of black magic because they employ characters, incantations, and adjurations in the preparation of their astrological images. These dangerous-appearing accessories [36] to the valid science of images may be defended upon two grounds. Roger Bacon finds that words are the natural instrument of the soul and that miracles have been performed through the use of them. " When words are uttered with deep thought and great desire and good intention and firm confidence, they have great virtue. For when these four qualities unite, the substance of the rational being is strongly excited to radiate its own species and virtues from itself into its own body and foreign matter." The voice, influenced by the rational soul, makes itself felt upon the atmosphere and all objects contained in it; and since the air and objects are receiving at the same time the influences of the stars, it follows that incantations " are words brought forth by the exertion of the rational soul, and receive the virtue of the sky as they are pronounced." [37] Words may be said, therefore, to reinforce by the power of rational soul the energy radiated from the stars and fixed in the image. Constantinus Africanus, on the other hand, presents an argument less tinged with suggestions of black magic. Since the time of the Greeks, says he, physicians have known that the humours of the body are directly related to the dispositions or virtues of the mind; the complexions of the body, indeed, determine in large measure the cast of the disposition. For example, the complexion in which cholera predominates so reacts upon the mind that the subject is easily angered; the sanguine man, on the other hand, is of a joyous and sunny disposition. And *econverso*, that which strongly affects from the outside the state of a man's mind causes a reaction upon the humours of the body and a consequent change in the com-

plexion. It is evident, therefore, that if a physician can
so employ amulets, and charms, and astrological images
— whether they have any inherent power or not — as to
put his patient's mind at rest from terror, to inspire confidence, and to arouse an intense desire for health, then
the humours of the body will be affected and health
probably restored.[38] As a thorough-going mental thera-
pist Constantinus would not hesitate to employ astrological images with or without incantations, characters, and
adjurations.

Returning now to the case of our hypothetical patient
whose continuous fever is broken on Friday and for
whom it becomes necessary to make an astrological image, we may create under the direction of Thebit and
Arnoldus such an image for this present situation. We
may suppose that the Doctor has already gone through
the preliminary processes of forming an Aries-image:
" Take the purest gold and melt it while the Sun is
entering Aries; and while shaping it into a round seal,
say these words: *Exurge lux mundi Iesu vere Agnus, qui
tollis peccata mundi, & illuminas tenebras nostras,* and
repeat the Psalm beginning, *Domine Dominus noster
. . .* ; and when you have made it, lay it aside." [39]
The physician presumably has this with him. He now
engraves on one side the figure of a ram and above it the
name of the ascendent (" Aries "), the name and unfortunate position of the lord of the ascendent (" Mars
cadent in Libra "), and the name and favorable position of Luna (" Luna exalted in Cancer "); in the circumference he writes, *Arabel tribus Iuda, 5 & 7.* On
the reverse side he engraves the following most sacred

words in the circumference: *Verbum caro factum est, & habitauit in nobis,* and in the central part, *Alpha & omega, & Sanctus Petrus.*[40]   Having secured this most powerful image somewhere upon the head of the already convalescing man, your physician may return home assured that the celestial influences, which have been instrumental in curing his patient and which are now fixed in the image, will continue to protect him from further attacks of continuous fever.

With all these complexities in the theory and practice of medicine Chaucer's Doctor of Physic is, as we have seen, doubtless conversant.   His speaking acquaintance with surgery, however, is probably confined to certain fundamental and elementary principles dealing with the influence of Luna in the twelve signs when the case requires blood-letting or perhaps cauterization.   He knows, of course, that the parts of the body are attributed respectively to the various signs of the Zodiac, i.e., that the bodily parts partake of the complexions or qualities of the signs; that, for example, the head has the complexion of Aries, the neck of Taurus, and so on.   He observes that when Luna is in Gemini, the sign corresponding to the shoulders and arms, it is unwise to let blood from the arms by cupping and that scarification with a scalpel or with any other iron instrument is likely to prove fatal.   This is true because when Luna is situated in any sign corresponding to a member, there is danger that the confluence of humours to such a member may cause serious infection.[41]   He is also skilled, no doubt, in the gathering of herbs and in the preparation of his medicines under certain favorable aspects of the stars.[42]

And it is indisputable that he has made an exhaustive study of dietetics,[43] for here at least he follows his own prescription:

> Of his diete mesurable was he,
> For it was of no superfluitee,
> But of greet norissing and digestible
> (*C. T.*, A, 435 ff.).

Surely no one could find anything to "pinche at" in either the preparation or learning [44] of Chaucer's Doctor of Physic; he seems to be an outstanding representative of the theoretical and practising physicians of his time. But as to his character — that is another matter.

II

Chaucer's forty-four lines of tantalising description devoted to the Doctor of Physic constitutes not so much a satire upon the principles of mediaeval medicine as a character-sketch of contemporary physicians. The poet would scarcely presume to criticise a historically respectable body of scientific principles, though covert references might seem to indicate a healthy skepticism regarding empirical remedies. But the student of human nature undoubtedly has a discerning eye fixed merrily upon the pompous and fraudulent practitioners of his time who bungle the handling of these principles; he may even have in mind a particular physician of his acquaintance, as has been conjectured, such as possibly John of Burgundy. Whether he gathers his material from observation of the individual or the class, however, the artist is interested primarily in the complex char-

acter growing under his hand. While the outline of the
Doctor's knowledge and preparation is comparatively
easy to follow, a clear understanding of his personality,
presented for the most part by means of sly suggestion
and innuendo, is exceedingly difficult to arrive at. Indeed, after one has considered that the whole passage
probably represents by way of indirect discourse the Doctor's own estimate of himself and his abilities, that he
and his apothecaries have been combined these many
years for the purpose of fleecing the public, and that his
study is but little upon the Bible, one begins to question
whether he is ever quite sincere and frank with his patients and whether his learning is as broad and accurate
as he would have it appear.

For the good Doctor I suspect talks too much. He
is exceedingly, though perhaps not abnormally, well
pleased with himself and with his profession, and seems
determined that the Canterbury Pilgrims shall be properly impressed by his successes in the recent pestilences.
One has the impression that he discourses rather ostenta-
tiously upon the occult philosophy of medicine, the influence of the stars on the elements and consequently
on the humours in the human body, upon the mysteries
connected with image-making and the confining of
powerful astral influences in bits of gold and silver, and
upon the great importance of "ascendents," "hours,"
and such. If anybody is interested, he doubtless lectures
with a show of wisdom upon diets, illustrating his points
by reference to his own personal habits in that matter;
everybody, of course, waits breathlessly to learn what
so eminent a medical man has for breakfast in January,

for dinner in March, or for supper in April. The names of fifteen illustrious physicians — Greek, Arabian, and modern — roll impressively from his tongue as if they were selected on the spur of the moment and at random from a much larger reading-list. It does not particularly matter that he fails to present them in strict historical order; his hearers are laymen and will not discover the difference. And his relations with his apothecaries are no doubt referred to as an indication of his astuteness as a business man, of which his general appearance and bearing suggest that he is inordinately proud. He is perhaps to be classed with those other physicians of whom John of Salisbury speaks: "They soon return from college full of flimsy theories to practise what they have learned. Galen and Hippocrates are continually in their mouths. They speak aphorisms on every subject, and make their hearers stare at their long, unknown, and high-sounding words. The good people believe that they can do anything because they pretend to all things: When I hear them talk I fancy that they can raise the dead. . . . They have only two maxims which they never violate: Never mind the poor; never refuse money from the rich." [45] At any rate, in all this world there has never been a man like Chaucer's Doctor (or the poet) for *speaking* of physic and surgery.

He is a cold-blooded rationalist, moreover, a strictly scientific man who boasts that his study is but little upon the Bible. This bit of information on the part of the reporter is neither accidental nor incidental; it indicates, I suspect, that the Doctor belongs to that class of physicians who find rational causes at the root of all maladies

and who depend exclusively upon their own skill in the
manipulation of natural laws for the working of cures.
John of Salisbury complains at length of such godless
men: " But the physicians, while they attribute too much
authority to Nature, cast aside the Author of Nature,
notwithstanding the faith.   Not that I would charge
them all with errors, though I have heard many of them
disputing otherwise than faith would have it about the
soul, its energies and working, about the growth and decline of the body, and its resurrection, and about the
creation of bodies both natural and spiritual.   Sometimes they talk about God Himself,

   ' As if earth-born giants were to attempt the stars,'

and by their empty toil appear to be anxious to deserve
the fate of Enceladus and to have placed upon them the
fiery burden of Etna. . . .   It is of little moment if
some physicians sell an imaginary benefit, and that they
may appear the more honest take no fee before the patient is well.   But such are dishonest in that they give
themselves the credit for a recovery which is due to time,
or rather to the gift of God; for it is due to God and
to the natural power of his constitution that the sick man
is raised up.   Few are they who act in this way, for you
will always hear physicians advising one another as follows: Take your fee while the patient still feels it." [46]
A later writer, Ahasverus Fritschius, is still more violent
in his condemnation of such impious and inflated physicians who confide more in their own skill than in divine
grace, arrogating to themselves the credit for cures which
belongs rightfully to God: " Quando medicus felicem

curam sibi adscribens exclamat: Hoc ego feci! tunc
fiunt feces Impious is such a physician, and he who
thinks and speaks after this fashion insults his Creator." [47]   Yet one may strongly suspect that Chaucer's
Doctor is this sort of man, trusting to his own intellect
in understanding and to his skill in managing the laws
of nature, relying upon his power to compel the influence of constellations according to the principles of natural magic, and leaving out of account God, the Author
of Nature, and His will as it is made manifest in the
Bible.   He would probably hold in supreme contempt
such pious incantations as those which accompany Arnoldus de Villa Nova's making of astrological images.
Arnold, it will be recalled, acknowledges God and repeats a Psalm while creating every several image for
the twelve signs.   For example further, for the seal in
Taurus he says, *Exurge Domine Deus meus, adiutor
meus,* and repeats entire the Psalm beginning, *Confitebor
tibi Domine, in toto corde meo, narrabo omnia mirabilia
tua.* . . .   But what has the Doctor of Physic to do
with such nonsense?   He is of the opinion, doubtless,
that to call upon God when Nature is sufficient is a confession of weakness or an indication of fragmentary
knowledge; superstition is reprehensible whether it is
connected with religious faith or with the practices of
black magic.   He stands complacently upon the principles of natural magic; he is conscious of eminent success in his profession; and, moreover, his digestion is excellent.   Therefore his study is but little upon the Bible.
  This particular Doctor and his apothecaries, moreover, are guilty of certain frauds and abuses of privilege

which net each of them a substantial profit. How is this
end accomplished? I have been unable to find any law
or edict promulgated in England before 1511 — the
date of Henry the Eighth's "Act for Appointing of Physicians and Surgeons" — designed to regulate the practice of physicians and control the traffic of chemists; [48]
and, in the fourteenth century, literary allusions to
abuses prevalent among the medical fraternity are scant.[49]
But a brief review of the violent controversy waged
about the middle of the seventeenth century between
Christopher Merritt and his opponents regarding the
malpractices of physicians and apothecaries may throw
some light upon the condition of affairs in Chaucer's
day; abuses deep-rooted and guarded by tradition may
well persist for three hundred years or more. Mr. Merritt, in *A Short View of the Frauds and Abuses Committed by Apothecaries* (London, 1669), charges among
other things that the chemists of his time load medicines
with honey and other cheaper ingredients and leave out
those of greater value, that they repeat long courses of
physic unadvisedly and needlessly when nothing or very
little is necessary to be done, and that they put what
rates they please upon their simples and compounds.
"But their principal Art of all," he continues, "is to
cry up and bring to patients such unworthy Physicians,
who through covetousness do, or through meanness of
parts or want, must comply with the Apothecaries Interest; and such Practisers they extol and cry up for good
Physicians, which some of them call more expressly good
Apothecaries Physicians; and such without doubt the
whole Company will raise unto a fame and practice.

But such as write only for the good of the patient, and not for the benefit of the Apothecary . . . they will endeavour to prevent their calling in, or shuffle out. Now this good Apothecaries Physician they describe by his frequent though needless visits, but especially the multitude of his Bills by his visiting twice a day or oftener (a very painful and careful Dr.) and by his writing new Medicines . . . making an Apothecaries Shop in the Patient's House, planting the Cupboards and Windows with Glasses and Galley-pots, and not a quarter of the whole made use of. He prescribes a medicine for every slight complaint, and never goes away from the Patient, or the Patient from him, without a Bill, for fear of the Apothecaries grumbling." [50]

Another writer, the anonymous author of *The Accomplisht Physician, the Honest Apothecary, and the Skilful Surgeon* (London, 1670), quite agrees with Dr. Merritt. He finds " that Physicians all, or most, being tied to particular Apothecaries, prescribe their Bills in terms so obscure that they force all chance patients to repair to their own Apothecaries, pretending a particular secret, which only they have the key to unlock; whereas in effect it's no other than the commonest of Medicines, disguised under an unusual name, on design to direct you to an Apothecary, between whom and the Physician there is a private compact of going snips. . . . The consequence hereof as to your particular patient is a double fraud; and as to Apothecaries in general, their number bearing the proportion of at least ten parts to one of noted Physicians, to whom allowing each his Covenant Apothecary, who constituting but one part of the ten, the remaining nine parts of the number are compelled either to sit still or to Quack for a livelyhood. . . . All Accomplished Physicians are likewise exposed to the manifest injuries from those Covenant Apothecaries, who being sent for by the Patients, after the short essay of a Cordial will overpower them by persuasions to call in a Doctor who shall be no other than his Covenant Physician, by which means the former Physician . . . shall be passed by. And should it happen, the sense of gratitude of the Patient should engage him to continue the use of his former Physician, yet this Covenant Apothecary shall privately cavil at every Bill and impute the appearance of every small pain . . . to his ill address in the Art of Physic, and shall not give over before he hath introduced his Covenanteer, whose authority in the fraud of a physic Bill he supposes to be most necessary." [51] This anatomy of seventeenth century abuses doubtless describes more or less accurately — perhaps with a degree of understatement — the relations existing between Chaucer's Doctor of Physic, such an Apothecaries' Physician, and his selected chemists, Covenant Apothecaries. And their friendship has been of long standing.

And finally, Chaucer suggests that his good Doctor so loves gold that he is inclined to prescribe *aurum potabile* upon every convenient occasion, not necessarily for the good of the patient (though "gold in phisik is a cordial") but because a little of it greatly increases the price of the medicine. Our Dr. Merritt notes a like practice: "To advance the prices, you shall hardly ever see a Bill without *Bezoar* or *Pearls* in it, to make peo-

ple think them very chargeable; whereas there is sometimes not above a grain or two of these dear ingredients
in it, and a few grains of these or Ambergrise doubles
or trebles the price of the Medicines, and are sure never
to be omitted in their Bills, besides the guilding of their
Pills, and covering their Boluses and Electuaries with
gold (which have only an imaginary and no real use in
Medicines so used) much inhanseth their prices, and a
rich *Cordial* inserted exceedingly advanceth most of
their Bills." [52]   So by gilding his cheap pills and charg-
ing high prices for them, by covering the electuaries [53]
received from his Covenant Apothecaries with a film of
gold, and by putting a few drops of *aurum potabile,* the
Elixir of Life, into his cordials, Chaucer's Doctor is
provided with such wealth that he is able to make a
holiday-pilgrimage to Canterbury, arrayed in clothes of
a blood-red and bluish-grey color lined with taffeta and
thin silk.   He is your complete fourteenth century physician.

Thus Chaucer's Doctor of Physic is, as we have seen,
a curious compound of contradictory elements which
make his character second only to that of the Wife of
Bath in complexity.   He acknowledges that he is acquainted with the works of sundry great medical authorities of ancient times, but one might suspect that the medical treatises with which he is thoroughly familiar are
perhaps as mythical as those of the old Esculapius; he
may be grounded in astrology, but it is to be feared that
his observance of "hours" and his astrological images
are potent somewhat less because he understands how to
control the power of the stars than because he knows

how to play upon human credulity; he comprehends the
mysteries of alchemy and the virtues of *aurum potabile*,
maybe, but one is privileged to doubt whether the gilding of his pills and electuaries is meant to be as powerful in working cures as in transmuting the base metal in
his purse to pure gold; perhaps the pleasant association
with his apothecaries is so much in the nature of a closed
corporation that the patients are practically excluded
from sharing in the profits; he *may* be a pious man who
has no time for reading the Bible or a rank materialist
who contemns religion — we are not sure.   In fact, we
cannot be absolutely sure about anything in the Doctor's
character.   Chaucer has created him so.   And it is this
very uncertainty as to his honesty, his honor, his sincerity,
and his learning which lends a certain life-like complexity to his character and actions; it is this human contra-
dictoriness which the author — doubtless with much
twinkling of eyes and thrusting of tongue in cheek —
seizes upon and develops by suggestion.   The result is
not merely a description of any particular man or of a
professional type, but a work of art — that very human
and complex Doctor of Physic himself.[54]

CHAPTER TWO

THE SUMMONER AND THE COOK

AMONG the Canterbury Pilgrims there are two, the Summoner and the Cook,[1] who bear upon their diseased bodies the marks of vicious living. Although the Summoner appears to stand in no awe of the Archdeacon's curse on account of his spiritual degeneracy, he may well consider the advisability of consulting the Doctor of Physic, or some other practising physician, regarding his aggravated physical disease. For all symptoms indicate that he is a dangerously sick man. Says the poet:

> A Somnour was ther with us in that place,
> That hadde a fyr-reed cherubinnes face,
> For sawcefleem he was, with eyen narwe.
> As hoot he was, and lecherous, as a sparwe;
> With scalled browes blake, and piled berd;
> Of his visage children were aferd.
> Ther nas quik-silver, litarge, ne brimstoon,
> Boras, ceruce, ne oille of tartre noon,
> Ne oynement that wolde clense and byte,
> That him mighte helpen of his whelkes whyte,
> Nor of the knobbes sittinge on his chekes.
> Wel loved he garleek, oynons, and eek lekes,
> And for to drinken strong wyn, reed as blood.
>
> (*C. T.*, A, 623 ff.)

If one may put faith in the accuracy of Chaucer's observation and description of the case, together with his

suggestion of the possible causes of the ailment and his
intimation of the remedies which ordinarily might be
expected to work a cure, and if a layman might venture
upon a diagnosis, by the card, according to the medical
lore of the Middle Ages, it would seem that the Summoner has been afflicted with a species of morphea known
as *gutta rosacea*, which has already been allowed to develop into that kind of leprosy called *alopicia*.

He who would seek to unravel the utter confusion of
terms applied by mediaeval medical writers to different
contagious and non-contagious skin diseases, sets for himself an almost impossible task.   Each author classifies
and reclassifies, divides once and again to suit his own
pleasure, so that in the end a perplexed reader can
scarcely distinguish psora from leuce, albaras from
melos, or impetigo from morphea.   Lanfrank attempts
to bring order out of chaos,[2] but his fraternal enemy,
Guy de Chauliac, impatiently finds his conclusions far
from satisfactory.   In spite of wide differences of opinion, however, I gather that morphea — by whatever
name it may be designated — is a skin disease resulting
from certain impurities in the blood, and that there are
three or four species of it corresponding to the four
natural humours of the body.   That " cursed monk dan
Constantyn " — whose work Chaucer mentions (*C. T.*,
E, 1811)[3] — says: " Morphea is a corruption of the
blood from which the skin of the body is nourished, or it
may be an affection of the intercutaneous flesh.   The general cause of it may be found in the weakening of the digestive virtue; for when the digestive virtue is exhausted,
the blood which should nourish the skin is corrupted."[4]

Gilbertus Anglicus — Chaucer's " Gilbertyn " (*C. T.*,
A, 434) — is of the opinion that the immediate or " antecedent causes are the four humours. The type that
has its origin in blood, *ex sanguine*, is more akin to
leprosy. Each several humour imparts its own color to
the skin: the morphea which comes from a corruption
of blood is of a reddish color; that which originates in
cholera is of a citron color; in salt phlegm, *de salso
flegme*, of a golden-yellow color; in natural phlegm, of
a white color; and that which proceeds from melancholia
is black." [5]

Now we may suppose that the type of morphea which
is produced *de sanguine* and which covers the skin of the
face with livid red pustules is to be identified with the
gutta rosacea of various authors. Bartholomaeus de
Glanvilla suggests as much. " Morphea is specks in the
skin, and originates from a corruption of meat and
drink. And that which is leprosy in the flesh is morphea
in the skin; though morphea is in the skin alone, and
leprosy is in both the flesh and skin. Morphea is in-
curable if the skin does not bleed when it is pricked with
a needle; but if it bleeds, then it is curable. This infection differs but little from what is called *gutta rosacea*,
which covers the face with small and soft pimples." [6]
And Bernardus de Gordon, whose account is similar to
that of Bartholomew, leaves no doubt as to the identity
of the two diseases: " And if it (morphea) has its origin
de sanguine and appears in the face, it is called *gutta
rosacea.*" [7]

Still further and more detailed descriptions of this
malady, together with discussions of causes and remedies

for effecting cures, may be found in almost every medical work of any importance dating from Chaucer's century. Lanfrank says: " *Gutta rosacea* is a malady which turns the skin of a man's face from its natural color and makes the face red. It originates in the corruption of humours in the skin." [8]   Andrew Boorde, in a description of a " Sawceflewme Face " found in his *Dietary*, remarks: " *Gutta rosacea* are the Latin words that designate this malady; in English it is called ' a sauce fleume face,' and the symptoms of it are a redness about the nose and cheeks together with small pimples; it is a privy sign of leprosy. . . . This infection comes of evil diet, and a hot liver, and the disordering of a man's complexion in his youth, of late drink and great surfeiting." [9]   And a still further account is given by the later writers, Willan and Thomas Bateman, under the head of Acne *rosacea*, to which is appended the note, " This is the *gutta rosea*, or *rosacea*, of authors " : " This form of Acne differs in several respects from the preceding species (Acne *simplex*, *punctata*, and *indurata*). In addition to an eruption of small suppurating tubercles, there is also a shining redness, and an irregular granulated appearance of the skin of that part of the face which is affected. The redness commonly appears first at the end of the nose, and afterwards spreads from both sides of the nose to the cheeks, the whole of which, however, it seldom covers. In the commencement it is not uniformly vivid; but is paler in the morning, and readily increased to an intense red after dinner, or at any time if a glass of wine or spirits be taken. . . . This species of Acne seldom occurs in early life . . . ; in general it does not appear before the age of forty; but it may be produced in any person by the constant, immoderate use of wine and spiritous liquors. The greater part of the face, even the forehead and the chin, are often affected in these cases; but the nose especially becomes tumid, and of a fiery red color. . . . At this period of life, too, the colour of Acne *rosacea* becomes darker and more livid; and if suppuration take place in any of the tubercles, they ulcerate unfavorably, and do not readily assume a healing disposition." [10] This is a rather accurate description, I take it, of the Summoner's appearance in the earlier stages of his disease; but not even the most violent case of *gutta rosacea* can account for his "scalled browes blake and piled berd," nor for his "narwe" eyes, nor for the "whelkes whyte" and the "knobbes" sitting on his cheeks. Though there is, of course, actually no relation between any of these skin diseases and leprosy proper,[11] Chaucer is evidently following the medical opinion of his time in supposing that the "sawce-fleem" has already developed into that type of leprosy which is produced *de sanguine*.

In all the works of medical writers from the ancient Greeks and Arabians on down to the authors who may be said to have laid the foundations of modern medicine, the general signs of elephantiasis or leprosy are found to be about the same.[12] Says Bernardus de Gordon: "The infallible signs are these: A falling out and a scabbiness of the eyebrows, a roundness (*rotunditas*) of the eyes, and an enlargement of the nostrils externally and a contraction internally. Breathing becomes difficult, and the patient speaks as if through the nose;

on the face there is a kind of pallor verging upon the
deathly, and the appearance of the face is terrible with
its fixed look. . . .   The secret signs in the beginning
are these: the color of the face is reddish inclining to
blackness, the breathing begins to alter, and the voice
becomes hoarse." [13]   Bartholomaeus de Glanvilla agrees:
" In those afflicted with leprosy the flesh is perceptibly
corrupted, the eyes and eyelids are corrugated or wrin-
kled (*corrugantur*) and have a certain glitter; the nostrils are constricted; and the voice becomes raucous." [14]
And John of Gaddesden — Chaucer's "Gatesden"
(*C. T.*, A, 434) — definitely associates the general
symptoms with *gutta rosacea:* " In the first place you
must note if the usual red color of the face tends toward
a black hue, and if the patient suffers from *gutta rosacea*
in his nose and face . . . if he sweats much and his
hair begins to get thin and sparse. . . .   In these cases
the color of the body tends towards black; the patient is
afflicted with laboured breathing and a husky voice
(*strictura anhelitus et vocis*) . . . thinness and falling
of the hair, *rotunditas* of the eyes, and a greasiness of the
skin." [15]   Even the general signs of elephantiasis agree,
it will be observed, with the physiognomical characteristics which Chaucer has attributed to the Summoner.

It must also be noted that the earlier of our modern
writers on the science of medicine describe the elephantiasis of the Greeks merely as a species of lepra, of which
they are acquainted with four types: namely, the ele-
phantia, leonina, alopicia, and tyria, each being associated with one of the four various humours of the body.
This arrangement dates first from Alsaharavius.[16]   For

example, as Bartholomaeus has it: " In foure manner wise Lepra is diuerse, as the foure humours be passingly and diuersely medled. One manner Lepra commeth of pure Melancholia, and is called *Elephancia,* and hath that name of the Elephant, that is a full great beast and large. For this euill grieueth and noieth the patient passing strongly and sore. The second commeth of melancholy and fleme, and is called *Tiria,* or Serpintina; and hath yt name of an adder that is called *Tirus.* For as an Adder leaueth lightlye his skin and his scale, so he that hath this manner Lepra is oft stript and pilled and full of scales. The third manner of Lepra commeth of melancholy, infecting of blood, and is called *Alopicia,* and *Vulpina.* . . . The Foxe hath a propertie, that his haire falleth in Summer for heat of bloud in the liuer; so oft his haire that hath this euill falleth from his browes, and from other places. The fourth manner Leperhood commeth of red Cholera, corrupt in the members with melancholy, and is called *Leonina.*" [17]

Now in our discussion of the Summoner we are concerned only with the third species, *alopicia,* which is a disease of the flesh growing out of an infection of the humour, blood, and ordinarily associated with the skin disease, *gutta rosacea,* which we have found to be a kind of morphea originating *de sanguine.* Arnoldus de Villa Nova — Chaucer's " Arnold of the Newe Toun " (*C. T.,* G, 1428) — describes it at considerable length: " Alopicia is a species of leprosy which is produced *ex sanguine adjusto.* This type is marked by a complete depilation of the eyebrows and beard. The eyes of the patient become inflated (*inflantur*) and exceedingly red.

Pimples of a reddish color appear in the face and even on the whole body, from which runs corruption mixed with blood; the veins are visible on the breast; and the odor of these and the perspiration and of the breath are loathsome. The cheeks swell up." [18] Gilbertus Anglicus, after giving a like account of the origin of the name and of the cause of the malady — " sit autem ex sanguine corrupto et superabundante, et negligentia diete et flommie " — continues: " Moreover, reddish-yellow spots full of phlegm appear upon the skin. . . . The eyes are watery and bloodshot; the eyebrows and eyelashes scale off, and the eyelids are turned wrong side out and thickened (*inversantur et ingrossantur*). . . . Nay, even the whole body and the face are spread with reddish spots and pimples, and the excessively tender flesh is always smeared over with a kind of whitish flatulence." [19] Surely when one looks closely at the Summoner, there can be no doubt that he is suffering from *alopicia.* The small pimples which might once have indicated *gutta rosacea* have developed into great matter-infected pustules — " whelkes whyte " and " knobbes " — of true leprosy. His eyebrows have nearly all fallen out,[20] and in place of them there is discovered a scabby, scurfy mark of black color; his beard, too, has the scall to such an extent that it is thin and slight. His eyes are swollen and inflamed to a violent red, and the lids, already deprived of lashes, are enlarged and corrugated so that he is able to see only through narrow slits between them. His eyes, as Chaucer says, are " narwe." It is not to be wondered at that children are afraid of such a face! And if one might broadly interpret, in the light

of the foregoing material, the " stif burdoun " which
he bears to the Pardoner's little love song (*C. T.*, A,
673) and his crying out as if he were mad after a drink
of blood-red wine, his voice has possibly that rough and
husky quality spoken of by medical men as an infallible
sign of the leper.

Chaucer has indicated, moreover, the two principal
causes of the disease: the Summoner is " lecherous as a
sparwe," and is accustomed to the eating of onions, garlic, and leeks and to the drinking of strong wine red as
blood. The rascal is either criminally ignorant or fool-
ishly indifferent. He might have learned from any physician of his time, or before, that leprosy may be contracted by illicit association with women infected with
it [21] (in mediaeval medicine lepra is possibly confused
with syphilis), that garlic, onions, and leeks produce
evil humours in the blood, and that red wine of all
others is the most powerful and heating of drinks. Bartholomaeus, for example, fathers the opinion that leprosy " commeth of fleshlye lyking, by a woman soone
after that a leprous man hath laye by her. . . . And
sometimes it commeth of too hot meates, as long use of
strong pepper, and of garlike, and of such other. And
sometimes of corrupt meates, and of meates that be soone
corrupt, as of meselyd Hogges, of flesh that haue peeces
therein, and is infected with such poison and greines.
And of uncleane wine and corrupt." [22] The reckless
Summoner might have found by consulting the *Isogoge*
of Joannitius that " certain kinds of vegetables produce
evil humours: for instance, nasturtium, mustard, and
garlic beget reddish bile; lentils, cabbage, and the meat

of old goats and beeves produce black bile." [23]　Paulus Aegenita might have informed him that the " onion, garlic, leek and dog-leek, being of an acrid nature, warm the body, attenuate and cut the thick humours contained in it; when twice boiled, they give little nourishment, and when unboiled they do not nourish at all.　Garlic is more deobstruent and diaphoretic than the others. . . . And regarding pot-herbs in general, the raw, when eaten, furnish worse juices than the boiled, as they have more excrementatious juice." [24]　Boorde might have warned him that " onyons doth prouoke a man to veneryous actes and to sompnolence " and that " he that is infectyd wyth any of the four kynds of lepored must refrayne from al maner of wynes, and from new drynkes, and stronge ale; let hym beware of ryot and surfeytynge." [25]　For as Bartholomaeus puts it, " Red wine that is full redde as bloud is most strong, and grieueth much the head, and noieth the wit, and maketh strong dronkennesse," [26] or according to Paulus, " Wine in general is nutritious but that which is red and thick is more particularly so; but its juices are not good." [27]　The Summoner, however, has either not read or has treated with contempt the medical authorities.　Having once contracted *alopicia* by riotous and lascivious living, by the immoderate use of unwholesome meats and wines, he further aggravates it by the same foolhardy practices.

Finally, it must be observed that Chaucer has apparently lifted the remedies, which he suggests have already been used in this case without effect, directly from the medical books.

> Ther nas quik-silver, litarge, ne brimstoon,
> Boras, ceruce, ne oille of tartre noon,
> Ne oynement that wolde clense and byte,
> That him mighte helpen of his whelkes whyte.

Lanfrank's prescription for the cure of *gutta rosacea* includes " litargiri, auripigmenti, sulphuris viui, viridis eris, oleum tartarinum, argenty viui," [28] and Guy de Chauliac would treat the same disease with " aigre de citron, ceruse, argent vif, borax, soulphre et alun, avec huil de tartre." [29]   For the more violent cases of skin disorders and for leprosy, Guy recommends the careful and judicious use of " le medicament corrosif " or perhaps of " le medicament caustique," [30] the chief ingredient of which is arsenic — and to which Chaucer clearly refers when he speaks of the " oynement that wolde clense and byte."   The poet is to be highly commended for his wisdom in ignoring the empirical remedy, composed largely of an adder variously prepared, which most of the medical men of his time employ.

That drunken reprobate, the Cook, is also afflicted with a kind of cutaneous eruption, which is less malignant than that of the Summoner but perhaps more offensive to the eye.   Chaucer professes an appreciation of his culinary art but cannot help observing, rather ruefully, the unsightly physical impediment calculated to suppress any too violent gustatory ardor:

> But greet harm was it, as it thoughte me,
> That on his shine a mormal hadde he.
>   (*C. T.*, A, 385 ff.).

It is generally agreed, it seems, that the " mormal "
from which the Cook suffers is to be identified with what
mediaeval medical writers call *malum mortuum.*[31]   This
disease, which is considered under separate headings by
most of the authors whom I have consulted, must not be
confused with cancer or gangrene; it appears to be a
species of ulcerated, dry-scabbed apostema produced by
corruption in the blood of natural melancholia or sometimes of melancholia combined with *salsum phlegma.*

As to the causes and appearance of the malady Theo-
doricus is explicit: " *Malum mortuum* is an infirmity
infecting the arms and shins of the patient.   It consists
of dry ulcers, slightly generative at times of bloody
matter, which are produced sometimes from a corruption
of pure melancholia and sometimes from melancholia
mixed with salt phlegm.   If the disease have its origin in
pure melancholia, it is recognised by black pustules without itching; but if salt phlegm be involved, the apostema
becomes livid with itching and gripings." [32]   Bernardus
de Gordon — Chaucer's " Bernard " (*C. T.*, A, 434)
— gives a still fuller account: " *Malum mortuum* is a
species of scabies, which arises from corrupted natural
melancholia or from melancholia mixed with salt
phlegm.   The marks of it are large pustules of a leaden
or black color, scabbed, and exceedingly fetid, though
suppuration and discharge do not occur; and it is frequently accompanied by a certain insensibility in the
places affected.   In appearance it is most unsightly, coming out as it does on the hip-bones and often on the shin-
bones.   Moreover, the cause of this scabies is much consuming of melancholic foods, retention of catamenia,

and the like." [33]   And John of Gaddesden concludes
his discussion " De malo mortuo " with the remark:
" And it is caused by the consumption of melancholic
foods, such as the flesh of cattle and salt fish, and by
intercourse with a woman *menstruata* or leprous or
wormy." [34]   One may suspect that the Cook's " mormal " is of the type which is produced from a corruption of melancholia mixed with salt phlegm and that he
is continually troubled with a severe itching, for as Lanfrank says: " Icchinge and scabbe cometh of salt humours, and nature hath abhominacioun therof, and put-
teth hem out of the skyn, and this falleth ofte of salt
metis and sharpe metis and of wijn that is strong; and
it falleth ofte to hem that wakith and traveilith and
usith no bathing and werith no lynnen clothis.   And this
is oon of the siknes that is contagious." [35]

To understand the prurient nature and particularly
the causes of *malum mortuum* and of *alopicia* is to have
a rather intimate acquaintance with the personalities and
probable secret lives of Roger Hogge of Ware and the
Summoner.   It would be exceedingly precarious to assume that in creating these characters Chaucer intends
them to be considered as types or representatives of physical diseases or even that medical material has furnished
the main source of inspiration for his artistic production.
These knaves of fourteenth century England are far
too sentient and vitally human to have been constructed
in accordance with any mechanical principle; they
breathe, enjoy life, suffer pain, and carry on their nefarious practices with motivated reactions as precisely ad-
justed as those of ordinary mortals.   Nor can they be

thought of merely as life-sized portraits of particular men known to the poet; they are faithful transcripts from life, to be sure, but they are too inevitably themselves in their own right to be considered as descriptive replicas of actual historical personages. The materials used in the creation of these characters are drawn, as is usual with Chaucer, from an inexhaustible wealth of observations of men and their ways, of their emotions and contradictory desires, their hidden motives, impulses, and cross-purposes; and out of the fusion by the creative imagination of otherwise incoherent elements emerges the miracle, the unified and unique personalities respectively of the Summoner and the Cook. The character of each is individual and, as it were, all of a single piece; and every separate element of it is inextricably bound up with and affected by the ravages of physical disease. As in real life, the symptoms of these maladies appearing upon the face and body become the infallible indices of inward character.

In the General Prologue information is given to the effect that the Cook is preëminent in his profession, that he knows what a draught of London ale is like, and that he is afflicted with a mormal (*C. T.*, A, 381–387). This meagre characterization appears at first to be merely indecisive sketching, but the items concerning London ale and the mormal contain in solution, so to speak, all the elements of personality afterwards revealed. When it is recalled that *malum mortuum* is caused in the first place by uncleanly personal habits, such as lack of frequent bathing and the continuous wearing of soiled clothes, by the eating of melancholic foods and the drinking of strong wines, and by disgraceful association with diseased and filthy women, then no one need be surprised at Roger Hogge's display of inebriety, slack morals, and predilection for salacious stories. A cook with a mormal is precisely the sort of person who might be expected to devour all tainted meats and spoiled victuals which he cannot palm off on long-suffering patrons of his art. Our Host directly charges him with bad dealings:

> For many a pastee hastow laten blood,
> And many a Jakke of Dover hastow sold
> That hath been twyes hoot and twyes cold.
> Of many a pilgrim hastow Cristes curs,
> For of thy persly yet they fare the wors,
> That they han eten with thy stubbel-goos;
> For in thy shoppe is many a flye loos.
>
> (*C. T.*, A, 4346, ff.).

The Cook confesses good-naturedly enough that it is true, but remarks, " Sooth pley, quaad pley." On the drab morning following a strenuous night of debauchery — the Host suspects that wine and women are involved — his dilapidated appearance is perhaps not less repulsive than his mormal. His face is haggard and pale, his eyes dazed because of drunkenness and lack of sleep, and when he gapes his sour breath so infects the air that the Maunciple is nauseated and reproves him sharply. In fact, Roger is so drunk with " wyn ape " that his rage against his critic is speechless; having fallen from his horse, he has to be helped up again; and in spite of the Host's sympathetic understanding and defense of his infirmity, he is not put in good humor again until given another long drink of wine (*C. T.*, H, 25–85). His disease might indicate, moreover, that he is just the kind of man likely to claw the Reeve on the back for joy of a dirty tale (*C. T.*, A, 4326), and to begin one of his own featuring a jolly hero given to gaming, rioting in taverns, and reveling in stews, and a heroine who under cover of keeping a shop " swyved for hir sustenance " (*C. T.*, A, 4366 ff.).   His acquaintance with such persons has probably been too intimate for his own good.   Such is the Cook who suffers from a mormal and who knows a draught of London ale.

Likewise, the Summoner of boorish action and speech is in some measure the Summoner who has brought upon himself a terrible disease.   His naturally cunning and grasping mind is at times dulled and his moral sense apparently atrophied by the ravages of *alopicia* and by the unabated malpractices which originally produced it. He continues to devour raw and innutritious vegetables and to swill quantities of wine red as blood, crowning himself in drunken foolery with a garland and in mockery arming himself with a buckler made of a cake.   And as the fiery intoxicant courses through his veins, he parrots the few Latin terms which his numbed intelligence has been able to catch from the jargon of Ecclesiastical Courts.   He is out upon a hilarious excursion, to be sure, but he doubtless runs true to form.   In exchange for sundry quarts of wine it has long been his custom to wink at the blatant immorality of those able to buy immunity from the exercise of his authority.   The Friar's indignant generalization regarding summoners is doubtless only too applicable in this instance:

Pardee, ye may wel knowe by the name,
That of a somnour may no good be sayd; . . .
A somnour is a renner up and doun
With mandements for fornicacioun,
And is y-bet at every tounes ende

(*C. T.*, D, 1280 ff.).

Though Chaucer does not say so, our Summoner's tainted
blood strongly indicates that the Archdeacon's messenger has called too promiscuously upon certain erring
women of the diocese with other than the professional
purpose of haling them into Court. This is the man
who makes shocking revelations regarding the untidy
dwelling-place of friars in Hell (*C. T.*, D, 1685–
1708),[36] and who entertains the Canterbury Pilgrims
with an unsavory but cleverly told story about a friar's
attempt to acquire a justly proportionate share in an
evanescent legacy. This is the cunning and observant
rascal who surmises that the Archdeacon's absolution
and *significavit* are effective only as a fraudulent means
of extracting money from the offender's purse, and who
by passing on this knowledge to his acquaintances teaches
contempt for the Court and no doubt secures for himself a steady income (*C. T.*, A, 655). Such in brief
is the Summoner who is afflicted with leprosy. The
disease emphasised does not make the man, but it is indicative of much that the poet leaves unrecorded and
consideration of it throws into high relief the elements
of character portrayed.

CHAPTER THREE

THE PARDONER'S SECRET

APPARENT inconsistencies in Chaucer's portrayal of the Pardoner have, up to this time, received no quite satisfactory explanation. Offering contemporary historical evidence, J. J. Jusserand arrives at the conclusion that in the presentation of this character " there is not the slightest exaggeration in Chaucer, that he knew well the Pardoners of his time, and described them exactly as they were, and that he did not add a word, not justified by what he saw, in order to win our laughter or to enliven his description." [1] Professor Tupper, in developing his theory of Chaucer's architectonic use of the Seven Deadly Sins *motif* in the composition of the *Canterbury Tales*, asserts in one place [2] that the " rascal is formally illustrating " the Sins of Gluttony and Avarice, in another,[3] that he is " exemplifying only the vices of the tavern," and in still another,[4] that he must be considered " a typical glutton or tavern-reveler." And Professor Kittredge, in his attempt to harmonise certain conflicting elements in both character and story, seeks a pleasant but unconvincing solution of the problem in the supposition that this " one lost soul among the Canterbury Pilgrims," acting for the most part from the basest of motives, suffers for a single moment from a " paroxysm of agonized sincerity." [5] Still in spite of these illuminating investigations, I cannot help feeling that the Pardoner's character in its relation to his personal appearance, his impudent confessions of moral delinquency and fraud, and his apparently unreasonable anger against the Host need further treatment.[6]

Critics have heretofore given too little attention, perhaps, to the possible significance of those supposedly accidental items of personal appearance which Chaucer is so fond of introducing, seemingly at random, in the presentation of his characters. The Prioress, to be sure, with her blue eyes, her soft, red mouth, and broad forehead has been said to represent the conventional mediaeval type of feminine beauty;[7] Chaucer's pronouncement that the joined eyebrows of Criseyde constitutes her only blemish has been considered the result of an inherited literary taste.[8] These are beginnings of investigations along right lines. But to our modern minds the Pardoner's physical peculiarities are not, at first sight, vitally related to his immoral character; they may seem, after we have become acquainted with him, entirely appropriate and perhaps rather humours, but not essential. It will be recalled that he has long, straight hair as yellow as wax, which hangs thinly spread over his shoulders, each hair to itself; his eyes are wide open and glaring like those of a hare; his voice is high-pitched and as " thin " as that of a goat; he is entirely without any indication of a beard; and, if we may judge from the description which he gives of himself in the act of delivering one of his powerful sermons, his neck is long and scrawny:

> Than peyne I me to strecche forth the nekke,
> And est and west upon the peple I bekke,
> As doth a dowe sitting on a berne
>
> (*C. T.*, C, 395 ff.).

What did these physical characteristics signify to the mediaeval mind? Before we can grasp the full meaning of the poet's purpose in his careful delineation of the Canterbury Pilgrims or offer adequate criticism of the product of his artistry, it becomes necessary to acquire as nearly as possible the point of view with which the fourteenth century Englishman looked upon the world. It is not by chance that Chaucer, the artist, hits upon these particular items of personal appearance rather than upon others; nor does he fortuitously invest the Pardoner with them rather than the Cook or the Summoner. Here, as usual, Chaucer knows what he is about. His selection of both form and feature given to many of his characters is determined in large measure or at least influenced, I believe, by that universally popular class of " scientific " literature known to mediaeval readers as the physiognomies. Now physiognomy is nothing more than the art of discovering the characteristic qualities of the mind or temper of a man by observation of his form and the movements of his face or body, or both. Since, as we have seen, celestial influences are powerful in determining the physical constitution and in fashioning the mental complexion of a human being, the science or art of physiognomy is bound up with and is firmly grounded upon the principles of astrology. For Chaucer and for every educated man of his time this physiognomical lore made it possible to judge with a certain degree of accuracy and with approximate infallibility the inner character of a man from a study of his form and features. According to well defined regulations they might interpret every line of the face, every shape and color of the eyes, and any tone of the voice. What, then, could be more natural than that Chaucer, who has before him a mediaeval audience no doubt familiar with physiognomical and astrological principles at least in a popularised form, should consult the physiognomies for suggestions as to the physical characteristics most appropriate for the men and women whom he wishes to introduce to his special audience?

With this idea in mind, let us proceed to examine what the physiognomies might have to say regarding the Pardoner's features in relation to his character. Antonius Polemon Laodicensis,[9] the most famous of the ancient physiognomists and perhaps the founder of the science, says of glaring eyes prominently set that they indicate a " man given to folly, a glutton, a libertine, and a drunkard ";[10] and an early anonymous author, whose work is evidently based upon that of Polemon, informs us that the person with " outstanding, bright eyes from which the eyelids have a tendency to withdraw, and with a high-pitched or shrill voice, is impudent and most dangerous." [11] The Middle English version of the *Secreta Secretorum,* which was certainly known to Chaucer (*C. T.,* G, 1447), also agrees that among other tokens of a shameless man are " ryst opyn eighyn and glysinge," and adds the significant remark that " tho that haue the voyce hei, smale and swete and pleasaunt, bene neshe and haue lytill of manhode, and i-likened to women." [12]   Here, precisely as in Chaucer's portrayal of the Pardoner, we find that the high, thin voice together with glaring eyes are directly associated with shameless impudence, gluttony, and licentiousness. Long and soft hair, immoderately fine in texture and reddish or yellow in color " indicates an impoverished blood, lack of virility, and effeminacy of mind; and the sparser the hair, the more cunning and deceptive is the man." [13] Goclenius is of the opinion that a " long, slim neck is a sign of garrulity, haughtiness of spirit, and of evil habits " and that " a man beardless by nature is endowed with a fondness for women and for crafty dealings, inasmuch as he is impotent in performing the works of Venus.   Yet repeatedly he exhibits a rare and singular intellectual cleverness.   Examples are in evidence." [14] The Pardoner is an example.   That he is an abandoned rascal delighting in hypocrisy and possessed of a colossal impudence, no one can doubt after hearing his shameless confession and witnessing his attempt to hypnotise the Host; that he is a glutton and a perhaps typical tavern reveler is revealed by the fact that he calls for cakes and ale before he can properly relate a " moral tale "; that he is a man of no mean ingenuity and of considerable cleverness is proclaimed by the great amount of his yearly income from the practice of chicanery and fraud; and that his lack of beard and his goat-like voice indicate impotence, or at least effeminacy, Chaucer plainly affirms:

> A voys he hadde as smal as hath a goot;
> No berd hadde he, ne never sholde have,

As smothe it was as it were late y-shave;
I trowe he were a gelding or a mare.

(C. T., A, 688 ff.).

In this passage the poet suggests the secret of the
Pardoner; he is most unfortunate in his birth. He carries upon his body and has stamped upon his mind and
character the marks of what is known to mediaeval physiognomists as a *eunuchus ex nativitate.* The Sophist Admantius (*ca.* the middle of the fourth century) devotes
one whole section to eunuchs of this type: " Those who
are eunuchs by fault of nature possess certain evil characteristics which distinguish them from other men; they
are usually cruel, crafty, and vicious, but some are more
so than others." [15] The Greek version of Polemon gives
a similar account, but draws a sharp distinction between
the *eunuchus ex nativitate* and the *eunuchus qui castratus
est:* " Eunuchs who are the result of defective procrea-
tion are generally of the same type of mind, crafty and
vicious, though some indeed merely execute other men's
trickery. But he who has been made a eunuch differs in
one respect: while he is brave and daring in whatever he
may attempt, he has a more noble nature and is without
the power of sustained effort." [16] Rasis, an eminent
Arabian physician of the tenth century,[17] adds a few
details regarding physical appearance: " A eunuch is always a man of evil habits; he is foolish, lustful and
presumptuous. He, however, who *castratus non fuit, sed
sine testiculis natus vel parvissimos habens eunuchus ap-
paret* and who never has a beard,[18] is worse." [19] The
anonymous author mentioned above, discussing the signifi-

cance of wide-open, glaring eyes, says further: " Eyes
wide-open, glaring, and moving slowly with an ingratiat-
ing air correspond with the description which Polemon,
the great author himself, gives of a eunuch said to have
been famous in his time.   He assigns other physical characteristics to this person as follows: a prominent forehead, thin neck, a feminine voice and womanly words.
He says that this man, because of the impatience of the
lust he endured, was also foul-mouthed and audacious,
continually planning evil deeds, for he was said to have
sold deadly poison secretly." [20]

Explanations of such physical phenomena are not lacking.   Bartholomaeus Anglicus, speaking of the hair, remarks: " Also gelded men are not balde, and that is for
chaungynge of theyr complexyon, and for maystery of
colde, and closith and stoppth ye poores of skyne of ye
heed and holyth togideres ye fumosite yt it maye not
passe and be wasted.   But in wymen and in gelded men
other heer fallyth and faylyth." [21]   He is also perfectly
familiar with the reason for the " acute " voice: " Males
haue stronger synewes and stringes than chyldren, and
vngelded haue stronger than gelded. And for febylnes
and synewes ye voys of theum yt ben gelded is lyke ye
voys of females." [22]   Nor is he at a loss for an explanation of the growth of beard.   " And therfore," he continues, " the berde is nedefull helpynge for chekes and
token of vertu and strengthe of kendely heet.   And therfore a man hath a berde and not a woman; for a man is
kyndly more hote than a woman.   And therfore in a
man ye smoke that is matere of heer encreasyth more
than in a woman.   And for kynde suffiseth not to waste

that smoke, he puttith and dryueth it out by two places, in the heed and in the berde. And therfore somtyme wymen hote and moyste of complexyon haue berdes. And in lyke wyse men of colde and drye complexyon haue lytyll berdes, and therfore in men yt ben gelded growe noo berdes. For they haue loste the hote membre that sholde brede the hote humour and smoke, the matere of heer." [23] Whatever may be said of Chaucer's knowl- edge of physiognomy, it is quite apparent that he is per- fectly at home in the medical science of his time. His Pardoner is, in respect to hair and voice, scientifically correct.

Most of the authorities cited above, it will be observed, give Polemon as the authority upon the subject of eunuchs. It may be well, therefore, to present here in full the original sketch from which later writers evi- dently drew their material. Polemon pretends to be describing a celebrated eunuch of his own time, whose name, he affirms, he does not know. One anonymous author remarks, however, that " he is understood to have had a certain Favorinus in mind." [24] That being the case, this may be Favorinus of Arles — a contemporary and a political opponent of Polemon — whose infirmity is ridiculed in Lucian's *Eunuchus* and whose life is touched upon by Philostratus in his *Lives of the So- phists.*[25] The whole passage as it appears in the Arabic and Latin versions of Polemon is as follows: " When the eye is wide open and, like marble, glitters or corus- cates, it indicates a shameless lack of modesty. This quality of the eyes is observed in a man who is not like other men, *ut eunuchus qui tamen non castratus est, sed*

sine testiculis natus. I have known, however, only one
man of this kind. He was lustful and dissolute above
all moderation — and his eyes were as I have described
above. He had a prominent forehead, a long, thin neck,
and his cries were like those of a woman. He took particular care of his person by nurturing his abundant hair,
rubbing his body with medicated unguents, and by employing every expedient that might excite a desire for
sexual pleasure. He was given to scornful jesting, and
whatever came into his mind he acted upon immediately.
Being learned in the Greek language, he was accustomed
to use that tongue most. He frequented cities and mar-
ket-places, meditating injustice and gathering men together in order that he might display evil. Above all
he was a very astute wizard, practising feats of legerde-
main and claiming the faculty of predicting life and
death for men; wherefore he so influenced people that
vast crowds of men and women flocked to him. Moreover, he persuaded men that he was able to force women
to them just as they sought women. And surreptitiously
he caused to transpire that which he had predicted. As an
instructor in the doing of evil he was a past master; he
collected all kinds of deadly poisons. And all the power
of his ingenuity was directed toward the performance
of these things. Whenever, therefore, you see eyes such
as I have described at the beginning of this disputation,
you may understand that their possessor is similar to this
kind of eunuch." [26]

Analysis of this particular passage reveals a marked
likeness in the characters, modes of thought, and bodily
characteristics of Favorinus and Chaucer's Pardoner.

Indeed, the parallelism is so close that it may well seem as if Chaucer may have had this account, or perhaps one of the wide-spread anonymous versions of it, before him as he wrote. The eyes of Favorinus are wide-open and shining or glittering like marble, his neck is long and thin, his voice like that of a woman, and he takes great pride in his abundantly long hair to which, as to his whole body, he makes frequent applications of ointments; the Pardoner's eyes are glaring like those of a hare, he stretches forth his thin neck like a dove on a barn, and he is so inordinately proud of his long, perfectly straight hair — probably greased to make it hang smooth — that he prefers to wear simply a cap rather than the hood of his profession (A, 675). Favorinus is, moreover, sensual, lustful, and dissolute above all measure; the Pardoner is lecherous — at least in thought and imagination — and a typical tavern reveler (C, 452). The former speaks Greek in his public harangues; the latter " saffrons " his " predicaciouns " with Latin in order to stir men to devotion (C, 345 ff.). Both rascals possess a remarkable knowledge of mob-psychology: crowds of men and women throng the forums and public places where Favorinus pursues his nefarious practices; thousands of unsophisticated people flock to hear the Pardoner's sermons and to behold and perhaps purchase his marvellous relics of saints. The Sophist is a most astute magician who, professing to have received his power from the occult world, proclaims an uncanny knowledge of, and control over the mysteries of life and death; a self-announced sorcerer with evil mind and polluted imagination who affirms his ability to force women to men even as men now seek women. The Pardoner is a shameless and impudent fraud who, bringing his spurious bulls and pardons all hot from the supreme spiritual authority at Rome, claims to exercise the power of life and death over the human soul; a colossal cynic who, cursed with a concupiscent mind and armed with false relics, offers to men a certain cure for jealousy — even though their wives are strumpets — and to women an easy absolution from the horrible sin of infidelity to their husbands. Both spit out venom under the hue of honesty or holiness (C, 420); both alike, urged on by a consuming avarice and cupidity, reap a golden harvest from their practices of villainy and fraud (C, 388, 455). Their minds not less than their bodies belong to the same type; their actions spring from like impulses; their purposes are formed and executed in a similar spirit. Only their fields of activity are different.[27] To Chaucer belongs great honor for having combined in the person and the tale of his Pardoner a complete psychological study of the mediaeval *eunuchus ex nativitate* and a mordant satire on the abuses practised in the church of his day.[28]

Considered in the light of the material presented in this investigation, certain problems which seem to have perplexed the critics become straightway clearer. After the Doctor has completed his pathetic account of Virginia, it will be remembered, the tender-hearted Host is so overcome with pity for the maid that he must either have a drink or listen to a merry tale to ease his pain of heart. He demands some " mirthe or japes " from the Pardoner, who appears quite willing to accommodate

him. Instantly, and unexpectedly, a protest comes from
the people of high rank:

> Nay! lat him telle us of no ribaudye;
> Tel us some moral thing, that we may lere
> Som wit, and thanne wol we gladly here.
>
> (*C. T.*, C, 324).

Why should the " gentils " suppose that when the Host
calls for a " merry tale," the Pardoner will relate a
filthy or obscene story? Professor Kittredge is of the
opinion that " what the Host wants is a ribald story "
and that the gentlefolk are justified by their association
with the noble " ecclesiaste," who is on his vacation, in
expecting it.[29] As a matter of fact, however, neither a
" merry tale " nor a " jape " is necessarily synonymous
with a ribald story in Chaucer. Sir Thopas is a "tale of
mirthe "; the extravaganza of Chauntecleer and Pertelote is called a " merry tale "; and the Host's little
pleasantry regarding Chaucer's shapely figure is a
" jape " (B, 1890). Nor is there any positive evidence
which would indicate that the Pilgrims of high rank
have had during the journey any close association whatever with the Pardoner. He has remained completely in
the background up to this time. But now when he comes
forward with alacrity at the call of the Host and speaks
of seeking inspiration for his story in a near-by tavern,
the gentlefolk, who are doubtless well acquainted with
the current physiognomical lore,[30] recognise the type immediately. They are able instantly to translate his physical peculiarities into terms of character. What only

could be expected from a *eunuchus ex nativitate?*
" Nay! " they cry, " let him tell us no ribald story."

The Pardoner's character having been given, however, Professor Kittredge's exposition of the dramatic
fitness of his cynical confession and excellent tale is admirable (*Chaucer and his Poetry,* pp. 214 ff.).   But that
the reprobate, near the end of his story, is so overcome by
the power of his own eloquence that he is betrayed into
a moment of sincerity, is unbelievable.   " The Pardoner," says Professor Kittredge, " has not always been
an assassin of souls.   He is a renegade, perhaps, from
some holy order.   Once he preached for Christ's sake;
and now, under the spell of the wonderful story he has
told and of recollections which stir within him, he suffers a very paroxysm of agonized sincerity."   But it
can last for only a moment.   Regaining his wonted
impudence after the unexpected " emotional crisis," he
offers his pardons and relics for sale to the Pilgrims
themselves, suggesting that the Host be first to come
forward.   Harry Baily, not understanding that the rascal has had a " moral convulsion," answers with a
" rough jocularity " which precipitates the furious anger of the rebuffed Pardoner.   It is, let us say, a beautiful theory.   We should like to believe that even this
" lost soul " may be touched by the beautiful and the
tragic.

But unfortunately, knowing his secret as we now do,
we are forced to a different interpretation of his concluding remark:

> . . . and, lo, sirs, thus I preche.

And Jesu Crist, that is our soules leche,

So graunte yow his pardon to receyve,
For that is best; I wol yow nat decyve (C, 915).

We see in this only a preparation for his proposed mas-
ter-stroke of deception. He has already revealed with
amazing frankness the fraud which he is accustomed to
practice upon his hearers; he has illustrated with eloquence and dramatic power the manner in which results
are obtained in his profession. He is evidently proud of
his skill. To hypnotize the Pilgrims into buying relics
after he has declared their worthlessness and his own
perfidy, would constitute the crowning success of his
career. Turning suddenly to them, he says in effect:
"Lo, sirs, this is the way I preach to *ignorant* people.
But *you* are my friends; may God grant that *you* may
receive the pardon of Jesus Christ; I would never de-
ceive *you!* Come, now, and kiss this relic." This
is, moreover, the correct manner in which to conclude
a well-constructed oration; having no customary audience, he is compelled to make shift with an appeal to the
Pilgrims themselves. But he reckons without his Host!
That he should be taken for a fool somewhat angers
the estimable inn-keeper, who replies in his momentary
heat with a direct allusion to the Pardoner's infirmity:

I wolde I hadde thy coillons in myn hond
In stede of relikes or of seintuarie.

It is small wonder that the Pardoner begins to redden at
this unmannerly probing of his secret and that he should
be speechless with rage when the Host continues with
withering sarcasm and scorn,

Lat cutte hem of, I wol thee helpe hem carie.
(*C. T.*, C, 951 ff.).

When we remember that the Pardoner is physically
unfortunate, " *natus sine testiculis vel parvissimos habens*," this rude speech on the part of the Host seems
to be something more than " rough jocularity." Again
as the Flemings say, "Sooth pley, quaad pley." And to
make matters worse the whole company laughs! The
good-natured Host, however, declares he will not play
with an angry man, and at the request of the Knight
consents to make peace with a kiss. The incident is
closed.

That the Pardoner is extremely sensitive upon the
matter of his weakness is evidenced by his pathetic attempts to conceal it. He goes about singing in concert
with the Summoner a gay little song, " Come hider,
love, to me " (A, 672), and boasts with brazen af-
frontery that he will drink wine " And have a jolly
wenche in every toun " (C, 453). He sings and brags
like a real man; but one suspects that most of his
affaires d'amour result in chagrin and disappointment
like that in which he engages with Kitt the Tapster
in the *Tale of Beryn*. It is significant that in this
pseudo-Chaucerian story the " Pardoner " appears in his
true colors. Recognising his weakness, the Tapster upon
seeing him for the first time determines to make him her
dupe. He is perfectly harmless, and she knows it. She
leads him on, permits him to come into compromising
situations with her, and finally hands him over to shameful treatment at the hands of her paramour.[31] At any

rate, Chaucer's Pardoner probably takes many of his potations of wine and ale in order to arouse an atrophied desire. He is almost as pitiable a figure as the aged January, who sits up late on the first night after his marriage with May, drinking strong wines hot with spices " t 'encreesen his corage " (*C. T.*, E, 1807). Being feeble in body, though not necessarily entirely impotent, he permits his polluted imagination to revel in thoughts of lust and fleshly delights.

The physical stamina of the Wife of Bath has his unbounded admiration. Her eloquent sermon against virginity and in favor of the proper use of God-given powers of body for the promotion of carnal pleasures (D, 95–150) meets with his enthusiastic approval. He even interrupts her steady flow of language to applaud:

> ' Now dame', quod he, ' by god and by seint John,
> Ye bee a noble prechour in this cas! '
>
> (*C. T.*, D, 164).

There is one part of her discourse, however, which strikes him with panic. Being naturally of a passionate disposition, she affirms that her husband will always be her slave and thrall. He shall pay his debts, sanctioned by the Apostle, both morning and evening. As long as she shall be his wife, he must have tribulation of the flesh and must make his body subject in love to her desire (D, 150–160). This is too much for the Pardoner. If this is the true and proper relation between husband and wife, he has just escaped being plunged into a most horrible situation:

I was about to wedde a wyf; alas!
What sholde I bye it on my flesh so dere?
Yet hadde I lever wedde no wyf to-yere.
(*C. T.*, D, 166 ff.)

At this unexpected interruption the Pilgrims do not even smile. Perhaps they remember his former anger and are content to let him play his little farce in peace. At any rate, this is the Pardoner's last boast. In it may be plainly seen his painful consciousness of his physical incompleteness and perhaps a bit of wistful sadness because of his misfortune.[32]

If this interpretation of the Pardoner's character has anything of truth in it, he is to be pitied rather than censured. Born a eunuch and in consequence provided by nature with a warped mind and soul, he is compelled to follow the urge of his unholy impulses into debauchery, vice, and crime. Being an outcast from human society, isolated both physically and morally, he satisfies his depraved instincts by preying upon it. His character is consistent throughout both with itself and with nature as described in the physiognomies. And Chaucer, the artist and man of deep human sympathy, has shown by the infinite care with which he has developed the Pardoner's character that he is able to appreciate, without judging too harshly, the point of view of even a *eunuchus ex nativitate.*

CHAPTER FOUR

THE REEVE AND THE MILLER

A MEDIAEVAL audience's comprehension of the personalities attributed to those delightful rascals, the Reeve and the Miller, must have been greatly facilitated by virtue of the fact that Chaucer has bodied them forth with the evident aid of physiognomical principles. It could not be maintained that the poet has created these personages mechanically according to certain rules and regulations known to his audience, but in presenting an exact correspondence between personal appearances and characters he has, while apparently detracting nothing from the lifelike qualities of the personalities introduced, succeeded in rendering them more vivid, natural, and significant to anyone with the mediaeval point of view.

Though the description of the Reeve's person is meager enough, it doubtless sufficed to indicate to the well informed men and women of the fourteenth century most of what Chaucer wanted to develop in the Reeve's character:

> The Reve was a sclendre colerik man,
> His berd was shave as ny as ever he can,
> His heer was by his eres round y-shorn,
> His top was dokked lyk a preest biforn.
> Ful longe were his legges, and ful lene,
> Y-lyk a staf, there was no calf y-sene.
>
> (*C. T.*, A, 587 ff.)

Now, may we ask again just what did these few items of personal appearance, perhaps only amusing to modern readers, signify to the mediaeval audience? The Reeve's custom of shaving his beard and of wearing his hair closely cropped need not detain us; it merely indicated in Middle English times a man of low caste or, more especially, an obedient and humble servant. This ostentatious display of humility affected by the Reeve was doubtless a part of his general programme of hoodwinking his young lord and of privately increasing his own store of goods; he could so " plesen subtilly " that, in addition to what he stole during the year, he had the confidence and thanks of his lord together with special gifts of coats and hoods besides. Everybody in Chaucer's time, it may be presumed, knew something about the four complexions of men, so that the artist thought it necessary to suggest only two characteristics of the choleric man in his description of the Reeve. The Middle English *Secreta Secretorum,* some version of which the poet certainly knew, has this to say: " The colerike (man) by kynde he sholde be lene of body; his body is light and drye, and he shal be sumwhat rogh; and lyght to wrethe and lyght to peyse; of sharpe witt, wyse and of good memorie, a greete entremyttere; he louyth hasty wengeaunce; desyrous of company of women moore than hym nedyth." [1]   A large part of the delineation of the Reeve's character, in the General Prologue, is taken up with illustrative material bearing out the fact that he is of " a sharpe witt, wyse, and of good memorie." He understands the art of husbandry; the raising of cattle, chickens, poultry, and swine is a congenial and profitable occupation; and, it is said, he has been accustomed to tampering so skilfully with the annual reports made to his lord that, in spite of his rascality, no man might bring him in arrears. Many of the under-servants have known him for a thief all along, of course, but according to his choleric nature he is generally so " hasty " of his " wengeaunce " that they have maintained a discreet silence:

They were adrad of him as of the deeth (A, 595).

The Reeve is a choleric man and, therefore, cunning and crafty. So Chaucer presents him in the General Prologue to the *Canterbury Tales.*

When we come to the Reeve's Prologue, however, Oswald the Carpenter seems, upon first acquaintance, to be quite another man; at any rate, emphasis is there placed upon other, different elements of his character. Without further preparation, apparently, than the suggestion that " in his youth " he learned a good trade, we suddenly find that he is an old man, easily angered and as easily appeased, indulging in certain preachments upon old age and the follies of youth — to the disgust of the Host (*C. T.,* A, 3865). He is here revealed in his true colors; he is a lecher of the worst sort, a churl, a pitiful example of the burnt-out body in which there still lives a concupiscent mind. Youth with its follies is past; his hairs are white with age and perhaps from illicit association with women; [2] he is like rotten fruit. Yet he still boasts of having a " coltes tooth," and though the power to gratify his physical desires is gone, he still mentally hops to folly while the world pipes.

And worst of all he shamelessly publishes the vicious-
ness of his imagination:

> For in oure wil there stiketh ever a nayl,
> To have an hoor heed and a grene tayl
> As hath a leek; for thogh our might be goon,
> Our wil desireth folie ever in oon,
> For when we may nat doon, than wol we speke;
> Yet in our asshen olde is fyr y-reke
>
> (*C. T.*, A, 3878 ff.).

This unexpected change in the character of the Reeve
might well seem to be a serious blemish upon the poet's
artistic workmanship; Oswald, an aged reprobate reveling in memories of follies committed in youth and
prime, appears to come into direct conflict with the cunning and wide-awake Reeve of the General Prologue.
But Chaucer is, for the most part, the conscious artist.
Rightly understood, he rarely leaves out any element that
might be considered essential to the unity and consistency
of his characterizations.   In the General Prologue —
precisely where it should be — there is the emphatic
statement that the Reeve has exceedingly small legs.
This apparently innocent observation contains by implication most of what the poet later develops in the
Reeve's hidden personality.

For it must be remembered that whenever Chaucer
takes the trouble to impress upon his reader's notice the
special physical peculiarities of his Pilgrims, we may rest
assured that he intends for them to be straightway interpreted in terms of character.   What, then, should small
legs like those of the Reeve signify?   The physiogno-

mists do not leave us in doubt. Aristotle himself affirms [3] that " whoever has thin, sinewy legs is luxurious or voluptuous by nature and is to be referred to birds." Polemon, the greatest and probably the father of most of the mediaeval physiognomists, is still more explicit in his discussion, " De signis crurum ": [4] " And if, moreover, the legs are slender so that the tendons are visible, such persons should be judged as being given to much cupidity and lust." An anonymous author of the eleventh century — and a follower of Polemon — is of a like opinion: [5] " People who are of a white color and have slender legs as if the tendons were stretched are lustful and intemperate in their sensual desires "; and the Middle English *Secreta Secretorum* says that " tho men whyche haue smale legges and synowye bene luchrus." When we remember, moreover, that one of the chief characteristics of the " colerik " man is that he is " Desyrous of the company of women moore than hym nedyth," it is apparent that Chaucer has made in the General Prologue ample preparation for the revelations which come in the Reeve's Prologue. His personal appearance betrays the Reeve to any ordinary observer — with the mediaeval point of view — , and his later confession need cause no surprise.

The Miller, indeed, takes his measure immediately. As Professor Tupper has already shown, the Miller and the Reeve are professional and traditional enemies; [6] it is even possible that they may have met before, it seems. At any rate, when the drunken Miller rises to a point of personal privilege and demands that he be permitted to " quyte the Knightes tale " with a story of a

cuckold carpenter and a faithless wife, the Reeve —
who is also a " wel good wrighte " (A, 614) — recognizes that he is about to be attacked and voices a
protest :

> stint thy clappe,
> Lat be thy lewed dronken harlotrye.
> It is a sinne and eek a greet folye
> To apeiren any man, or him diffame,
> And eek to bringen wyves in swich fame (A, 3145).

The battle is on! The *Miller's Tale* is not so much an
attack upon carpenters as a class as it is a direct thrust
at this particular Reeve. And the ribald Miller has already divined the weak spot in the *amour propre* of his
ancient enemy; namely, his advanced age. Professor
Tupper says: " The obvious parallel between the Reeve
and the victim of the Miller's Tale lies not in their
common trade . . . but in their like cuckoldry, the traditional fate of eld mated with youth. The story . . .
is eminently successful as a fabliau of futile jealousy of
age." [7] In other words, the Miller in his description of
the carpenter of the Tale is drawing material from his
personal observations of the Reeve. In like manner, as
we shall see later, the Reeve retaliates by attributing to
the miller of *his* story personal characteristics which his
enemy possessed, but which Chaucer has failed to put
into the picture of his Miller in the General Prologue.
Neither the Reeve nor the Miller, therefore, is complete without reference to his prototype. Since the
whole of the Miller's Tale is a shaft aimed at the old
age of the Reeve, we are prepared, as we should not
otherwise have been, for the sermon which the latter

preaches in the Prologue to the *Reeve's Tale.* He is
there angered that his feeble condition should have been
held up to the ridicule of the whole company in such a
manner; perhaps he is indeed a cuckold. At least he
feels that he must defend himself, and in doing so he is
betrayed into revealing his life of harlotry and into boasting that, though his hair is gray, he is still not so impotent and so worn out in doing " Venus workes " as
he may seem. He still has a " grene tayl "; his " coltes
tooth." is yet to be shed (A, 3865.). He proves himself
guilty of three, at least, of the four Sins which he says
" longen un-to elde ": boasting, covetousness, and anger.

The mildness of his anger, however, is somewhat surprising when we remember that the under-servants at
home are as afraid of him as of the pestilence. Chaucer
says that most of the company laughed at the Miller's
story, and that no man professed to find it unbearably
obscene except Oswald:

A litel ire is in his herte y-laft,
He gan to grucche and blamed it a lyte (A, 3862).

As a matter of fact, Oswald is really what the physiognomists would list as a timid man. Aristotle writes
that the " signs of a timid and faint-hearted man are
these: soft hair, extreme weakness of the body, small
legs, delicate members and joints, slim hands, and lank
loins," [8] to which the *Secreta Secretorum* might add that
" longe leggis " indicate a man of " ill Complexcioun."
While the Reeve may rule with a tyrannical hand the
underlings at home, he is, as his small legs indicate, a
coward at heart; he is especially afraid of the bluster-

ing, bragging Miller, who rides blowing and sounding upon his bagpipe at the head of the " route " (A, 566). Consequently he withdraws himself from the other Pilgrims and no doubt from the Miller in particular and, as Chaucer says,

> And ever he rood the hinderest of our route
> (A, 622).

Forced later to come into the very presence of his burly enemy, however, the Reeve discreetly represses his anger; he has only a " litel ire " in his heart and blames the Miller's tale only a " lyte." He could, if he wanted to speak of ribaldry, tell a story about a certain miller — but he is too old; " me list not pley for age " (A, 3865). And partly because his pride has been hurt, as we have seen already, but mostly because he is afraid of the Miller, Oswald launches forth into a sermon on old age in general and on his own sad case in particular. Under the circumstances, it is a neat and effective subterfuge. But being rallied by the Host, he allows his indignation to get the better part of prudence; he suddenly decides that, after all, he *will* tell " right in his cherles termes " a story about a proud miller called " deynous Simkin."

Nothing could be more natural than that the Reeve, who has just expressed the fervent wish that the Miller's neck might be broken (A, 3918), should give in the description of the unfortunate hero of his Tale items of character and personal appearance taken directly from the man who stands before him. Just as the carpenter of the *Miller's Tale* is none other than the Reeve himself, so far as age and cuckoldry are concerned, so the character and person of Simkin, in the first eighteen lines of the *Reeve's Tale,* are in reality those of the Miller. Both, it will be observed, are excellent wrestlers, proud boasters and swaggerers, and consummate harlots; both reap a rich harvest from the practice of bold theft. The Miller, therefore, as we shall discuss him, is a composite of Simkin and of Chaucer's Canterbury Pilgrim. Of him, as of Simkin, may be said:

> Round was his face, and camuse was his nose.
> As piled as an ape was his skulle (A, 3935).

And only when we consider these lines in connection with the description in the General Prologue can we gain an accurate and full picture of the Miller:

> The Miller was a stout carl, for the nones,
> Ful big he was of braun and eek of bones . . .
> He was short-sholdered, brood, a thikke knarre,
> Ther nas no dore that he nolde heve of harre
> Or breke it, at a renning, with his heed.
> His berd as any sowe or fox was reed,
> And ther-to brood, as though it were a spade.
> Up-on the cop right of his nose he hade
> A wert, and ther-on stood a tuft of heres,
> Reed as the bristles of a sowes eres;
> His nose-thirles blake were and wyde . . .
> His mouth as greet was as a greet forneys
> > (A, 545 ff.).

To all of this must be added the fact that, in his own drunken raving, he cries out with a rumbling, raucous voice, which is otherwise called a "Pilates vois." (A, 3124).

In the above description I take "short-sholdered" to mean not only, as Professor Skeat suggests, "short in the forearms"; it evidently has reference also to the fact that the Miller's broad, knotty shoulders are square and high-upreared so that, his short bull-like neck scarcely appearing at all, the head seems to rest upon them.   Of such a stocky figure Aristotle says: " The signs of a shameless and immodest man are vigorous shoulders raised upward, figure not erect but slightly bowed, rapid movements, a red body and sanguine complexion, a round face, and a chest thrust upwards." [9] Rasis, whom Chaucer certainly knew, also remarks: " The shameless man has elevated shoulders, a red complexion, round face; he is chicken-breasted and very garrulous." [10]   Not only is a man of the Miller's build known to be shameless, immodest, and loquacious, according to the physiognomists as in Chaucer, but he is apparently bold and easily angered.   Says Aristotle: " The signs of an irascible person are these: a broad figure with shoulders large and wide, powerful and strong extremities, a courageous appearance, and a florid complexion," [11] to which Rasis adds that " He is a bold man whose hair is coarse and bristly and whose figure is erect, bones large, and limbs and ribs strong.   His chest is well-developed, his stomach protruding, shoulders broad, his neck strong and thick.   Such a person is clearly wrathful, always conserving his wrath." [12]   Our anonymous author would say that the Miller might be referred to the bull, because " The Bull is an animal having a large head, wide mouth, broad nostrils, and gross flanks. . . .   Men who are referred to this species of animal are violent, lacking in wisdom, base in speech and action, fit to be ruled rather than to rule." [13] Already it appears from these passages that a man of the Miller's figure and with his round face, sanguine complexion, and red, bristly beard, his short neck, great mouth, and broad nostrils may be pronounced upon sight a man easily angered, shameless, loquacious, and apt to stir up strife. So Chaucer presents his Miller:

He was a janglere and a goliardeys,
And that was most of sinne and harlotryes (A, 560).

We have already seen how, in his drunkenness, he thrusts himself forward immediately after the Knight to tell his tale, and how he picks a quarrel with the Reeve.

But it is only from a study of these physical traits in detail that we are able to get the full significance of them in terms of character. Of short arms, such as the Miller has, the pseudo-Aristotelian *Secreta Secretorum* says, " If the arms are short, the possessor of them is a friend of evil and foolish, being of evil understanding and wicked in his practices." [14] Nor does the Middle English *Secreta Secretorum* dissent: " Whan the shuldres bene moche vprerid, thei tokenyth orribill kynde and vntrouthe; . . . and whan the armes bene ful shorte thay tokenyth lowe of dyscorde." Nor must the bull-like neck be left out of consideration in connection with the item " short-sholdered," for as Rasis has it, " He who has a neck thick and strong and hard is wrathful and hasty," [15] or according to the *Secreta Secretorum*, " a crafty trickster, astute, deceitful, and voracious," or

in the words of the M. E. *Secreta Secretorum,* " a fole
and a gloton, a gyloure and a decyuoure."

This most unfortunate Miller has, moreover, a round
face (probably fleshy, with puffed-out cheeks) covered
with a red, bushy beard. Of such a face Aristotle says,
" Those who have a fleshy face are easily aroused to
lust ";[16] Polemon affirms that " If there is much flesh
in the cheeks it signifies drunkenness and baseness "; [17]
the author of the *Secreta Secretorum* continues, " A man
fleshy in the face is impudent, ignorant, untruthful,
foolish, and of a gross nature "; [18] and the M. E. *Sec.
Sec.* concludes that " who-so hath a face ouer fleshy and
ouer grete, he is vnvyse, enuyous, a lyar, and bene dy-
sposyd to consupyscence of fleschy lustes." (P. 228.)
This estimate of the Miller's character is further borne
out by the physiognomical interpretation of his red
beard. As the M. E. *Sec. Sec.* has it, " Tho that bene
red men, bene Parceuynge and trechrus, and full of
queyntise, i-liknyd to Foxis," which may contain some
explanation of Chaucer's description, " His berd as any
sowe or fox was reed." As far back as the time of the
Proverbs of Alfred this distrust of the red man, i.e.,
rufus, subrufus, is felt and expressed:

> þe rede mon he is quede
> for he wole þe þin iwil rede,
> he is a cocher, þef and horeling,
> Scolde, of wrechedome is king (702 ff.).

In the description of the Miller's skull the term
" piled " is defined incorrectly by Professor Skeat, who
says that it means " deprived of hair, very thin." Rather

Chaucer intends to say probably that the hair of the Miller's head is thick (most likely bristly), and especially that it comes far down over his wide, " villainous low " forehead. (See the picture of the Miller from the Ellesmere MS.) It is such a head and forehead as Giraldus Cambrensis attributes to the wicked Geoffrey, Archbishop of York, who is said to have had " a large head with the hair extending, like that of an ape, over the forehead even to his eyelids." [19] This quotation explains quite clearly, it seems to me, the meaning of Chaucer's " piled as an ape." Our anonymous author on physiognomy informs us that one of the signs of the proud-minded man is " hair of the head coming far down upon the forehead," and continues with the information that " thick hair overhanging the forehead declares an excessively base mind." [20] What he is trying to say, I think, is better expressed by a later writer, Richard Saunders — of whom more anon — in his discussion of the man with a depressed and low forehead: " For a man that is so," says he, " hath a low and abject soul, is fearful, surville . . . cowardly, and carried away with many words of a great talker, for there is not much assurance in his words, yet he is overcome by the speech of the most simple man that he stands in fear of." [21] From these indications we learn that, in spite of his enormous physical strength, his jangling and babbling, and for all his boasting, the Miller is still a bully, a coward at heart. For, it must be observed, when his blustering demand to be heard in the rôle of story-teller calls forth a display of considerable animus on the part of the Host (A, 3135), he is quick to ac-

knowledge with a show of weakening courage that he is
drunk (A, 3138); and when so slender a man as the
Reeve protests against his telling a libelous tale about
a carpenter and a faithless wife, he hastens to mollify
the irate little man with gentle assurance of his absolute
faith in — or perhaps his indifference to — the chastity
of married women (A, 3151 ff.). He would not for
the world cast reflections upon the Reeve or upon any
woman; why should " leve brother Oswald " be angry
with him (A, 3157)! His braggardism has received a
sharp and effective check. With respect to his strength,
the Miller may indeed be " referred " to the bull; but
with respect to his low forehead, he must be referred
to the ape, which is " an animal malignant, ridiculous,
and base." The man who is referred to the ape, says
Goclenius, " is likely to be given to scurrility and dis-
simulation." [22]

That a mouth as large as a " greet forneys " is sufficient to brand the Miller as a glutton, a swaggerer, a
sensualist, and an impious fornicator who might be expected to swear by God's " armes and by blood and
bones " (A, 3125), is attested by the best physiognomists.
" He who has a large mouth," say Rasis and others,
" is pugnacious, gluttonous, audacious; breadth of mouth
and thickness of lips signify desire and voracity of the
stomach, while at the same time their possessor is harmful and clearly irreverent. A large mouth, which is as
it were deep-set, is vicious and is the index of the love of
ill-will and of murder, and of lust and copulation." [23]
Saunders, as usual, states the matter in clear and pic-
turesque English: " He that hath a greet and broad

mouth is shameless, a great babler and lyar, a carrier of
false tales, very foolish, impudent, courageous, but per-
fidious withal. . . . Indagine and Corvus say, they
were never deceived by this sign." [24] Nor does this sign
fail in the case of the Miller. His " Pilates vois " is,
moreover, still another indication of an evil and malignant nature. According to Aristotle and others the
man who has a great, rough voice is " injurious, law-
less, the servant of his own stomach, wrathful and
hasty, and of an evil nature, performing wicked deeds
gladly." [25] The Miller's deep, rumbling voice must be
carefully distinguished from the loud, sonorous voice
such as has Emetrius, King of Inde:

His voys was as a trompe thunderinge (A, 2174).

For as Polemon tells us, " When you hear a deep, grave,
sonorous voice, you may attribute to the owner of it
great agility and bravery, sincerity and truthfulness." [26]
Chaucer seems to be quite aware of the fact that, of
all parts of the body, the nose is a most infallible indica-
tor of character. He is careful, therefore, to tell us
that the Miller's nose is " camuse," i.e., flat, low and
concave, a pug-nose, with wide distended nostrils, and
with an unsightly wart on the top in which there is a
tuft of red hairs. Such an ape-like nose, say the physiognomists, indicates " lustfulness, desire for coition,
and a love of things Venerian." [27] All of the physiognomists further agree that the man with wide open nostrils is easily angered — " For whan a man angryth his
noose thurles oppenyth " —, that he is a jangler, a liar,
and given to filthy luxurious practices.[28] Any discus-

sion of the Miller's wart, however, must necessarily lead
us into a consideration of that division of physiognomy
known generally to the Middle Ages as metoposcopy,
which, in addition to treating of the significance of the
lines of the forehead corresponding to the celestial
bodies, deals with warts, moles, and other natural marks
found upon the face.   It is based, as are the kindred
sciences of geomancy and chiromancy, together with the
science of dreams and medicine, upon astrology.   That
Chaucer's knowledge of medicine, in its technical as
well as in its astrological aspects, was wider and more
accurate than critics once supposed,[29] we have already
demonstrated in our discussion of the Doctor of Physic;
and that he was also well acquainted with the " symmetrical proportions and signal moles of the body," is
revealed in his description of the Miller's wart.   From
the time of Ptolemy on down to the age of Chaucer, I
understand, astrologers were accustomed to " attribute "
to the various planets sundry corresponding parts of the
human body: to the Sun, for example, the nerves, the
sinews, and the brain; to Jupiter, the hands, .the liver,
and the blood; and, what concerns us especially at this
point, to Venus, the nose, the mouth, and the corresponding instruments of generation.[30]   A full discussion of
this question may be found in the works of Albohazen
Haly, or of Baptista Porta, or of Cardan,[31] or of the
Grecian Melampus, or of Mr. Richard Saunders.   Now
this Saunders, who has apparently familiarized himself
with the works of most of the above-mentioned ancient
writers, seems to be the authority *par excellence* on all
things physiognomical, chiromantical, metoposcopical, a

self-styled " student of astrology and physic," *semetip-sissimum*. He complains of his sources that they were so " depraved with manual Errors, that no light of truth could I derive from these Fountains; but whatsoever shews of truth did therein appear, I have found them rather mistaken fallacies than real verities." But after sifting all the material at his disposal and comparing it with his own personal observations, he at last arrives at the truth of the whole matter.

We are interested, therefore, to hear what Saunders has to say about warts on the nose. " Now let us treat of the Nose," says he, " which, as before I observed, relates to the Genitals or Secrets. When a Mole is on the root of the Fore-head, in the hollow between the Nose and the Fore-head, there is another on the Foreskin of the flesh; but Haly saith, a Mole on the Forehead another on the stones; but he explains not in what part of the Forehead, when as he means the lower part of the Forehead, next the beginning of the Nose. Haly again saith, He which hath a Mole or mark on the Nostril, hath another on the privy parts on the circumference of the genitals, and another on the ribs and that side of the breast; but by the nostrils there should be understood the top of the nose; but I attribute this mistake to his interpreter, who might easily mistake the *Arabick*, and render *Naris* for *Nasus*. Melampus renders judgment that if a Mole appear on the Nose or near the eye, that person is beyond measure Venereal . . . ; a Mole on the Nostrils gives another on the Stones, between which and the nostrils there is great sympathy." [32] We are delighted to get these opinions

of Haly, no doubt Albohazen Haly filius Abenragel, a
noted astrologer of the eleventh century, and to note
the trifling nature of the " manual Errors " of which
he stands convicted, because we may now accept Saunders as a more or less accurate authority on the science
as it must have been understood in Chaucer's time.   He
is correct, moreover, in his quotation from Melampus,
who says, " If the mark is on the nose of a man, and
if the color of it is yellowish, then he will be insatiable
in love; you may say also that there is another mark in
a secret place." [33]   And this reminds us of the fact that
Chaucer knows what he is about when he makes the
Wife of Bath own to having somewhere about her person " the prente of sëynte Venus seel " (D, 604), and,
on account of having been born when Taurus was in
the ascendent with Mars posited in it, lament:

> Yet have I Martes mark up-on my face,
> And also in another privee place (D, 619).

But let us return to the Miller's wart.   The exact
location of it is, for an interpretation of the Miller's
character, of considerable importance.   Chaucer says,
" Up-on the cop right of his nose he hade a werte,"
which may be interpreted in either of two ways: it is
right on top, i.e., directly or exactly on top (or, for aught
I know, on the very point), or on top of the nose a little
to the right side.   I am inclined to think that Chaucer
had the latter meaning in mind when he wrote the
passage.   But in either case the significance of it is
not flattering to the Miller.   " If the mark (or mole)
is placed on the middle of the nose," says Melampus,

" it signifies that a man because of women, or a woman because of men, shall be subject to homicides and given to shameful fornication." [34]   Saunders is still more explicit: " A mole in a man or a woman appearing under the very point of the Nose toward the middle . . . describes another on the fore part of the Privy member, and denotes the man to be inclined to filthy infamous luxury, and subject to a violent gout, or worse, which he gets by women's company; . . . if it appear red, he is principally pained in the extreme parts of his body, as Hands, Arms, Legs, and Feet . . . ; if it appear as a Lentil (i.e., a wart), he is in most danger of the secret Privy parts; let him take heed thereof." [35]   If the wart or mark is on the top of the nose, a little to the right, Melampus says: " Always, if the mark is placed on the middle of the nose and on the right side, it produces quarrels and miseries between the sexes." [36]   Saunders again assents, adding further complications: " A man or woman having a Mole on top of the bridge of the Nose, inclining to the right side a little, indicates another on the top of the Yard or privy member, and discovers the man to be an enemy to his own peace, to sow discord between himself and his wife; . . . if it appear of a honey colour, contentious brawlings shall most perplex him; if red, he is most afflicted with envious hostility; if it is like a wart or Lentil, he is a principal Artificer in his calling." [37]   And finally, as to the red tuft of hairs that stands out from the Miller's wart, Saunders would probably say, " He that hath the nose hairy at the point, or above, is a person altogether simple hearted." [38]

From the material presented in this chapter we may

safely deduce the obvious conclusion, I think, that in the creation of the Reeve and Miller Chaucer has made ample use of the science of physiognomy. The character of the Reeve is made to seem a consistent and unified whole when his personal appearance is interpreted, and the Miller's dissolute and abandoned personality is to be realized in full only by reference to the physiognomical significance of his physical peculiarities. The real Miller is presented in large measure by suggestion. Chaucer expresses, indeed, some compunction of conscience at being compelled to delineate so much of the Miller's character as he does (A, 3170); but he is not backward in heaping up bodily signs, which to the initiated speak louder than words. When it appears that the Host is finally unable to dissuade dear brother Robin — whom we now know to be much worse at heart than Chaucer has described him in so many words — from telling his filthy story, the poet reluctantly and with some misgivings, apparently, concludes to rehearse " his cherles tale in his manere." " And therefore I pray every gentle person," says he, " for God's love, not to judge that I speak with evil intent, but that I must rehearse all their tales, be they better or worse, or else falsify some of my matter. And therefore whoever does not want to hear it, let him turn over the leaf and choose another tale; for he shall find enough of other stories dealing with gentility and morality and holiness. Do not blame me if you choose amiss."

The Miller is a cherl, ye knowe wel this;
So was the Reve, and othere many mo,
And harlotrye they tolden bothe two (A, 3171 ff.).

CHAPTER FIVE

THE WIFE OF BATH

HE who would enter upon anything like an adequate explanation of the remarkably complex and contradictory character of Chaucer's Wife of Bath must
expect heavenly guidance and receive aid from the stars.
Though one may not be entirely prepared to accept the
opinion that she " is one of the most amazing characters . . . the brain of man has ever conceived," [1] still
she is so vividly feminine and human, so coarse and
shameless in her disclosures of the marital relations with
five husbands, and yet so imaginative and delicate in her
story-telling, that one is fascinated against his will and
beset with an irresistible impulse to analyze her dual
personality with the view of locating, if possible, definite
causes for the coexistence of more incongruent elements
than are ordinarily found in living human beings.
When I first proposed casting the Wife of Bath's horoscope, it was with the supposition that rules of natural
astrology might be used exclusively in the interpretation
of certain data, concerning planets and their influence,
which Chaucer has furnished us; but it is not entirely
so. In the full presentation of the Wife's " fortune "
— her character, personal appearance, and the location
and significance of mysterious " marks " about her body
— constant reference must be made to what the mediae-

val mind believed to be truths found in the " sciences " of celestial physiognomy, metoposcopy, and perhaps of geomancy.

That startling revelation of a woman's experiences in love, the Wife of Bath's Prologue, reaches its climax, I suppose, at the point where Jankin, the unsophisticated clerk of twenty, is selected by Dame Alisoun, aged forty, to fill the recently vacated place and to take up the labors of her fourth husband who has just been packed off to the church-yard. She has wept a little for decency's sake, it will be remembered, and has worn the mourning veil for at least a month out of respect for custom; but her heart has never been in the grave of her husband. Even while following the bier, she tells us, she kept an appraising eye upon the excellent shape of Jankin's leg — she always had a " coltes tooth."

Gat-tothed I was, and that bicam me weel;
I hadde the prente of sëynt Venus seel.
As help me god, I was a lusty oon,
And feire and riche, and yong, and wel bigoon . . .
For certes, I am al Venerien
In felinge, and myn herte is Marcien.
Venus me yaf my lust, my likerousnesse,
And Mars yaf me my sturdy hardinesse.
Myn ascendent was Taur, and Mars thereinne.
Allas! allas! that ever love was sinne!
I folwed ay myn inclinacioun
By vertu of my constellacioun;
That made me I coude noght withdrawe
My chambre of Venus from a good felawe.
Yet have I Martes mark up-on my face,
And also in another privee place

(*C. T.*, D, 600 ff.).

Now from this passage it appears that, to the mind of Chaucer, the cause of Dame Alisoun's peculiarly contradictory character lies not so much in herself as in her stars; possibly she is not to be held morally responsible

PLATE IV

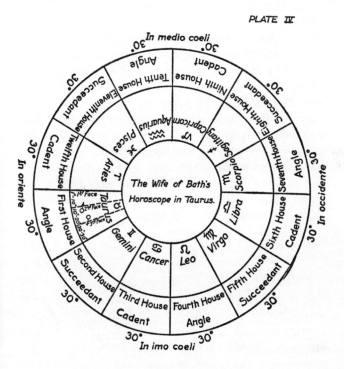

The Wife of Bath's Horoscope in Taurus.

for all her actions. For at her birth the sign Taurus, one of the " houses " or " mansions "[2] of Venus, is said to have been in the ascendent over the horizon, hers being what the exponents of natural astrology would

call " the horoscope in Taurus." Her dominant star or
ruling planet is Venus — she speaks proudly of the wisdom taught her by " my dame," the love-star (D,
575) [3] — which, being posited and at home in its own
house Taurus, may be considered " well-dignified " or
particularly beneficent in aspect toward the " native."
Most unfortunately, however, the combined good influence of the ascendent sign and the dominant star is
vitiated by the presence in perhaps platic conjunction of
Mars, one of the most "malefic " and evil of planets
(see Plate IV). Both Mars and Venus — and if one
may put faith in astrologers, the sign Taurus — have
left their " marks " upon her body as well as upon her
character. With one eye upon this configuration of
stars and with the other upon mediaeval astrological
and physiognomical lore, which must have been familiar to Chaucer,[4] let us read and interpret the Wife of
Bath's horoscope.

II

Mediaeval astrologers are exceedingly careful in setting up and in drawing figures of the heavens representing horoscopes in all the various signs of the zodiac.
Ioannes Taisnier finds that, when Taurus is just rising
in oriente, Aquarius is discovered *in medio coeli,* Scorpio
in occidente, and Leo *in imo coeli,* and shows what particular influence each sign in this position exerts upon the
native:

" If the horoscope is in Taurus (says he), it may be
interpreted in this manner: the native shall be an industri-

ous person, prudent, energetic in acquiring wealth, gaining and losing it with ease, triumphing over enemies.

" Aquarius *in medio coeli* assures favor with princes and presages public acts and offices, perhaps affairs which have to do with water, since this sign is of a watery nature.

" Scorpio *in occidente* indicates that the native will be sagacious, serviceable, and dutiful; he shall lose his wife, if he be masculine, and, if feminine, she shall be deprived of her husband and son.

" Leo *in imo coeli* assures the appropriation of inheritances, which shall be gained in spite of insidious obstacles and the claims of children born after the will was made." [5]

So far one may follow with some confidence the technical directions of natural astrology, but no farther; Chaucer has failed to give data concerning the exact positions of sun and moon, and has not indicated the exact hour of the day — whether morning, afternoon, or night — and the day of the year of the nativity in question, all of which is absolutely necessary. But writers on metoposcopy are not silent regarding the supposed influence of Taurus on women — and men — born under that sign. For example, Philippi Finella says:

" When Taurus is discovered in the ascendent, the woman born under that sign shall be exceedingly large of face and forehead, rather fleshy with a great number of lines or wrinkles, especially in the forehead, and florid of complexion. She shall have bold eyes, a mobile head inclined more to the right than to the left side, long black hair widely spread over broad shoulders and breast.   She shall be slow in her movements, but equipped to perform a maximum of labor with a minimum of aversion.   When the first face of Taurus is in the ascendent, she shall be lightly given to affairs of the heart, having a lover for the greater part of her life; often in her amorous affairs she is followed by the reproach of her parents. . . .   She shall be inconstant, changeable, speaking (or gossiping) with fluency and volubility, now to this one now to that. . . .   This sign shall give her a mole or mark on the neck near its juncture with the shoulders; when this mark is located on the right side, a happy fate may be conjectured, but if on the left side one may reasonably predict dangers. . . .   When the line of Venus is observed to be joined to that of Mars, she shall be exceedingly virile, and sagacious in matrimony." [6]

A later writer concerning these matters assures us that " those born under Taurus are of a cold and dry constitution, inclined to melancholy; one that loves pleasure; . . . once provoked, seldom reconciled; of short stature, but well set; short legs, big buttocks, a bull's neck, wide mouth, and black hair." [7]   And the most scholarly of the students of celestial physiognomy, Baptista Porta, reporting faithfully the opinions of Albohazen Haly, Maternus, and Leopoldus, presents in a passage too long to quote, " De Tauri formae constitutione, moribus, & physicis rationibus," [8] much the same conclusions as those cited above.

Still fuller and far more detailed are the prognostications which may be made with certainty regarding the physical form and the disposition of those so fortunate as to be born when Venus, posited in either of her two houses, Taurus and Libra, is the ruling star in a nativity. In a passage headed " De Veneris forma ad Astrologis descripta," Porta records the following: " Venus mistress of a nativity (says Maternus) gives to the native a tall, elegant, white body, pleasing eyes sparkling with splendid beauty, and thick hair agreeably fluffy and sometimes curly or charmingly waving. Venus is similar to Jupiter (says Haly) except that it is her particular province to bestow more charm, greater beauty, and a better conceived, more finely formed, and more alluring and seductive body (seeing that Venus is responsible for that grace and elegance peculiar to women); a woman so born is milder and gentler. Others say that she is frail and slender, having dark eyes, delicate eyebrows joined together, tender lips, a full face, a magnificent breast, short ribs, well developed thighs; her general appearance is most attractive, and her figure is refined and elegant. She wantons with her eyes, believing this to be attractive; and her hair is somewhat curly. And Messahala says she has black eyes, in which the dark appears more than in those of other people, beautiful hair, and a face becomingly round and plump but not too full." [9]

Nor does the same author leave us in doubt as to the exact disposition and character of the person born when Venus reigns well-dignified and undisturbed by evil influences in the ascendent sign Taurus. In the section called " Mores quos Venus largiatur " he continues quoting from his authorities:

" When Venus is the ruling influence in a nativity
(says Haly), alone and in a favorable position, the native will be quiet and gentle in disposition, morally upright in character and not in the least depraved or
wicked, reflecting always upon right things. She loves
to dance and sing, abhors brawls, disputes, and contentions of all kinds; she delights in dictatorships and in-
trigues, fine forms and good manners, in truthfulness,
and in delicate fancies. She succeeds in making herself loved and esteemed by men; and since she is a devout and pious person engaged in doing right, she is
fortunate and happy. Venus makes her children attractive (Maternus agrees), joyous and cheerful of disposition, devoid of constant debaucheries or even of ex-
cesses, worthy of love, agreeable, affable, and altogether
charming. They are usually lovers of the opposite sex,
passionate and voluptuous by nature but religious and
righteous. They drink much and eat little; they have
a good digestion, which provokes passion and an ardent
desire for coition — but they are noble in life and
cleanly in act. They cleave with delight to the spirit
and practice of music and the arts. They rejoice in
sweet-scented baths and in perfumes and fragrances of
all kinds, and in poetry inspired by the Muses enriched
by choral dance and song. They have finely formed figures, especially the young women, achieve many amatory
affairs and happy weddings; temperamental by nature,
they show displeasure easily and indulge in complaints,
employ crafty devices, and refresh themselves by a return to peace and affection. They have a mutual es-
teem, the one for another, a fine sense of duty, a ready

faith, and a supremacy in good breeding, refinement, and
kindliness of heart. Venus makes singers and charming
people (says Haly further), ardent lovers of flowers and
elegance, taking great care of their fine bodies and
splendid, delicate skin and complexion. They are strenu-
ously diligent in the propagation of offspring and in the
perpetuation of the race, but are religious and sympathetic. They delight in feminine ornaments and are
given to adorning their bodies with elegant and smart
attire, most often white in color, have the genteel manners of a courtier, and take pleasure in luxurious flavors
and savors. They easily become rulers, performing
whatever they undertake with facility. They are given
to games and various diversions, to laughter and joyous
living, rejoicing in the companionship of friends and
in eating and drinking, relying upon others to the point
of being often deceived. They are benevolent and utter
soft and gentle-voiced words with a small, sweet mouth;
they are tender by nature and prone to shed tears." [10]
To this significant passage may be added a pertinent ex-
cerpt from the four full pages which Helvetius devotes
to the same subject. "They like to wander and so-
journ in strange lands" says he "in order that they may
enjoy the acclaim of foreign peoples or be accounted
cosmopolitan. They love smart, elegant wearing apparel of white, blue, and even black materials, and
jewelry of Phrygian workmanship made of gold, silver,
and precious stones for the adornment of their bodies,
according to their conception of style and length of
purse. In practices and experiences of love, however,
they often exceed the measure of good form, and as ex-

hibited in secret their (amatory) services are eager, exceedingly ardent, and glowing with passion. In the marriage relations they are to a high degree volatile, capricious, and inconstant, especially when they are not maintained sumptuously and in grand style; and they are certainly more contented and happy if they are permitted as many separations and divorces as there are numbered principles of love. Their amorous actions bring it about that, while they serve themselves by deceptions and cajoleries, they are pleasing and attractive at the same time, forcing the fascinated will of the lover to surrender." [11] And still further items may be gleaned from Indagine's account of the influence of Venus when she dominates in the roots of nativities of phlegmatic natures — and she is found only in such nativities: " Venus makes her children playful, passionate, joyous, beautiful, loving and fearing God, just; . . . they shall be great drinkers, musicians, players upon musical instruments, and singers. They will love the manual arts, such as painting and other things which are made neatly and without sweepings." [12]

I have ventured to give at considerable length these prognostications regarding the influence of Venus in Taurus, because in any correct interpretation of Chaucer's Wife of Bath it is necessary that one realize what she might have been. Such a fascinating personal appearance and attractive disposition might have been assured her at birth [13] had not fate — or perhaps her creator — decreed that she should sink i' the scale by virtue of the malignant influence of the war-planet, Mars, at that time in platic conjunction with Venus in

Taurus. At the conclusion of a long discussion of the beauty and charm of one born under the dominion of Venus, Indagine remarks: " But if Mars mingles his occult influence with hers, he changes all these prognostications into vain words and lies, and into that which is according to his nature." [14] Let us consider, therefore, the power and nature of Mars.

All the writers on these occult matters whom I have consulted agree with convincing unanimity that Mars, either in his own houses or in those of other planets, is a powerful worker of evil. Porta, in his discussion of Mars in the various zodiacal signs, quotes Haly and Maternus as follows: " Mars in the third face of Taurus (says Haly) gives a form marvelously foul and ugly, and a repulsive countenance; the native shall be a jester, delighting in merriment, incantations, and vices. If Mars is discovered anywhere in Taurus (says Maternus) the native shall be most loathsome of aspect, given to jesting continually, also greedy and rapacious, rash, reckless, criminal, rejoicing in causing unhappiness." [15] And Taisnier, adding further harrowing details, is in substantial agreement: " When Mars is found in the house of Venus (e.g., in Taurus), the native shall be voluptuous and a fornicator, perpetrating wickedness with women of his own blood, becoming guilty of incest, or committing adultery with women whom he has seduced by promises of marriage; he shall suffer damages and loss because of women. If Mars is posited in Taurus particularly, it signifies that all voluptuousness and wickedness shall be combined." [16] Still, one is delighted to learn that the case of a phlegmatic nature —

such as that of the Wife of Bath — is not so desperate as that of the melancholic and the choleric: " Mars in the nativity of a phlegmatic nature " says Indagine " is evil enough; he produces a native with a mean and violent disposition, strong, adventurous, a great babbler and liar. He burns the hair on the top of the head, makes the face coarse, enlarges the head; the native shall be cruel, casting his eyes aside, exceedingly courageous, a boaster, a traitor, fiery, arrogant, a maker of noises, a pillager, a beater of people, slayer of his father and mother, worthy of being beaten himself, and secretly boresome to his friends. Nevertheless all these characteristics are not so strongly marked in the phlegmatic as in melancholic and choleric natures, because the phlegmatic humour foams and cools the heat." [17]

Thus the power of Mars, situated alone in Taurus or posited at all in the nativities of phlegmatic natures, is exerted for evil; but when he mingles his influence with that of Venus, the situation is, according to Guido Bonatus and Cardan, indeed deplorable: " He that has Mars in his ascendante shall be exposed to many dangers, and commonly at last receives a great scar in his Face. When Mars is Lord of a Woman's Ascendant, and Venus is posited in it, or Venus is Lady of it, and Mars in it . . . 'tis more than probable that she will Cucold her Husband. When Venus shall be too powerful in a Geniture, and in place of the Infortunes (i.e., in conjunction with Mars, for example), inconveniences are to be feared from unlawful Loves. If in a Woman's nativity Mars shall be under the Sun Beams, she will be apt to play the Harlot with her Servants and mean fellows; but if Venus be there, then she will trade discreetly with nobles and Gallants of Quality." [18] And William Lilly has it that " Mars with Venus denote the Wife full of spirit, movable, an ill Housewife, prodigall, and that the native is or will be an Adulterer." [19] But it is Albohazen Haly who gives the best account of the combined influences of Mars and Venus in good and bad positions: " If Mars is in harmony with Venus and in a good position (says he), they create a native who is in agreement with men, one who is credulous but a deceiver of friends, one who loves a vicious and depraved life. Such a native delights in quiet simplicity and loves to sing and dance. He is a reveler, is transported by love, and has unlawful and sinful relations with the opposite sex; he is sensitive, a mocker and a deceiver, but none the less happy, a deep thinker, a waster, easily angered. But if these planets are in positions opposite to that of which we have spoken (e.g., in conjunction in Taurus), they make the native of a passionate disposition, desiring to lie with women without any consideration or sense of shame, seeing that he is exceedingly irresponsible in his actions; he is meretricious, a dishonorer, a teller of lies, and a deceiver of friends and others; successful in satisfying his desires, seducing and corrupting good women and virgins, wise in perpetrating frauds and betrayals. He is a perjurer, a scoffer and reviler, a reprobate in habits of thought, busily engaged in conceiving corrupt acts and in the practice of abominable fornication." [20] So far as the personal appearance of the native is concerned, however, Maternus is of the opinion that " When Mars participates with Venus in a nativity, he lays aside the utmost ardor of his evil. The person born when Mars is in conjunction with Venus has a complexion pleasingly red mixed with white; a face rounded but not too full with cheeks appropriately plump; lovely eyes a little too dark for greatest beauty but not black enough to be called ugly; a becomingly medium stature; and a body not fat to the point of being obese but, as one might say, semi-fat." [21] Such a person one might expect the Wife of Bath to be.

Not all the astro-physiognomical material that may aid in the correct interpretation of her constellation has been presented, however, until some explanation has been offered of the mysterious " prente of sëynt Venus seel," located somewhere about her person, and of " Martes mark " which is found upon her face and " also in another privee place." What is the nature of these " marks," and precisely where are they placed? It is a marvellous truth, we are told by the celestial physiognomists,[22] that every human being has printed upon his body, at the hour of conception or perhaps at birth, the " mark " of at least the ascendent sign and of the dominant star which are supposed to rule his fortunes. These marks are found in those parts of the body that are referred or " attributed " to the various signs and planets; and whether they are placed before, behind, or to the left or right side depends upon the " face " [23] of the sign just appearing above the horizon. If there should be another planet in conjunction, moreover, and if the Sun should be in the ascendent, then the native will have an additional set of marks on those parts of the body which correspond to these stars. Thus it comes about that a person may have four marks, each one of which may possibly be duplicated in another place. The mark of the ascendent sign, it must be observed, is usually the highest, that of the Sun lower — if he happens to be rising —, that of the dominant star still lower, and that of the planet in conjunction lowest of all.

For example, the Wife of Bath's horoscope is in Taurus, but Chaucer has unfortunately neglected to inform us as to which face of the sign was in the ascendent at the time of her birth. We may locate, therefore, the mark of this sign somewhere on the neck; but whether it is on the throat, or on the side, or on the nape of the neck cannot be determined. M. Belot says in this connection: " When a person is born under the sign Taurus, he has a mark on the neck; if the first face, which the Arabians call *Adoldaya*, is just rising, the mark is found upon the throat in the form of a small strawberry or of a little red spot something like the foot-print of a cat; this is an evil sign. If the person is born under the second face of the sign, i.e., from ten to twenty degrees, the mark is on one of the two sides of the neck; and if he is born under the third face of the sign, the mark is on the back of the neck, but in this case it is most often in the form of a small bulbus mole." [24] Le Sievre de Pervchio furnishes additional information and interpretation: " The head of Taurus (from one to ten degrees) dominates in the middle of April; its mark is impressed upon the neck in the form of a red spot, denoting birth in that season.

It indicates a person courageous, honest, endowed with a lovable disposition, but given to anger and lasciviousness, having a good color and long hair. . . . The heart of Taurus (from ten to twenty degrees) presides at the end of April and places its mark upon the side of the neck. . . . The tail of Taurus (from twenty to thirty degrees) is powerful at the beginning of May, at which time are born those who have the mark on the back of the neck." [25] And Rosa Baughan says that " When Taurus is rising at birth, the native bears a mark in the front of the throat; sometimes in the form of a rasberry or red-coloured mole, which mark is always ill in its effects." [26] Since there is no indication in Chaucer's text of the relation of the Sun to the Wife of Bath's constellation, one may safely conclude that she has escaped being branded on the left arm by that planet.

But, as we have already seen, she is stamped with the print of Venus's seal. If one may credit Le Sievre de Pervchio, " Venus, when she is discovered in the ascendent, imprints upon the native's left arm a red mark, a sort of scar decorated with a tint of vermilion." [27] Or according to M. Belot, whose opinion differs slightly from that of Pervchio, " When Venus is the dominant star in a nativity, her marks are found upon the loins, testicles, thighs, or perhaps upon the neck because Taurus, the first house of Venus, rules in that part; the form of these marks may be either bulbus or flat and the color either violet or whitish. They signify nothing but a lascivious nature." [28] On the whole I am inclined to think that M. Belot is the more trustworthy

authority and to accept his location of the mark of
Venus, especially so since all astrologers and physiognomists agree in attributing the secret parts of the body
to that planet. Nor is that all. The good Wife has
Mars's mark somewhere in her face and — because, as
we have seen in the discussion of the Miller's wart,
every mark or mole on the face is certainly reduplicated
in a corresponding part of the body — also in another
" privee place." M. Belot says: " If Mars is powerful
in a nativity, his marks are found on the right side and
most commonly in the front parts of the head [i.e., in
the face or somewhere about the forehead, though one
cannot be sure as to the exact position], or [he might
have said, " and also "] on the ' little stomach ' near the
secret parts. These marks are red or purple, most often
as large as small roses or drops of wine, moles colored
like strawberries or cherries." [29]

It should be quite apparent by this time that Chaucer, the artist, considered it necessary only to make suggestions, in connection with the constellation in question,
concerning certain planetary marks, being confident that
his educated and cultured — from the mediaeval point
of view — hearers or readers would instantly understand
their exact nature, color, shape, size, location, and significance.

III

With the above astrological principles and interpretations in mind, one is practically forced to the conclusion that Chaucer's Wife of Bath is in some measure the living embodiment, both in form and in character, of mingled but still conflicting astral influences.

That she herself is aware — and makes capital — of this conflict started within her nature at birth is suggested by her somewhat pitiful lamentation:

> For certes, I am al Venerien
> In felinge, and myn herte is Marcien.
> Venus me yaf my lust, my likerousnesse,
> And Mars yaf me my sturdy hardinesse . . .
> I folwed ay myn inclinacioun
> By vertu of my constellacioun.

Instead of having the naturally beautiful and well-proportioned figure — stately and tall, plump but never stout, graceful, with white skin touched delicately to pink — which might have been hers under the free, beneficent influence of Venus, she is endowed by the Mars-Venus combination with a stockily built, more or less ungraceful, buxom form of medium height. That strength which should have accompanied grace and beauty of body has been distorted into a powerful fecund energy; her large hips indicate excessive virility.[30] In place of the attractive face — round but not too large, with finely chiseled features, resplendent black eyes and delicately arched eyebrows, and with a lovely peach-bloom complexion set off by thick, curling hair of a dark shade — which Venus might have given, she has inflicted upon her by the malignancy of Mars a slightly heavy face inclined to fatness, characterised by perhaps coarsened features and certainly by a suspiciously red or florid complexion, which indicates that the woman is immodest, loquacious, and given to drunkenness. Let no such woman be trusted, say the physiognomists.[31] Her voice, which should have been sweet, low, and well-modulated, is harsh, strident, and raised continually, as one might expect, in vulgar jest and indelicate banter. Such a voice is especially significant in its betrayal of the Wife's voluptuous and luxurious nature; one has suspected for a long time that she knows only too well how to " laughe and carpe " in fellowship with the most dissolute rakes among the pilgrims. It is not surprising, therefore, to find that her physical characteristics and her disposition correspond in a remarkable way with the " Signa mulieris calidae & quae libenter coit," which are these: " She reaches maturity at the age of twelve years; has small breasts becomingly full and hard, and coarse hair. She is bold in speech, having a keen, high-pitched voice, proud in mind, red of face, erect in carriage, given to drink; she loves to sing, wanders much, and delights in adorning herself as much as possible." [32] And the Love-star might have given her small, sharp teeth, white as alabaster and evenly set in gums like coral; Mars is perhaps responsible for the long, spike-like teeth, set far apart with gaps between, which she possesses. Unfortunately the good Wife is " gat-tothed," which interpreted as meaning " gap-toothed " may signify that she is " envious, irreverent, luxurious by nature, bold, deceitful, faithless, and suspicious." [33]

Not less remarkable than this more or less distortion of the Wife of Bath's body is the warping of her character which results from the Venus-Mars conjunction in Taurus. One may still find everywhere traces of the Venerean disposition — never essentially evil or vulgar, but *inclining* sometimes to be so — intensified or turned

awry or metamorphosed by Martian influence into something resembling a caricature — or even into what is
quite the contrary — of that which she might have been.
The children of Venus, as we have already seen, are
naturally of a happy, joyous disposition, amiable and
therefore charming and universally attractive, delighting
in the dance and in all forms of innocent amusement,
but withal characterised by a gentleness, a refinement,.
and by a calm dignity which results in a well-developed
hatred of brawls and strife of any description. They
are religious by nature, just in their dealings with men,
leaders of noble lives, and — this is most important —
of an artistic nature which expresses itself in an appreciation of song and instrumental music, in a love for
delicate and pleasant odors, and which revels in the
colors of elegant wearing apparel and in precious jewels.
Being tender-hearted, bountiful, and benevolent, they
are particularly happy in their social intercourse with
people of culture and with those who have a taste for
the artistic. Endowed with the warmest and most affectionate hearts, they are lightly prone to violent *amours*
with the opposite sex, though it must be observed that
their amatory relations need not of necessity lead to
vice; they may be pleasure-loving and even voluptuous
by inclination without being touched by wantonness, passionate without being sensual or lustful, and full of a
consuming and perhaps entirely human desire without
a trace of licentiousness. Their nature demands that
variety of scene and the spice of exotic life which comes
only through travel in foreign countries and through
the association with people of unlike customs and manners. The children of Venus are your true aristocrats.

Such a woman the cloth-maker of Bath might have been. But how different! The natural cheerfulness of her disposition resolves itself into a sort of crude and clamorous hilarity, an overflow of superabundant animal and intellectual spirits, which makes of her a *bonne vivante* and a fitting companion for such tavern revelers as the Pardoner and her fourth husband. Her religious instinct has been debased to the extent that she goes to vigils and to preaching for the sole purpose, apparently, of showing her finery and arousing the envy of less fortunate women as she parades to the offering before everybody else; she attends miracle plays and follows the routes taken by devout pilgrims to the shrines of saints in order that she may satisfy an idle curiosity or find another lusty husband, no doubt; her readings — or the passages she most easily remembers having heard read — from the Bible or from St. Jerome are significant texts dealing with marriage and other complex sex-relations. The artistic temperament which should have been hers has been cheapened by the influence of the War-star, so that she flashily decks herself out in gaudy colors — in scarlet dresses and hose, to say nothing of brand new shoes and silver spurs — and adorns herself on Sundays with coverchiefs weighing ten pounds and on the pilgrimage with a hat as large as a buckler. Even this strikingly overdressed woman shows a certain feeling, all the more pitiful because it is uncultivated or perverted, for the beautiful in dress; she is at least delightfully neat and trim for a middle-class woman of her time. But worst of all, Mars has played havoc with the luxurious impulses — the " likerousnesse " — which come from her mistress, Venus; she has always had a

" coltes tooth." Whatever else she may be, in the Prologue to her tale she appears as an unusually healthy and frank female animal, human and sexually attractive, whose dominating idea seems to be the glorification of fleshly delights and the gratification of physical desire. Mars has given her a " sturdy hardinesse " and a body so full of "ragerye " that even at the age of forty she is still " faire and yong and wel bigoon." She has married five husbands at the church door — besides other " companye in youthe," which may mean almost anything —, has enjoyed them with varying degrees of animal pleasure, and has laid them to rest after their marital labors were ended. Welcome the sixth; eight would be all too few. With the most brazen and shameless lack of modesty she reveals her exciting experiences abed, omitting neither the feigned appetite which secures for her whatever funds she needs for the decking of her person, nor the passionate love-making — an excellent example of misdirected tenderness — with which she wins the services of her three old husbands. She is not so much a restless wanderer as a gadder about in search of excitement — until her fifth husband puts a stop to her going and her gossiping for a season. And it is Mars who impels her to gain at all costs the dominating power over her husbands and who makes of her a scold, a wrangler, and a striker of blows — worthy of being beaten herself — until she attains her purpose. Truly, whatever one may say of Venus's influence it is turned into a baser order when Mars is discovered in conjunction. So the Wife of Bath appears in the Prologue to her tale: a fair Venerean figure and character imposed upon and oppressed, distorted in some measure and warped, by the power of Mars.

No one must suppose, however, that this worthy woman is entirely depraved or that she is unattractive; after the worst has been said, she still has Venus for her mistress. Everybody knows that, even in the Prologue to her tale, she is pursued by the melancholy conviction that the type of life she has led is not the best possible; her laughing and carping, and perhaps her coarseness, are assumed in part as a mask to hide the bitterness which has been forced upon her by an unholy constellation. She knows better, at least, and still has the grace to cry,

> Allas! allas! that ever love was sinne.

Consequently, there need be no occasion for surprise when we come to her tale to find that her creator, not only a genius but among the most sympathetic of men, should lift the veil for a moment from the secret places of her nature and should have permitted her to tell a story of the most delicate beauty and grace. It is an artistically woven tale of faery,[34] centering, to be sure, about the Wife's original contention that women should have dominion over their husbands but nonetheless imaginative and free from the slightest touch of vulgarity, and containing a long and nobly expressed sermon on what constitutes true " gentilesse " of heart and life. So excellent a critic as Ten Brink, not understanding the artistic side of her character and finding something dramatically inappropriate in such sentiments from the lips of a clothweaver, is moved to say: " The thoroughly sound moral of the long sermon given by the wise old woman,

before her metamorphosis, to her young, unwilling husband, comes more from the heart of the poet than from
the Wife of Bath." [35]   But it does not seem so to me;
both the story and the sermon may be considered as
highly characteristic of the unfortunate teller.

Professor Root gives, with a remarkably keen and
sympathetic insight into the complexities of the character
under discussion, a more or less correct description of —
though not the " key " to — the whole contradictory
situation. " I conceive of the Wife of Bath," says he,
" as endowed originally with strong passions and vivid
imagination, with what we are wont to call the poetic
temperament. Had she been born in a palace, she might
have become your typical heroine of romance, her inevitable lapses from virtue gilded over with the romantic
adornments of moonlight serenades and secret trysts.
But born an heiress to a weaver's bench, there was
no chance for her poetic imaginativeness to develop.
Laughed at by others for her fine-spun fancies, she
would certainly grow ashamed of them herself. I can
believe that her excessive coarseness of speech was originally an affectation assumed to conceal the natural fineness of her nature, an affectation which easily became a
second nature to her. Her strong passions demanded
expression; and denied a more poetic gratification, and
quite unrestrained by moral character, they express
themselves in coarse vulgarity. It is only when called
upon to tell a story, to leave the practical every-day
world, in which she is forced to live, for the other world
of fantasy, that the original imaginativeness of her nature finds opportunity to reveal itself." [36]   Precisely!

The key to her character, however, lies in the fact, as I have already indicated, that the fineness and delicacy which achieves expression in the story is but the resurging, as it were, of the artistic Venerean impulse, an outcropping of the poetic temperament which somehow has been kept, subconsciously no doubt, pure and untainted from the blasting and warping influence of Mars and circumstance. Or perhaps she has guarded faithfully as a kind of sacred possession this love of the beautiful, which no one about her could understand; it may be that in moments of world-weariness she sought the fairy realm of the imagination given to her by her mistress, and found refuge for a time from the coarseness inflicted upon her by the War-star. The unsatisfied yearning for that gentility and nobility of character which might and should have been hers, but for the power of an evil planet, is pathetic; the struggle which has kept unmarred a bit of her original nature in the midst of sordid conditions of life and in the face of adverse circumstances is heroic. The poet may, after all, have considered her his most tragic figure because — as is certainly the case — she is the most nearly completely human.

How does such a character grow? Any dogmatizing by a layman upon the workings of an artist's mind in the act of creation is hazardous in the extreme, but speculation is always fascinating and perhaps harmless. It may be conceived by some that Chaucer is here drawing, to the best of his ability, the portrait of an actual middle-class person of his time, whom he has known on intimate terms of association.[37] In that case he has no

doubt noted carefully and recorded faithfully the significant speech and actions, the mannerisms and emotional reactions of the woman under observation, and
has interpreted these external indications of inward personality in terms of character. The idea is intriguing;
but since it is manifestly impossible for even the most
cunning artist to penetrate the mystery of another person's individuality, to sound its depths and shallows, and
to discover the mixed sources of action and feeling in
any given instance, such a process of imaginative interpretation from the outside must inevitably remain
largely descriptive, resulting in a character-sketch and not
a character-creation. The Wife of Bath is a character-
creation. Or again, most critics hold that the original " model " for Chaucer's " portrait " of the clothweaver may be found in the figure of an old harridan,
La Vielle, taken from the *Roman de la Rose.* Professor W. E. Mead is of the opinion that, though the poet
" did not attempt to copy the portrait of La Vielle as a
whole, he took from her the general suggestions for the
outlines of the Wife of Bath. But he modified the figure of La Vielle by making her younger and more vigorous, by giving her as keen an interest in life as she had
ever had, by representing her as still ready for matrimony whenever opportunity should offer. Furthermore,
Chaucer transformed the somewhat morose and broken-
spirited old woman, entirely out of sympathy with life,
into a witty and frisky shrew — good-natured in a way,
but still a shrew. Where did Chaucer pick up the hint
for that? " Quite likely, concludes Professor Mead, he
borrows again from the French poem some characteris-

tics of a jealous husband, Le Jaloux, whose scolding is somewhat similar to that indulged in by the Wife of Bath.[38] But granting that Chaucer has borrowed from the *Roman de la Rose* and from other literary sources certain ideas, or outlines, or human qualities, or personal characteristics, as it were, literary scraps and fragments, we are still but little nearer the solution of the problem. A figure consisting merely of a composite of many elements, a mosaic of human qualities and characteristics, is — to use the terms of scholastic philosophy — a monstrosity of " accidents " without " substance." The Wife of Bath is essentially " substance."

And finally, the present writer — influenced by the material presented in this chapter — once entertained the perilous theory that Chaucer may have fashioned Dame Alisoun in accordance with astrological principles. Being continually exercised over the problem of foreordination — I have said elsewhere [39] — and apparently believing to some extent in the influence of the stars upon the affairs of men, he has, in the case of the Wife of Bath, assumed the prerogatives and the responsibilities of a creator, setting up carefully a horoscope, producing a human being to be ruled by it, and amusing himself — perhaps like some other Creator — with the inevitable actions and emotions of his living creature. But upon more mature consideration I have concluded that such a theory in application is so mechanical and so simple in its execution that the resultant figure is likely to be little better than a highly colored dummy galvanized into a semblance of activity and emotion by astral influences, and in no sense a complex human being. Under the spell of Chaucer's pen one rests under the illusion that the Wife of Bath is a complex human being. Endowed with passion, reason, memory, and imagination, she is discovered undergoing a succession of human experiences which compass many joys and ills this flesh is heir to, growing old with the passing of time like the rest of us, recalling her youth with a gusto not unmixed with regret and sadness, sending her imagination abroad and forward with that pathetic wistfulness characteristic of those whose pleasures are chiefly material but whose spiritual powers are sufficiently developed to afford glimpses of something better. I do not know how Chaucer has created such a character, but I suspect that the soul and personality of this woman was conceived in the poet's imagination as a complete whole; at least, he alone could understand fully the sources of her contradictory thinking, feeling, and action. And in order to body her forth he has evidently drawn upon a rich store of human materials gleaned here and there from observation, from the imaginative interpretation of the common experiences of life, and from the literary works of other men, assimilating these raw materials by the power of a creative imagination into the personality of the Wife of Bath. In this process of creation the astrological material has played only a relatively small part. But a full interpretation of the horoscope and a consideration of astral influences moving upon the character in question would seem to be necessary for a thorough understanding of the part's original conception.

CHAPTER SIX

THE KNIGHT'S TALE

CHAUCER'S *Knight's Tale* is a marked example of the author's genius for welding into a symmetrical and unified whole the literary and other materials, often within themselves incongruous, that may have come into his hands. While the story is based primarily upon the *Teseide* of Boccaccio with amplifying passages from the *Thebaid* of Statius, it may more properly be called an original paraphrase than a translation; the result is a distinct creation much more artistic and effective than either of the prime sources. As critics have shown, the poet has added to the general outline of the narrative certain extraneous elements gleaned here and there from mythography, legend, history, and medicine; he has made use of realistic touches, revealing the customs and manners of his own day; and so subtle is the contraction, amplification, and fusion that one scarcely realises how epic material has been transformed into a romance of the highest order.[1] In recasting the story for his mediae-val audience the artist has apparently found it necessary or perhaps expedient to discard much of the ancient mythological machinery, which would encumber his narrative to no purpose, and to substitute as a motivating force that formative and impelling influence of stars in which his age believed. It is the general aim of this chapter, therefore, to interpret the technical significance of the astrological references, and their implications, with which the poem abounds and to show that Chaucer, in order to furnish such a motivating force for the final stages of the action, has skilfully gone about transferring the power of the ancient gods of his sources to the astrological planets of the same name; that the real conflict behind the surface action of the story is a conflict between the planets, Saturn and Mars; that the kings Lycurgus and Emetreus are, respectively, Saturnalian and Martian figures introduced to champion the causes of the heroes; and that the illness of Arcite is a malady inflicted upon him by his planetary enemy, Saturn.

Already near the beginning of the story Chaucer has indicated that there may be a planetary influence working back of the misfortunes of the heroes. Palamon has just been stung to the heart by the sight of " fresshe Emelye " walking in the garden outside of the prison walls, and has cried out in pain; whereupon his fellow prisoner, Arcite, not yet understanding the source of the trouble, counsels patience in adversity and philosophises:

> Some wikke aspect or disposicioun
> Of Saturne, by sum constellacioun,
> Hath yeven us this, al-though we hadde it sworn;
> So stood the heven whan that we were born;
> We moste endure it; this is the short and pleyn.
>
> (*C. T.*, A, 1087).

Though Arcite's knowledge of astrology is apparently hazy and indefinite enough, still his analysis of his own situation is more true than he can be aware of; as we shall see later he does indeed lose his life through the malignancy of this same wicked Saturn. At any rate, his reference to the stars fortifies the reader's mind against surprise when later Chaucer, in describing the temple of Mars — for the most part the god — says:

> Depeynted was the slaughtre of Julius,
> Of grete Nero, and of Antonius;
> Al be that thilke tyme they were unborn,
> Yet was hir deeth depeynted ther-biforn,
> By manasinge of Mars, right by figure;
> So was it shewed in that portreiture
> As is depeynted in the sterres above,
> Who shal be slayn or elles deed for love.
> <div align="right">(<i>C. T.</i>, A, 2031 ff.).</div>

By the beginning of Part Three, then, there is felt behind the action of the story a mysterious, impelling power, the force of the planets in the affairs of men; perhaps the fortunes of Palamon and Arcite were written at birth among the stars.

All through Part Three may be seen Chaucer's process of substituting the influence of planets for the power of the gods. Tatlock says of the poet's manner in the *Franklin's Tale:* "Since Chaucer has set the poem in pagan times, he might have ascribed the marvel to the power of a divinity; but characteristically of his later manner he chose a means which brought the poem closer to real life, the astrological magic which the Middle Ages universally credited." [2] So it is in the *Knight's Tale.* During the fifty weeks which must pass before the coming of Palamon and Arcite for their final battle, Theseus busies himself with preparing the royal lists, over the gates of which he builds temples to the gods. The altar of Venus stands above the east gate, that of Mars over the west entrance, and northward in a tower above the wall is the oratory of Diane. The description of Mars's temple is translated out of Boccaccio and Statius down to line 2016; this represents Mars the god. But the succeeding lines, introduced independently by Chaucer, describe the power of Mars the planet:

> Yet saugh I brent the shippes hoppesteres;
> The hunte strangled with the wilde beres;
> The sowe freten the child right in the cradel;
> The cook y-scalded, for al his longe ladel,
> Noght was foryeten by th' infortune of Marte;
> The carter over-riden with his carte,[3]
> Under the wheel ful lowe adoun.
> Ther were also, of Martes divisioun,
> The barbour, and the bocher, and the smith
> That forgeth sharpe swerdes on his stith.
> And al above, depeynted in a tour,
> Saw I conquest sitting in greet honour,
> With the sharpe swerde over his heed
> Hanginge by a sotil twynes threed.
>
> > (*C. T.*, A, 2016 ff.).

" Tyrwhitt thinks," says Wright, " that Chaucer might intend to be satirical in these lines; but the introduction of such apparently undignified incidents arose from the confusion already mentioned of the god of war and the planet to which his name was given, and the influence of which was supposed to produce all the disasters here mentioned." [4] But here is no confusion, it seems to me; Chaucer is deliberately building up an as-

trological influence with which he is going to supplant
that of the divinities.

And in this instance his astrology is entirely correct;
in the Middle Ages Mars was supposed to produce just
such catastrophes. Albohazen Haly filius Abenragel,
who represents possibly the best in mediaeval astrology,
says of the nature and influence of the war-star: " Mars
is a planet by nature hot and dry, fiery, nocturnal, feminine, and violent; he is a destroyer and a conqueror, delighting in slaughter and death, in quarrels, brawls, disputes, contests, and other contraventions; he is stupid,
quickly moved to vehement and devastating anger, aban-
doning himself completely to the execution of whatever
he plans and never withdrawing his hand from accomplishing that which he begins. He is instrumental in
stirring up seditions; he inspires wars and battles and
rules over the ravaging and laying waste of lands, over
pillage, plundering, ruin, and destruction by land and
sea. He rejoices in the outpouring of blood, in the afflictions of the miserable, and in all kinds of oppression." [5]
One may doubtless ascribe to Chaucer's creative imagination, however, the particular illustrations which he produces of Mars's baleful influence, such as the burning of
ships, the strangled hunter, the scalded cook, and the
child devoured by a sow. The poet is correct, moreover,
in his enumeration of the classes of men in the profes-
sions to which Mars is supposed to be patron. William
Lilly gives an extended list as follows: " Generals of
Armies, Colonels, Captains, or any Souldiers having
Command of Armies, all manner of Souldiers, Phy-
sitians, Apothecaries, Chirurgions, Alchimists, Gunners,

Butchers, Marshals, Sergeants, Bailiffs, Hang-men, Theeves, *Smiths,* Bakers, Armourers, Watch-makers, Tailors, *Cutlers of Swords and Knives, Barbers,* Dyers, *Cookes,* Carpenters, Gamesters, Tanners, *Carriers.*" [6] Chaucer selects as representatives of " Martes divisioun," however, only the barber, the butcher, and the smith who forges swords, though he mentions also the cook and the carter. In addition, the statue of Mars is described as having two figures of stars shining above it,

> That oon Puella, that other Rubeus,
> > (*C. T.*, A, 2045),

which are, as Skeat has shown, two " figures " in geo-mantic astrology ascribed, as the poet thinks, to the planet Mars.[7] Both the temple and the statue of Mars, it seems, indicate that Chaucer intends to combine the form of the god with the power of the star.

Though there is little in the descriptions of the temples and persons of Venus and Diane to indicate that they are anything other than pagan goddesses, still it must be observed that prayers are made to them by Palamon and Emily in their respective " hours," i.e., in their unequal astrological hours. Tyrwhitt has al-ready sufficiently explained the meaning of " unequal as-trological hours." He notes that each hour of the day is attributed to some one of the planets, and successively in the following order: Saturn, Jupiter, Mars, Sol, Venus, Mercury, and Luna. " In the astrological sys-tem," says he, " the day, from sunrise to sunset, and the night, from sunset to sunrise, being each divided into twelve hours, it is plain that the hours of the day and night were never equal except just at the equinoxes. The hours attributed to the planets were of this unequal sort." [8] On Sunday morning, says Chaucer apparently after the most careful astrological calculation, when Palamon hears the lark sing, although it is not yet day by two hours, he prepares to make a pilgrimage to the temple of Venus "in hir houre" (2217); at the "thridde houre inequal" (2271) the sun rises, and Emily goes to pray in the temple of Diane; and "the nexte houre of Mars folwinge this" (2367) Arcite goes to do sacrifice to Mars. "To apply this doctrine (of astrological hours) to the present case," says Tyrwhitt, "the first hour of the Sunday, reckoning from sunrise, belonged to the Sun, the planet of the day; the second to Venus, the third to Mercury, etc.; and continuing the method of allotment, we shall find that the twenty-second hour also belonged to the Sun, and the twenty-third to Venus; so that the hour of Venus was, as Chaucer says, two hours before sunrise of the following day. Accordingly we are told that the third hour after Palamon set out for the temple of Venus, the Sun rose, and Emily began to go to the temple of Diane. It is not said that this was the hour of Diane, or the Moon, but it really was; for, as we have seen, the twenty-third hour of Sunday belonging to Venus, the twenty-fourth must be given to Mercury, and the first hour of Monday fell in course to the Moon, the presiding planet of that day. After this, Arcite is described as walking to the temple of Mars, l.2357, in *the nexte houre of Mars,* that is, the fourth hour of the day. It is necessary to take these words together, for the *nexte houre* would signify the *second* hour of the day; but that, according to the rule of rotation mentioned above, belonged to Saturn, as the third did to Jupiter. The *fourth* was the *nexte houre of Mars* after the last hour named." [9] From this analysis it appears that Chaucer has not *confused* the gods and the planets but that he is with painstaking accuracy calling attention to the fact that, in the action of the story, they will function as planets alone. It is significant that in securing this planetary rotation he has changed the order of the petitioners from that observed in the *Teseide:* in the *Knight's Tale* it is Palamon to Venus, Emily to Diane, Arcite to Mars; in the *Teseide* it is Arcite to Mars (vii, 23–28), Palamon to Venus (vii, 43–49), Emily to Diane (vii, 71–92).

Prayers and sacrifices having been finished, Venus (though she knows little of wars and battles) seems to promise success to Palamon in the coming contest; Mars already adjudges victory to Arcite; and Diane assures Emily that she shall wed one of the lovers who now suffer so much woe on her account. Here is a conflict of promises on the part of the " gods " ; surely both Palamon and Arcite cannot be victorious.

> And right anon swich stryf ther is bigonne
> For thilke graunting, in the hevene above,
> Betwixe Venus, the goddesse of love,
> And Mars, the sterne god armipotente,
> That Jupiter was bisy it to stente;
> Til that the pale Saturnus the colde
> That knew so manye of aventures olde,
> Fond in his olde experience an art,
> That he ful sone hath plesed every part.
>
> *(C. T.,* 2438 ff.).

The suggestion for this strife in the heavens Chaucer gets from the *Teseide* (vii, 67); but, the gods having been transformed into planets as we have seen, the conflict has now become one of planetary influences. Jupiter, the greatest of all the fortunate planets, is introduced as peacemaker; and Saturn, the most powerful of the infortunes, arises to resolve the difficulties apparently, but in reality, according to his nature, to furnish through malignant advice the final disaster. Chaucer is again wise in his selection of Jupiter as the bringer of peace. For, says Haly, " Jupiter abhors Saturn and his nature, prohibits and restrains him in all his works. The former teaches and fosters goodness, shrinks from evil, assists the poor, and governs whatever is commodious or agreeable. He is truthful in speech, honest in deed, and fortunate in all his activities and influences, loving councils of wise men, just ordinances, and discriminating judgments." [10]   And Alchabitius is still more complimentary and pertinent: " In his magisterial capacity Jupiter possesses adequate knowledge pertaining to law, delivers just decisions, and judges with integrity. When he beholds men engaged in altercations and litigations, he has the happy faculty of restoring peace and establishing concord among them." [11]

Saturn, as Chaucer presents him, is entirely the planet except that his being represented as the father of Venus suggests a myth connected with his godship. He is the " olde," wise, " pale Saturnus the colde," who stops the strife for the time being " al be that it is agayn his kynde " (2451). Finding that his daughter Venus, who is more powerful in matters pertaining to love and

peace than in war, cannot properly support her warrior
Palamon, he ranges himself upon her side and prepares
to fight her battles against Mars, the war-star. The
conflict, therefore, until the final catastrophe rages between Mars, the lesser infortune and supporter of Arcite, and Saturn, the greater infortune and protector of
Palamon. And Saturn is well equipped for such a conflict; for, says he,

> My cours, that hath so wyde for to turne,
> Hath more power than wot any man.
> Myn is the drenching in the see so wan;
> Myn is the prison in the derke cote;
> Myn is the strangling and hanging by the throte;
> The murmure, and the cherles rebelling,
> The groyning, and the pryvee empoysoning;
> I do vengeance and pleyn correccioun
> Whyl I dwelle in the signe of the Leoun.
> Myn is the ruine of hye halles,
> The falling of the toures and of the walles
> Upon the mynour or the carpenter.
> I slow Sampsoun in shaking the piler;
> And myne be the maladyes colde,
> The derke tresons, and the castes olde;
> My loking is the fader of pestilence.
>
> $\qquad$ (*C. T.*, A, 2444 ff.)

Confident in his strength he comforts Venus with the
assurance that her own knight Palamon shall have his
lady Emily, Mars to the contrary.

Saturn's boast of an overwhelming power for evil is
well authenticated by the best mediaeval astrologers. We
are informed in the *Compost of Ptolemaeus* that " Sat-

urne is the highest Planet of all the seven; he is mighty
of himself, and governeth all the great cold and waters;
he compasseth all the other Planets, for he is under the
first mobile. Saturne is so hye that Astronomers cannot well measure it; he is thirty years in running his
course." [12]   As to his general nature Alchabitius is
lengthy and explicit: " Saturn is masculine, evil, diurnal,
signifying extreme old age if he be in the West and the
beginning of old age if he be in the East. He controls
a certain heaviness of cold and dry, and from a combination of these qualities under his influence is produced
and fostered the wise man of melancholic complexion. He signifies darkness of counsel, profound silence, and ancient and precious things pertaining to
judgments. He is deserving of mistrust and suspicion,
moving men to complaints and mutterings. He is old,
changeable, and of evil taste; he has power over dirty
waters, long wanderings, prisons, chains, slowness of
labors, afflictions, and *almauerith,* that is, the substance of
dead men." [13]   He is malicious enough in any position,
but he is most powerful in the fixed signs, especially, as
Chaucer has him inform Venus, in the sign of the Lion.
Says Guido Bonatus: " If Saturn be in the fixed signs,
he is powerful in producing destitution and death for
those born upon the earth. But in Leo he is stronger,
hardier, and more persistent than in the other signs." [14]
Albumasar further remarks: " And if his position be
equidistant in Leo, it signifies that infirmities and death
will come upon women, that wars and misfortunes of all
kinds will transpire, and that bandits will be active.
If he be meridional, you may expect the rise of rivers

and floods of great waters; if he be retrograde, corruption of the air, mortality, and the vehemence of hot, destructive winds; if under the Rays of the Sun, conflicts, wars, fevers and other diseases bringing death to men, the working of poison, and the bite of serpents." [15] His indeed are the " maladyes colde," and his looking is the " fader of pestilence." When in Leo, says William Lilly, he is responsible for " all impediments of the right ear, teeth, all quartan agues proceeding of cold, dry, and melancholy distempers, leprosies, rheums, consumptions, black jaundies, palsies, tremblings, vain fears, fantasies, dropsie, the hand and foot-gout, apoplexies, dog-hunger, too much flux of the hemeroids, and ruptures." [16] And as we shall see anon, he visits one of his most malignant distempers upon the wounded Arcite. This, then, is the cold, dry, slow-moving Saturn, sending death by inundation and violent storms of pestilential winds, fomenting insurrections, dealing destruction by poison, in prison, and by means of disease, who is pitted against his natural competitor in evil, Mars. The lines are clearly drawn; the battle between Palamon and Arcite — and back of that the struggle between the planets for mastery — is, by the end of Part Three, imminent.

Chaucer has seen fit to provide his heroes with one champion each of transcendent prowess; with Palamon comes Lycurgus, King of Thrace, and with Arcite appears Emetreus, King of India. Twenty-seven lines of description (2128–2154) are devoted to the personal appearance and regalia of Lycurgus, while he has only four lines in the *Teseide* (vi, 14); [17] and it requires twenty-four lines to present properly the King of India.

For some time it has seemed to me an artistic impropriety on Chaucer's part to introduce these figures into the story with such pomp and to call especially attention to them with such description of their splendid appearance, only to drop them from the action of the narrative forthwith, except to remark later (2637–2646) that Emetreus strikes Palamon a powerful blow and that in the rescue of Palamon, who has been taken to the stake by the force of twenty, Lycurgus is borne down and Emetreus is unhorsed. But as usual Chaucer works with a sure hand. These two champions are, it may be supposed, personal representatives in the lists of the astrological forces working back of the story and centered, as we have seen, in Saturn and Mars. Emetreus, who comes to support Arcite the protégé of Mars, is a typical Martian figure; and Lycurgus, who aids Palamon, now under the protection of Saturn, is Saturnalian in form.

This Emetreus, who does not appear in either the *Thebaid* or the *Teseide* and who is almost entirely a creation of Chaucer's own,[18] not only comes riding " lyk the god of armes, Mars," but is in body a product of Martian influence.

> His crispe heer lyk ringes was y-ronne
> And that was yelow, and glitered as the sonne.
> His nose was heigh, his eyen bright citryn,
> His lippes rounde, his colour was sangwyn,
> A fewe fraknes in his face y-spreynd,
> Betwixen yelow and somdel blak y-meynd,
> And as a leoun he his loking caste . . .
> His voys was as a trompe thunderinge.
>
> (*C. T.*, A, 2169 ff.).

Of the Martial man, whose complexion is hot and dry, Claudius Ptolemaeus remarks: " When Mars is oriental, the man born under his influence will be of medium size, neither too fat nor too lean; his complexion will be of a pleasing red and white color; his eyes mottled or speckled (*varii*); his hair thick and of medium texture. If, however, Mars be occidental, the native will be of a red color." [19]   Alchabitius is of the opinion that such a man will have a " round, red face and red hair, and saffron-colored eyes (*croceos*); he will be bold, of a fearful and violent aspect, lightly scoffing at men." [20] But it is Albohazen Haly who gives the best account: " If Mars be oriental, the man born under his influence will have a red and white body of medium proportions, a large head with thick hair inclining to curl and of a reddish color, a round face with a few freckles or marks upon it, large nostrils, and a sharp and wrathful aspect." [21]   Baptista Porta quotes from Firmicus Maternus to the effect that the Martial man will have " red hair and eyes with blood-spots in them "; from Abdila, that " he will have a fat, round face of a red color mixed with black, not quite a pure red but rather a red darkened as if by sun-burn "; and from others, that he " will have a strong, firm voice and thick, curly hair." [22] Lilly is not quite convinced in his own mind, apparently, as to the color of the eyes: he says in one place, " Generally Martialists have this forme, namely, they are but of middle stature, their bodies strong, and their bones big, rather lean than fat; their complexion is of a brown ruddy colour, or of a high colour, their visage round, their haire red or sandy flaxen, and many times crisping or curling; sharp hazel eyes, and they piercing, a bold confident countenance, and the man active and fearless "; [23] but elsewhere he remarks, " A Martial man is many times full faced with a lively high colour like sunne-burnt, or like raw tanned leather, a fierce countenance, his eyes being sparkling or sharp and darting, and of a yellow colour; his haire both of head and beard being reddish (but herein you must vary according to the Sign); in fiery signs and aery where Mars fals to be with fixed stars of his owne nature, there he shewes a deepe sandy red colour, but·in watery signs he is of a flaxenish or whitish bright hayre; if in earthly signs, the haire is like a sad browne, or of a sad chestnut colour." [24] From what Mr. Richard Saunders has to say about Mars's influence in sanguine complexions I would judge Emetreus's temperament to be of that sort: " If Mars be in a sanguine nativity, which happens very seldom, the person will be very well featured, round-faced, flaxen-haired, green-eyed . . . the speech bold, proud, and menacing." [25] The Martial man's hair, then, varies in shades of color according to circumstances from dark brown to chestnut, reddish, red, yellow, sandy, or whitish flaxen, and it is crisp or curling; or as Chaucer says, " His crisp hair, curling in rings, was yellow and glittered as the sun." His complexion is a fine mixture of white and deep red, usually tanned as if by exposure to the sun; Chaucer merely states, " his color was sangwyn." His face is full and round, which Chaucer suggests, possibly, when he speaks of the " lippes rounde " — the usual full lips of the heavy man with a round face. His sanguine complexion is dark-

ened, however, not only as if by a healthy tan but by
the appearance of a few freckles — " forte in ea macu-
las "; or as Chaucer says, " He had a few freckles
sprinkled in his face, in color somewhat between yellow
and black." His eyes vary in color from *varius* to
croceus, hazel, yellow, or light green; Chaucer selects
the bright citron. His voice is firm and strong, or as
Chaucer has it, " as a trompe thunderinge "; his countenance is fierce, proud, bold, menacing, with sparkling
piercing eyes, or as Chaucer says, " as a leoun he his lok-
ing caste." Such is the man born under the influence of
Mars; and such, it would seem, is Emetreus, King of
India, champion of Arcite the protégé of the war-star.

Lycurgus, King of Thrace, is in physical appearance
striking and magnificent:

Blak was his berd, and manly was his face,
The cercles of his eyen in his heed
They gloweden betwixe yelow and reed;
And lyk a griffon loked he aboute,
With kempe heres on his browes stoute;
His limes grete, his braunes harde and stronge,
His shuldres brode, his armes rounde and longe . . .
His longe heer was kembed bihinde his bak,
As any ravenes fether it shoon for-blak.
(*C. T.*, A, 2130 ff.)

And this is the very form and fashion of the Saturnalian
man. Claudius Ptolemaeus says: " When Saturn is
oriental and the sole dispositor of a man's fortunes at
birth, the native's form will be of medium proportions,
his color like that of a quince; the hair of his head and
breast will be thick, black, and curling." [26] Albohazen

Haly adds further: " He who is born under the influence of Saturn has large eyes, one of which may be manifestly smaller than the other, and in both of them there are spots; his hair curls, and his face is large." [27] Porta quotes from Iulius Maternus to the effect that Saturnalian influence " makes a man of thin body and of a pallid, languid color "; from Messahala, that " he forms a man colored between black and yellow, with small eyes, thick lips, and a flat nose "; from Dorotheus, that such a man will be " extremely hairy on his body, having bushy, overhanging eyebrows joined together over the nose "; and from others, that " he will possess the black, bristly hair of melancholic men, have heavy eyebrows joined together, thick lips, constricted nostrils, and be moist and livid or bluish of complexion." [28] Of the corporature of a man of Saturn Lilly says: " Most part his body more dry and cold, of a middle stature; his complexion pale, swartish or muddy, his eyes little . . . black or sad haire, and it hard and rugged, great eares, hanging, lowering eyebrows, thick lips and nose . . . his shoulders broad and large . . . his belly somewhat short and lank "; [29] and again, " Saturn signifieth one of a swart colour, palish like lead; thicke and very hairy on the body, not great eyes; many times his complexion is between black and yellow, or as if he has a species of black and yellow jaundies." [30] And Mr. Saunders concludes: " First, he that is cholerick havinge Saturne in his radix ruling, is pale, having his eyes deep in his head; slow-paced, red eyes, or like those of a cat, and little. Secondly, if Saturn be in the nativity of a flegmatick radix of any person of either sex, he is naturally fat, the

colour of his eyes and the eyes themselves like lead, and
all about them there is as it were a bruisedness. . . .
But Saturn participating of the sanguine humour, which
is the royal one and best of the temperaments, the properties are these: They have the voyce sharp and strong,
they are merry and jovial; but there are very few that
have Saturn chronocrator, or are of a Sanguine humour;
as for the face, they have it fair enough, but the colour
like an olive, red eyes with bloody spots in them." [31] He
is also of the opinion that " when the hair hangs down
and is soft, it denotes a humid complexion and sanguine." [32.]

These, then, are the characteristics of the man born
under the influence of Saturn in various positions. His
hair, on the head and elsewhere, is always a deep black,
sometimes coarse, crisp or curling, but in the case of
the royal sanguine nature softer and hanging down
straighter; or as Chaucer says, " His beard was black,
and his long hair, black as a raven's feather, was combed
behind his back." His complexion is usually swartish
or maybe honey-colored, a mixture of black and yellow
as if from a touch of black and yellow jaundice, or in
the case of the sanguine temperament the color of a ripe
olive. His eyes are sometimes large, sometimes small,
but always deep set in the head, in color red like those
of a cat or, in sanguine natures, red with bloody spots
in them. Observe that Chaucer does not say that the
eyes are yellow and red, but that the " *circles* of his
eyes in his head glowed between yellow and red." This
curious effect is doubtless produced when the " red eyes
with bloody spots in them " of a sanguine Saturnalian

man are set deep in a dark yellowish complexion; the red eyes have yellowish circles about them. His eye-brows are exceedingly thick, rugged, joined over the nose, and hang lowering over the eyes; or as Chaucer remarks, after having described the circles of his eyes glowing between yellow and red,

> And lyk a griffon loked he aboute,
> With kempe heres on his browes stoute.[33]

And his body, though of medium stature, is well formed with broad shoulders and slender waist; or as Chaucer expands it; " His limbs great, his muscles hard and strong, his shoulders broad, his arms long and round." Such is the man born under the influence of Saturn; and such, it seems, is Lycurgus, King of Thrace and champion of Palamon, whose cause has been es-poused by the greater infortune, Saturn.

Monday having been spent in the offering of sacri-fices, in jousting, and in the arraying of both astrological and knightly forces, Tuesday brings in the day of the great combat. All day the battle is waged, wavering from side to side with varying success, until just before the " sonne un-to the reste wente " (2637) the strong king Emetreus strikes Palamon such a terrific blow that he is taken by the force of twenty knights and drawn, still unyielding, to the stake. In the attempted rescue Lycurgus is borne down, and Emetreus, for all his strength, is hurled out of his saddle a sword's length. Theseus stops the combat and pronounces Arcite the vic-tor (2658). Venus, seeing her knight thus overcome and being powerless to aid him, is so ashamed and pro-

voked that her tears fall into the lists.   But Saturn has
promised to support her.   " Daughter," says he, " hold
thy peace.   Mars has his will; his knight has all that he
asked for; and, by my head, thou shalt be comforted
soon " (2663–2670).   Accordingly, as Arcite parades
himself as victor before the now friendly eye of Emily,
an infernal Fury, sent by Pluto at the request of Saturn,
starts from the ground and frightens the horse of Arcite
so that the victorious knight is thrown and fatally injured (2679–2690).   It must be observed that, whereas
in the *Teseide* (ix, 4) this Fury is sent from Dis at the
request of Venus herself, here the accident is brought
about through the machinations of Saturn, who fights
for the cause of Venus and Palamon.   The fatal injury to Arcite, moreover, is delivered in the astrological " hour " of Saturn when he is most powerful.
William Hand Browne reviews the astrological situation
admirably: " The combat takes place on Tuesday, Mars'
own day, and Arcite is victorious.   Venus cries out with
vexation; but Saturn bids her be quiet and watch what
happens.   Now there are three hours in Tuesday in
which Saturn could act: the sixth, the thirteenth, and the
twentieth.   The sixth was too early; it came at noon,
when the combat was not yet decided; the thirteenth
began at sunset.   So Chaucer carefully notes the time;
just before sunset — ' er the sonne un-to the reste
wente ' — Palamon is overcome and bound, Theseus
stops the combat and proclaims Arcite victor, who rides
triumphantly around the lists.   The sun has set, and
Saturn's hour has come.   He sends a flash of fire from
the earth, frightening Arcite's horse, who throws his

rider, injuring him fatally." [34] Mars and Arcite have indeed had their little moment of victory, but now Venus and Palamon under the protection of Saturn have already seen the beginning of what will presently be complete success for their cause.

But Arcite is not yet dead. Immediately after being pitched from his horse, his breast injured on the saddle-bow, he is tortured by a congestion of blood in the face, which becomes as black as charcoal or a crow (2690). They remove him to the palace and try every remedy known to physicians for his recovery, but nature no longer has any dominion over his body; and where nature will not work, farewell physic! go bear the man to church (2760).

> Swelleth the brest of Arcite, and the sore
> Encreesseth at his herte more and more.
> The clothered blood, for any lechecraft,
> Corrupteth, and is in his bouk y-laft,
> That neither veyne-blood, ne ventusinge,
> Ne drinke of herbes may ben his helpinge.
> The vertu expulsif, or animal,
> Fro thilke vertu cleped natural
> Ne may the venim voyden, ne expelle.
> The pypes of his longes gonne to swelle,
> And every lacerte in his brest adoun
> Is shent with venim and corrupcioun.
> Him gayneth neither, for to gete his lyf,
> Vomyt upward, ne dounward laxatif.
>
> (*C. T.*, A, 2743 ff.)

Now before it can be shown that Saturn is responsible for complications which render Arcite's injury fatal —

as I hope to do anon — it is necessary to consider in some detail the nature of the so-called " virtues " and their functions in the human body.

Chaucer is technically correct, from the mediaeval point of view, when he says that in this case the virtue expulsive, or animal, cannot expel the poison from that virtue which is called natural. According to Constantinus Africanus the Reasonable Human Soul or, in its various manifestations, the *spiritus* gets its work done in the body through the mediate functioning of a general force called *virtus*. This *virtus* may be divided into three classes: *virtus naturalis*, whose seat of action is primarily in the liver; the *virtus spiritualis*, or *vitalis*, which functions chiefly in the heart; and the *virtus animata*, or *animalis*, working through the brain. The *virtus naturalis*, in turn, is further divided into (1) the *generatiua* (*ministrata*), which has two functions, (a) *mutabilis*, and (b) *formitiua*; and (2) the *nutritiua* and *pascitiua* (both *ministrans*), which together have four functions, (a) *appetitiua*, (b) *digestiua*, (c) *contentiua*, and (d) *expulsiua*. The *virtus spiritualis* is of two kinds: (1) *ministrans*, producing emotions such as anger, fear, or joy in the heart, and (2) *ministrata*, having to do with the contraction and expansion of the heart (*pulsus*). And the *virtus animalis* has two modes of expression: (1) *interior*, which includes reason, imagination, and (2) *exterior*, embracing (a) *sensus*, and (b) *motus localis*, or voluntary motion, both of which depend largely upon the action of the nerves.[35] From this scheme it appears that the " virtue expulsive " is one of the subdivisions of the *virtus naturalis*, and that, therefore,

Chaucer may be mistaken when he speaks of the " vertu expulsif, or animal " cleansing " thilke vertu cleped natural " from poison. But Chaucer is not mistaken; he is merely following the best medical authority of his time in that violent controversy which was waged over the location, in this scheme of the virtues, of that voluntary motion of the lungs, *anhelitus*, or that still more voluntary motion performed by the lungs and the surrounding muscles and nerves in the act of coughing.

Arnoldus de Villa Nova classifies *anhelitus* along with *pulsus* under *virtus vitalis*, because " in the contraction and expansion of the breast the other virtues are exercised "; but his commentator concludes, after considerable reasoning, that " although this is true, the movement involved in breathing is not *vitalis* but *animalis*." [36] Constantinus, indeed, finding that breathing is the most indispensable of the virtues, gives one whole chapter to it. " Anhelitus or breathing," says he in part, " is very necessary in order that the natural heat of the body may be tempered or regulated, the *spiritus uitalis* nourished, and the *spiritus animalis* generated. In the management of cold air it guards the natural heat, which is reduced to the proper temperature, and expels the smoky air thrown off by the blood. Thus from the frigidity of fresh air is the *spiritus uitalis* nourished and the *spiritus animalis* created." In other words, the action of the lungs in breathing draws in cold air which is sent to the heart to regulate the natural heat of it and from thence is distributed to all parts of the body as a purging and purifying influence. Thus *anhelitus* feeds continually and tempers the *virtus vitalis* out of which comes the spirit which rules the *virtus animalis.* And therefore, nothing is more needful than breath to keep and save life. A man may live for some time without meat and drink; but if the breath is stopped or hindered in any way, the heart becomes surcharged with an unnatural heat so that the man straightway strangles. " Consequently," he concludes, " this contraction and expansion of the breast, which is called breathing, is voluntary; it brings into play the nerves and the muscles, and every conscious exercise of the nerves and muscles is a voluntary motion." [37] And therefore, he implies, *anhelitus* belongs to the activities of the *virtus animalis.*

But it is Gilbertus Anglicus who, in his conclusive arguments regarding the inter-relation of the virtues in lung-actions, furnishes, I believe, the source of Chaucer's present medical theory. Gilbertus takes the cough as his point of departure in discussing the virtues. Though there is no universally accepted medical tradition upon the matter — differences of opinion are wide and well known, says he in effect — still, because the inter-relation of the virtues in producing voluntary action of the lungs is so easily comprehended, he states his proposition boldly and with conviction: " The cough is a movement resulting from the combined action of the *virtus animalis* and the *virtus naturalis.* It must employ naturally the instruments of that *spiritus* which is active in expelling superfluous and noxious matter from the body. The *virtus naturalis,* in which there is injury, may initiate an impulse to activity in the instruments of the *spiritus,* but it is not of itself able to complete the movement resulting in expulsion; it may incite but not consummate ejection except by employing the mediation of that virtue which has control over the nerves and muscles of the bodily members. It is necessary, therefore, that the initial impulse felt in the tubes of the lungs should receive aid from the *virtus animalis* before the fumes can be repressed and the noxious materials expelled." [38] He then proceeds to show that the *virtus animalis* has the power to move the cartilages of the lung-passages and to cast out that which is harmful to the *virtus naturalis* by employing two modes of action, *sensus* and *motus*.[39] Expressing itself in the capacity of *sensus*, the *virtus animalis* feels or apprehends the presence of that which is noxious to the *virtus naturalis*, and in the capacity of *motus* expels it. Above the *virtus naturalis*, then, stands the *virtus animalis* with its joint activities, *sensus* and *motus*, each having a special function to perform in keeping the *virtus naturalis* in a healthy and normal condition. The *sensus* or apprehension is therefore prior to *motus*, because without apprehension or consciousness of that which is harmful or beneficial to the *virtus naturalis* there can be no voluntary action in the expulsion or retention of it.

Gilbertus further conceives of the *motiua* as appearing under two distinct aspects, *imperans* and *imperata*: "*Imperans* is what gives commands to nerves and muscles in any action involving choice or rejection of that which is consistent or inconsistent with the body's wellbeing; the *imperata* is that which moves the members of the body through the contraction and expansion of their muscles," as in the movement of the bodily members from place to place, breathing, and such like. The *motiua imperans* is, therefore, said to have its seat of action in the brain and the *motiua imperata* in the nerves.[40] And after further detailed discussion, he sums up the whole matter as follows: " When anything harmful secures entrance to the lung-passages or injures in any way the muscles having control over the expansion and contraction of the breast, then on account of the presence of the *virtus animalis* the *sensus* takes cognizance of the disturbance, the *motiua imperans* calls for immediate relief, and the *motiua imperata* moves the appropriate latitudinal and transverse muscles and nerves to expulsion. Such a movement of the lungs and breast, so initiated and carried out, is called a cough. The *virtus naturalis* has, moreover, four activities, *digestiua, appetitiua, retentiua,* and *expulsiua,* which originate in the liver; since the seat of the *sensus* is in the brain, it is quite apparent that there can be no precise adaptation of the instruments to the work in hand unless nature gives the initial impulse. When, therefore, the mind becomes conscious of an injury in the *virtus naturalis* on account of the presence of something odious to nature, then the *virtus animalis* acts for the purpose of expelling the superfluous matter; the muscles and nerves are put to their normal functions, and expulsion is completed. Thus the cough is a movement resulting from the combined action of the *virtus animalis* and the *virtus naturalis.*" [41]

Now this, as it seems to me, might well serve as a basis for the correct, though rather technical, diagnosis of Arcite's malady occasioned by his injury. That virtue expulsive, in this case *animalis,* which is concerned with the action of the lungs in expelling superfluous and noxious matter by means of the cough, is unable to cleanse the *virtus naturalis* from that which hinders the exercise of its proper appetitive, digestive, retentive, and expulsive functions. The *sensus* doubtless apprehends the existence of a violent disturbance in the region of Arcite's breast, the *virtus motiua imperans* calls upon the nerves and muscles to remove the noxious humours; but the *virtus motiua imperata* is powerless to carry out the command because the " pypes of the longes " are swollen and the longitudinal, latitudinal, and transverse muscles — " every lacerte in his brest " — are broken or torn and " shent with venim and corrupcioun." In short, Arcite cannot cough at all, and in consequence cannot rid his lungs of the unnatural humours collecting there. The result is disastrous. Cold air not having free circulation in the lung-passages, the liver is straight-way disorganised by corrupted air; it sends impure blood to the heart and hence to all parts of the body, so that presently the " clothered blood . . . corrupteth, and is in his bouk y-laft." And the heart, since it is not properly and naturally tempered by cold air from the lungs and since it is oppressed by blood from the liver sur-charged with hot and dry humours — choleric and melancholic — becomes overheated and so strangles or smothers. The " vital strengthe is lost an al ago " — and the spirit of Arcite changes house.

From the mediaeval point of view, however, no diag-nosis of a disease can be quite complete or trustworthy unless it is based upon astrological observation. As we have already seen, medical men must know how the planets in certain positions and combinations cause particular diseases, which may be cured only under special astrological conditions. The planets must be consulted upon not only the best kinds of medicines to be administered but also upon the exact time most appropriate for giving them. Cupping and blood-letting are especially subject to planetary influence, certain hours being more favorable than others. When Arcite's malady is considered astrologically, therefore, it is found to have been caused by Saturn indirectly, as we have seen; and this same wicked planet is directly responsible for the internal complications which finally produce death. Richard Saunders explains in his work, *The Astrological Judgment and Practice of Physic,* that there are in the bodies of men four radical virtues — he refers to the functions of the *virtus naturalis* — " holding a due proportion by Nature, by the which health and strength of body is always maintained; and when any one of these four do predominate and get dominion over the other, then doth the body wax sick, and languish in pain, and so surprised and overcome by death." [42] Of these four there are two that are directly opposed the one to the other, the retentive and the expulsive; and when the expulsive faculty is hurt or weakened in any manner, then the retentive virtue becomes unduly strong and dangerous in proportion. Now the first stroke of Saturn, as we have noted, is to have injured the lungs and the surrounding muscles of Arcite so that the expulsive virtue, whose office is " to drive out and expell all superfluities in the veins or arteries that do annoy or are hurtful to Nature," cannot function at all. This presents his opportunity for acting directly and fatally.[43]   For all astrologers interested in medicine affirm that *the retentive virtue belongs to and is ruled over by Saturn.*[44] Thus the expulsive faculty having been injured, the greater infortune sets about deliberately working through the *virtus retentiua*, his own special field of action in the body, for the death of his enemy.

It is evident, therefore, that the final scene of conflict between the planets is in the body of Arcite.   Mr. Saunders says further: " Sometimes this expulsive virtue is hurt or weakened so that he cannot do his office in expelling the humours and excrements of the body as he should or ought to do, either by heat or drowth, or by both; by heat in respect of choler and blood; by drowth, in respect of choler and melancholy; but most of all it is impedited and hindered by drowth, either of choler or melancholy, superabundantly abounding in the body." [45]   And in Arcite's case the accumulation of hot and dry humours, choleric and melancholic, is the work of Saturn through the manipulation of the retentive virtue.   " Unnatural retention," proceeds Mr. Saunders, " is caused of unnatural melancholy, whether it be in the extreme parts, or in the inward parts; and by reason of this unnatural retention a man falleth into a consumption; when the consumption is either particular, or general, in one member or throughout the whole body, by reason of the unnatural melancholy impacted in the veins in some particular place, or spread abroad generally in the body, this kind of melancholy is more dry than that which is natural, and by reason of the dryness thereof, stoppeth the veins and passages, that the blood

cannot have free passage as it ought, to give nourishment to the body or to the members; and this unnatural melancholy overcometh the natural melancholy." [46]
This is precisely what happens in Arcite's malady. Physicians do all in their power to relieve his system from
the oppression of melancholic and choleric humours impacted in the veins and arteries by the malignancy of
Saturn, but without result. They have recourse to the
letting of blood from the veins by cupping,[47] probably by
the use of fire with or without scarification; but the
clotted and coagulated blood corrupts in his chest about
his lungs. They administer emetics and purgatives, and
no doubt digestives [48] of choleric and melancholic humours, but to no purpose. The expulsive virtue is powerless to act; the retentive virtue has absolute dominion
over nature. And in the continued exercise of this retentive virtue, Saturn is finally victorious.

After this manner, it seems to me, Chaucer has built
up back of the patent conflict between Palamon and
Arcite in the *Knight's Tale* the story of another struggle between the influences of two planets. With me-
ticulous care and with painstaking accuracy of detail he
has succeeded in transferring the motivating power in
the narrative from the pagan gods, who are to him probably little more than poetic fancies, to the planets of the
same name, in order that the unusual ending of the
story's action — victory to each of two knights who
fight for the hand of the same lady — might be made
reasonable to the readers of his own day, who believed
in astrology but not in the divinity of the ancient gods.
Since the conflict is between Saturn and Mars, Chaucer

has created a typical Saturnalian man, Lycurgus, King of Thrace, to champion the cause of Palamon, who is under the protection of the greater infortune, and a Martial man, Emetreus, King of India, to support Arcite, protégé of the lesser infortune. And, finally, he has let it be known that Saturn has conquered in the struggle by directly increasing the retentive virtue, over which he has control, in the injured body of his enemy, Arcite. The poet has thus motivated independently and anew the story received from Statius and Boccaccio. Thus certain passages, which at first sight may seem to be digressions or unassimilated elements of the narrative as Chaucer presents it, are discovered to be organic and absolutely essential to the technique of the finished story.

II

Upon precisely what source or sources the English poet drew for his astrological interpretation of the pagan gods, it would be hard to determine with certainty. But I have observed that he is original only in his artistic use of it in the motivation of a given story; the interpretation was common enough in his day. To thinkers of the Middle Ages, myths about the ancient gods were merely figments of the poetic imagination or creations of the philosophic mind put forward to express an esoteric meaning. There seems to have been in general two schools of interpretation: that of the natural philosophers, who sought to give rational explanations of these poetic imaginings according to the principles of natural philosophy or physics,[49] and that of the *mathematici*, or astronomers, and later of the astrologers. We are interested only in the latter.

As early as the twelfth century Albericus, *philosophus*, arranges the gods whose persons he is describing in their astronomical order and indicates by remarks, introduced independently of his sources,[50] that they are to be considered as planets and not as gods. He says, for example, that " Venus holds the fifth place among the planets, and on that account she is described fifthly," [51] that " Mercury comes sixth in the order of the planets, and therefore among the ancients he was said to be sixth among the gods," and so on. In a later and much fuller work, *Allegoriae poeticarum*, he gives a more or less complete compendium of opinion on the gods, their nature and appearance as painted by the poets, myths concerning them, philosophical interpretations of the mythical history, their nature and influence as planets, and interpretations of the fables according to the *mathematici*.[52] And always he assumes that the astronomical interpretation is correct. If Chaucer drew from this source his descriptions of the persons of Venus, Mars, and Diana in the *Knight's Tale* — and Skeat's suggestion to that effect seems plausible — it is reasonable to suppose that he may have received from this same source the idea of treating the gods as planets. Be that as it may, in 1366 Bartholomaeus Anglicus wrote his *De proprietatibus rerum*, in which he discusses the planets and explains by reference to their astrological natures certain myths concerning the gods of the same names. He notes, for example, that Saturn is the most sinister of all the planets, cold and dry, and that he is therefore

painted in fables as an old man with a crooked staff.[53]
Jupiter by his goodness abates the malice of Saturn when
they are in conjunction, and therefore poets feign that
he put his father out of the kingdom.[54] Mercury is a
planet whose influence is good with good planets and
evil with evil, so that when he is conjoined with Venus
their qualities mingle; therefore poets have imagined
that he did fornication with Venus. He makes men
studious and lovers of the sciences and all kinds of
knowledge; therefore poets speak of him as the god of
fair-speaking and of wisdom.[55] The Sun is red at dawn,
brightly shining in the morning, hot at noon, and pale in
the afternoon; therefore poets fancy that he had four
horses, of whom the first was red, the second bright, the
third burning, and the fourth pale or loving the earth.
In a nativity he makes men fair and swift; therefore in
fables he is painted with feathers and with Achilles's
face, and is called Phoebus.[56] Luna gives plenteousness
of seeds to the earth and waters them with dew that falls
from her body; therefore according to fables she is
called Proserpina, goddess of seeds. She also gives light
to beasts and wild things that gather their food by night
in woods and groves; she is therefore fabled as the goddess of hunting and is painted with a bow in her hand.[57]
This will doubtless be sufficient to show that by Chaucer's time the astrological interpretation of allegories
about the pagan gods was not unusual. It may be noted
that when Batman comes to translate Bartholomaeus's
work in 1397, he adds more myths and indulges in astrological interpretation at great length.[58]

Finally, Robert Greene's manner of treating the gods

as astrological planets must be emphasised in contrast
with that of Chaucer.   In the Introduction to *Planetomachia* (1585) Greene has much to say concerning the
astrological significance of ancient myths.   He conceives
of Daedalus, for example, as that perfect astrologer
who instructed his son in the mysteries of it.   " But
Icarus tickled forward with the heate of youth, and
trusting to much in his vnperfect skill, began at first to
search the depths of Astrologie, and to wade so far in the
intricate misteries thereof, that climing to hie he erred
from the truth, and fell headlong into the deepe Sea
of supernaturall conceipts; whereof the Gretians said he
was drowned in the Sea." [59]   Eneas was not really the
son of Venus, nor Mynos of Jupiter, nor Autolycus of
Mercury; these myths mean simply that these persons
had, respectively, these planets in their nativities.   Neither did Jupiter cast Saturn into bonds, nor throw him
headlong into hell, nor offer him those unnatural in-
dignities which the poets have imagined; but since Saturn is a planet very slow in his motion and so far
removed from our horizon that his movements may
scarcely be marked by men, he is consequently said to
stand as though he were in chains.   " Who so considereth
the sacred and misticall verses of Homer and Hesiod,
shall find their fiction did tende to the discoverie of
Astrologie.   For whereas he telleth of the Chaine of
Jupiter and of the Darts of Sol, I doe think he meaneth
their irradiations." [60]   But in order that the science may
be made more interesting, Greene has staged a mighty
dispute in the heavens — modeled perhaps upon that in
the *Knight's Tale* — between Saturn and his daughter

Venus. The other gods take sides, and Sol is appointed by common consent to act as sole arbiter. For some time the controversy rages over which is more wicked in the nativities of men, Saturn or Venus, in the course of which the author succeeds in bringing out the astrological nature of the gods and their respective influences in mundane affairs. " But," says he in an address to the Gentlemen Readers, " that I might not be to tedious to young minds, I have interlaced my Astronomicall discourse with pleasaunt Tragedies, that your profitable Haruest may be gleaned together with delightful paines." Consequently, after Venus has given an astronomical description of the wicked Saturn and has remarked upon the melancholy natures of Saturnists, she proceeds to narrate a tragedy in which, as Sol judges, the final catastrophe is brought about by Saturn's malefic influence; [61] and Saturn, in turn, gives a story in which the tragic ending is occasioned by the power of Venus in the nativities of the chief characters.[62]

In other words, Greene is resorting to the literary device of illustrating the science of astrology with stories, in which the motivating power is the influence of Saturn and Venus. Now this is precisely what Chaucer does not do. He is not interested chiefly in astrology; the *Knight's Tale* is in no sense presented to illustrate the influence of Saturn and Mars in the affairs of the two heroes. On the other hand, Chaucer is immensely and primarily interested in the forward action of his story and in the conflicting passions of his characters. And in order that this action and these emotions may be rationalised for his readers of the Middle Ages, he has made of scientific astrology a handmaiden to his literary art.

III

But so far Chaucer has by no means finished adding to the original story of Palamon and Arcite sundry independent passages, by the assimilation of which largely his ancient source-material has been transformed into that marvellously unified fourteenth century narrative, the *Knight's Tale*. His age was not merely scientific; it was deeply philosophical, an age when philosophy must be made broad or elastic enough to compass all the sciences and nature itself. While Chaucer the artist may perhaps rest content with having accomplished the motivation of a story by reference to astral influences, Chaucer the thinker and inquirer into ultimate problems finds it necessary or expedient to consider the philosophical implications of his innovations. For the *Knight's Tale* is fashioned out of vivid life-materials, in which there is mingled much of human joy and distress, hope, grief, tragedy, and death. Since the tears and sorrows of old folk and folk of tender years are infinite and since in this world there is great pain, Chaucer will not permit these things to be left ultimately to the cold, unsympathetic direction of the stars; life would be unbearable if it were subject to these natural or mechanical processes alone. Consequently, he is impelled to introduce additional passages of philosophical import in which he attempts to solve in some measure the problem of humanity's variegated fortune in its relation to the destinal power of the planets and to Providence. His solution is evidently based upon the *Consolation of Philosophy* of Boethius.[63]

That part of Boethius's philosophical system which is pertinent to the *Knight's Tale* is comparatively simple, schematized, mechanical, and rigid. In general it deals with God's " simplicity " or one-ness in relation to the heterogeneity or multifariousness of His creations; in particular it treats of questions concerning the nature of Providence, the orders of destiny, the processes of fortune, and the significance of so-called chance or accident. How does a God infinitely removed intervene in the affairs of men dwelling upon this mundane sphere? This God, stable, indivisible, and benevolent, transmits the power of his will through successive stages of action, each one of which, as it is discovered to be farther and farther away from the unchangeable divine source, shows more and more diversity, change, and alteration than the one before. First, standing outside and aloof upon the " tower " of His simplicity or one-ness, God plans in His divine reason a universe as a complete and final whole, an entirely unified conception so infinite that it embraces every possible part — the creation of all things, the progressions of changing nature, all forms, causes, movements, that have been or can be. This ordinance, assembled and unified in the divine thought, is called Providence.[64] Secondly, in order that this conception may be realized in all its diverse particulars, Providence delegates executive powers to a blind force called Destiny, which administers in detail whatever Providence has planned. But because Destiny is somewhat removed from the absolutely stable center of divine intelligence, it necessarily becomes split up and divided into many manifestations; Providence is One, but he administers through Destiny in many manners and at various times that which as a whole he has ordained. Thus, whether Destiny be exercised by divine spirits (servants of Providence), or by some soul (*anima mundi*), or by all Nature serving God, or by the celestial movings of stars, or by virtue of angels, or by the machinations of devils, by any of these or by all of them together, the destinal ordinance is woven and accomplished.[65]

Thirdly, this Destiny so divided or distributed sends its influences outward and still farther away from the stable center until they move upon still another blind and capricious force called Fortune, whose function it is (being personified as a sort of goddess) to rule over the checkered careers of human beings in this world. And because this plane of activity is the farthest possible removed from the one-ness characteristic of Providence, the chief qualities of Fortune are mutability, change, instability, and irrationality. In other words, whatever comes to a man in this precarious existence — for example, birth, riches, power, happiness, grief, sorrow, reverses, friendship, love, death, anything and everything — is the immediate gift of Fortune. This unsympathetic, erratic force which continually whirls human beings from good to bad, from poverty to riches or from eminence to destruction, cares no more for one man than for another; its activities *seem* in their infinite capriciousness and diversity to be entirely illogical and chaotic.[66] But they only *seem* so to those who are ignorant or themselves blinded by success or adversity. For Fortune has two aspects; namely, (a) that " common " Fortune, which represents all common experiences of humanity such as birth, growth, disposition, love, death; and (b) that more personal Fortune, according to which an individual may be born at a certain time and place, grow up in this or that environment, perform a great variety of acts according to his disposition, love one person in particular, and die in youth or middle age by war or flood or poison. Thus any given experience of a man is likely to be the complex result of the combined influence of two or more destinal forces. Fortune as " common " comes from the moving of Destiny as Nature. Or to speak in poetic terms, God binds together the diverse elements of His creation and maintains their proper status by the universal bond of Love; planets follow their prescribed courses without faltering, for example; seasons follow each other in regular order, neither day nor night encroaches upon the province of the other, the sea remains within its limited bounds, men's lives progress in general from birth and youth to age and death, and people are joined together in the holy sacrament of marriage — all this because God has bound them by the chain of Love.[67] But Fortune in its more personal bearings may be the result not only of Destiny as Nature but also of other destinal forces such as, for example, that of the stars. It is Fortune in this latter aspect that is sometimes spoken of as chance or " hap " or " aventure of fortune " or accident.[68] But if accident be taken to mean that which comes to pass without cause or design, there is really no such thing. What

through ignorance is called chance is nothing more than
an occurrence whose causes are not understood. When,
say, a man digs in a field for the purpose of planting
seeds and finds a pot of gold, no one should say that
this chances without cause. The causes for this and for
everything else, though perhaps not perceived by finite
men, stretch back in an unbroken order through Destiny to the divine plan in God's mind. For all things
that are, or can be, are inescapably bound together and
unified in the ordinance of Providence. It is only because men are so short-sighted that they rail at the mutability of Fortune or the cruelty of Destiny (or Fate)
or even at Providence itself. But he who is philosophical of mind and stays his thought upon the stability of
God may rise in some measure above the vicissitudes of
Fortune.

Now of all the destinal forces manifesting themselves
in the affairs of men — " whether exercised by divine
spirits (servants of Providence), or by some soul, or by
all Nature serving God, or by the celestial movings of
stars, or by virtue of angels, or by the machinations of
devils, by any of these or by all of them together " —
that which seems to appeal most strongly to Chaucer as
artist is the celestial movings of stars. Time and again
he refers both character and action to planetary influences. For example, when Criseyde determines to return home after a visit with her uncle Pandarus, her going is prevented by Providence working through the
high heavens. " But O Fortune, executrix of fates,"
says Chaucer, " O influences of these high heavens, it
is truth that, under God, you are our shepherds, though

to us beasts the causes are hidden. She started home, but by the gods' will it was executed other than she desired. For because the bent Moon joined with Saturn and Jupiter in Cancer brought a deluge of rain, she was compelled to remain " (*T. C.*, III, 617). Again, in the *Marchant's Tale* the narrator is in light mood undecided what combination of destinal forces brings May to bestow her love upon Damian: " Whether it was by destiny or by chance, by the influence (of spirits), or by nature, or by the power of a constellation thus-or-so placed in the heavens that it was a favorable time for presenting a love-letter to a woman to get her love, I cannot say; let that great God above, who knows that no act is causeless, judge the matter." We have already seen elsewhere,[69] moreover, that the Destiny governing the Wife of Bath resides in a conjunction of Venus and Mars in Taurus; it is evident that the destinal forces hanging over Hypermnestra, in the *Legend of Good Women*, are lodged in the movements of Venus, Jupiter, and Saturn, and that Constance's fortunes in the *Man of Law's Tale* are in large measure subject to the power of Mars and Luna cadent from an angle in Scorpio and the eighth house.[70]

Now let us return to a further study of the *Knight's Tale*. Having demonstrated that the fortunes of Palamon and Arcite are to a great extent the result of destinal movings of stars, Chaucer now proceeds to philosophise the whole situation by referring this Destiny back to God. Throughout the story both Palamon and Arcite indulge in lamentations which indicate that neither is able to see clearly through Fortune, at least not farther than Destiny. When they are placed in prison, Arcite concludes at first that it is Fortune who has brought this adversity upon them, but he immediately traces these evil influences back to some ordinance written in the heavens, to some constellation in which Saturn is powerful (A, 1086). But for the most part he is so blinded by passion that, when he escapes from prison, his thought is only upon earthly things; he is distressed to imagine that " by some chance, since fortune is changeable " Palamon, being near his love, may attain his desire. This thought is as a death to him. Then he remembers that there is said to be a Providence which, working out the fortunes of men, often gives in many a guise better blessings than they could themselves conceive; he does not understand how or why it should be so, but he repents of having complained when he was in prison and comparatively happy, seeing that he is now free and utterly miserable (A, 1257). But Palamon revolts outright against the Fortune that has come upon him; he finds the gods, who are supposed to rule this world by their eternal word written in the " table of athamaunt," guilty of being cruel beyond measure or else senseless, since they seem to have no more compassion for a man than for a sheep. They torment the innocent, while the guilty often go free; he himself is in prison because of Saturn and is likely to be slain by the jealousy of Venus. He is perplexed in the extreme because his comprehension extends only to the changeableness of Fortune; he only knows that in this world there is great pain (A, 1303). Neither Palamon nor Arcite is wise enough to solve the problem of human suffering in relation to Des-

tiny and Providence, but their pitiful cryings in the dark
serve admirably to impress upon the reader's mind the
necessity for some solution.

Once Chaucer himself steps outside the story long
enough to remark that everything which may transpire
in this world is precisely as God planned it. Even so
slight an occurrence as Theseus's meeting with Palamon
and Arcite in the forest may be brought within the perfect scheme of things, though it may appear accidental.
" Destiny, the general minister which executes everywhere in this world the purveyance seen by God before,"
says he, " is so strong that, though the world had sworn
the contrary of a thing, yet it must come to pass if only
once in a thousand years. For certainly our appetites
here, whether concerned with war or peace or hate or
love, are ruled by the sight above " (A, 1663). It is
Theseus's nature to love hunting especially in May, and
partly on that account he meets Palamon and Arcite in
the forest. But it is the wise Theseus who, near the
end of the story, concludes the whole matter. Even the
Theseus taken directly from Boccaccio's *Teseide* has
known much of this world's transmutation, as he has
seen it changing up and down, joy after woe and woe
after gladness. Just as no man ever died who did not
first live, so no man ever lived who has not died (A,
2837–2846).[71] Everything must have an end — the
hardy oak decays at last, the hard stone wastes away,
and every man, be he king or page, must come to the
common end of all mankind (A, 3017–3034). Then
no one ought to mourn or complain at the passing of
Arcite, seeing that he died in the flower of life, sure of

his good name and fame; his friends ought rather to rejoice because he departed out of the prison of this life
with honor before the weakness of old age overtook him
(A, 3041–3065).[72] But it is Theseus of the *Knight's
Tale* who has studied Boethian philosophy and can pierce
beyond the mutability of Fortune in this world to the
stability of God. After Arcite has been dead for some
years and the mourning and tears have stopped, he sends.
quietly for Palamon and Emily. When they have come
and the place is hushed, he speaks: " When the first
Mover of the cause above made the fair chain of Love,
great was the result and high was his intent. He knew
why and what his purpose was. For with that fair
chain of Love he constrained the fire, the air, the land,
and the water within certain bounds so that they may
not escape. That same Prince and Mover has established in this wretched world certain days and duration
to all that is created, beyond which span of time they
may not pass though it may be shortened. Then by this
order men may well understand that this Mover is stable
and eternal. Well may men know, unless one be a fool,
that every part of creation is derived from the whole
(in God's mind); for Nature has not taken its beginning from any part of a thing, but from that which
is stable and perfect, descending thence until it is corruptible. And therefore, of his wise Providence he has
so fixed his ordinance that species of things and progressions (of birth, life, death) shall continue by successions
and not be eternal " (A, 2987–3015). Thus Arcite's
death, like that of every other man, belongs to the " common " Fortune of all corruptible things, is but an in-

cident in the progressions of Nature. And whatever may
have been the destinal cause of his more personal Fortune, that too may be included in the Providence of
God. "Who brings all these things about but Jupiter
the King — (i.e., God)? He is Prince and the cause
of all things, converting everything back to its proper
source from which it was first derived " (3035–3038).

In conclusion, it must be observed that in the *Knight's
Tale* Chaucer has used both astrological and philosophical material with admirable restraint and artistry. The
main question here is not whether he actually believed
in either astrology or Boethian philosophy — though I
have an idea he had faith in both — but whether he has
employed them successfully in the artistic reworking of
an ancient tale. Not being primarily a scientist, he has
used only so much astrological material as serves to
establish the destinal power of the stars, in some measure, over the fortunes of Palamon and Arcite; not being
primarily a philosopher, he employs only so much of the
Boethian philosophy as will direct all destinal forces
back to their original source. Under the guidance of
Boethius he might easily have solved the problems of
free-will, predestination, and the relation of innocence
or guilt to human suffering or happiness. But why
should he do it here? He is principally interested in the
story and not in philosophy. Consequently, having motivated his story by reference to the stars and having
traced destinal forces back to Providence, he leaves the
Knight's Tale a complete, well-rounded, homogeneous
piece of artistic workmanship.

CHAPTER SEVEN

THE MAN OF LAW'S TALE

NOT only in the *Knight's Tale* but also in the *Legend of Hypermnestra* and in the *Man of Law's Tale,* where the incidents of a story are already fixed and the elements of character largely determined, Chaucer introduces the motivating power of the stars. In these two narratives he attempts, I believe, to explain to his audience the action of a ready-made story and to rationalise a given character by the process of referring them to astral influence, by interpolating nativities which seem to govern and direct the prescribed action.

Introducing a nativity in the *Legend of Hypermnestra* is apparently something in the nature of an experiment on Chaucer's part. For the authentic incidents of the story he consults presumably every available authority, Ovid, Boccaccio, and possibly Gower; [1] and in all of them he finds that only one of the fifty daughters of Danaüs, who were married to the fifty sons of Aegyptus, failed to slay her husband at her father's command. Why? The story as it stands in the sources is entirely unmotivated and therefore not so artistic as it might be. Straightway Chaucer sets about supplying the missing motivating power in the form of a nativity, which to some extent explains Hypermnestra's character and hence her unusual actions.

Ypermnistra, yongest of hem alle;
The whiche child, of her nativitee,
To alle gode thewes born was she,
As lyked to the goddes, or she was born,
That of the shefe she sholde be the corn;
The Wirdes, that we clepen Destinee,
Hath shapen her that she mot nedes be
Pitouse, sadde, wyse, and trewe as steel.

The horoscope is general and indefinite enough, but it
will serve for an experiment. Chaucer continues:

For, though that Venus yaf her greet beautee,
With Jupiter compouned so was she
That conscience, trouthe, and dreed of shame,
And of her wyfhood for to kepe her name,
This, thoughte her, was felicitee as here.
And rede Mars was, that tyme of the yere,
So feble, that his malice is him raft,
Repressed hath Venus his cruel craft;
What with Venus and other oppressioun
Of houses, Mars his venim is adoun,
That Ypermnistra dar not handle a knyf
In malice, thogh she sholde lese her lyf.
But natheles, as heven gan tho turne,
To badde aspectes hath she of Saturne,
That made her for to deyen in prisoun,
As I shall after make mencioun (*LGW.* 2575 ff.).

Venus's influence, it would seem, is responsible for Hypermnestra's beauty of person and for the partial sup-
pression of Mars's malice; and Jupiter, joined in some
benevolent aspect with Venus, has been most powerful

in the creation of her gentle, sympathetic character and her marital fidelity. As the heavens revolve, however, the progress of Saturn into a position of evil aspect results in her untimely death.

Even a casual glance at any mediaeval astrology will show that Chaucer's interpretation of these planetary influences is scientifically correct. Baptista Porta gives a compendium of authoritative opinions regarding the beauty of person bestowed by Venus upon the fortunate native: " Venus mistress of a nativity (says Maternus) gives to the native a tall, elegant, white body, pleasing eyes sparkling with splendid beauty, and thick hair agreeably fluffy and sometimes curly or charmingly waving. Venus is similar to Jupiter (says Haly), except that it is her particular province to bestow more charm, greater beauty, and a better conceived, more finely formed, and more alluring and seductive body (seeing that Venus is responsible for that grace and elegance peculiar to women); a woman so born is milder and gentler. Others say that she is frail and slender, having dark eyes, delicate eyebrows joined together, tender lips, a full face, a magnificent breast, short ribs, and well-developed thighs; her general appearance is most attractive, and her figure is refined and elegant. . . . And Messahala says she has black eyes, in which the dark appears more than in those of other people, beautiful hair, and a face becoming round and plumb but not too full." [2] It must be remembered, however, that the children of Venus are in their marriage relations " volatile, capricious, and inconstant to a high degree, especially when they are not maintained sumptuously

and in grand style; and they are certainly more contented and happy if they are permitted as many separations and divorces as there are numbered principles of
love." Hence Chaucer is careful to qualify: "*Although*
Venus gives Hypermnestra her *beauty*, it is the partici-
pation of *Jupiter* with Venus that is responsible for her
tenderness and truth and fidelity to her husband and
wifely duty." For Jupiter is exceedingly beneficent
when he is alone in the nativity and entirely unoppressed
by evil influences: "If Jupiter is discovered lord of a
nativity," says Haly, "alone and in a good position, he
makes the native of great nobility of mind, honorable,
virtuous and pure, of fine reputation, just, morally upright and religious, frank and free, gentle of disposition,
quiet, unruffled, eschewing vain things; such a person
loves and is beloved by people who perform beautiful and
honest deeds, meditates and plans good actions while
wishing to have them secret and unnoticed, is diligent
in well-doing, and knows how to guard, serve, and re-
tain friends." [3] Now when these two planets, separately
so favorable, are discovered together, beneficently placed
in good aspect the one to the other and free from destructive influences, the resultant power for good is particularly strong: "If Jupiter is in agreement with Venus
and in a favorable position," says Haly, "the native is
likely to be illustrious and distinguished; — one who delights in beauty, has an earnest desire to acquire knowledge, approves of plays, games, and jests, is pleased with
benevolent deeds and characterised by honorable con-
duct; one who, having honest and pure inclinations and
virtuous desires, fears God, rejoices in right principles

and in keeping good faith, loves to defend the law, and delights in people of gentle disposition; one who derives pleasure from the examination and study of books, who is honest and upright in dealings with the opposite sex, and who observes righteousness, duty, and justice." [4]

These passages illustrate how much Chaucer the artist leaves to the imagination of his readers; he has only indicated the noble character of Hypermnestra when he says that she was born to all good manners, that the Destinies made her tender-hearted and compassionate, wise, earnest, stable, and true as steel. He is also careful — though without any attempt to deal in technicalities — to state that Mars is feeble in his influence, being dominated by Venus and suppressed by various and sundry afflictions of houses. Professor Skeat's learned note, in which he attempts to locate precisely the position of Mars (III, 384), is gratuitous. If Mars *had* been in power, however, Hypermnestra would undoubtedly have been able to use the fatal knife without a qualm. In the case of the Wife of Bath we have already seen the disastrous results when Mars rules in oppression over Venus. But here Chaucer is interested in emphasising the general influences of the several planets; it is quite sufficient for his present purpose to point out that Mars was feeble.

He says, however, that at some time in the course of the stars' revolution, Saturn's malignant power became directed against the freedom and life of Hypermnestra. As we have seen in the discussion of the *Knight's Tale*, Saturn is the most potent and evil of all planets; he is envious, covetous, jealous, a malicious dissembler, the servant of anger and the begetter of strife, delighting in destruction wherever he is able to accomplish it. He works havoc in every sign of the zodiac and in dominion over any of the other planets; " he has power over dirty waters, long wanderings, prisons, chains, afflictions, and the substance of dead men." [5] Albubather shows especially, in his observations " De natis incarcerandis," that Saturn brings about death by imprisonment, particularly when in aspect with Venus and Jupiter.[6] How, then, should Hypermnestra escape?

After this manner would Chaucer rationalise the life and character of Hypermnestra. Having provided a horoscope for her, he proceeds to lay great stress upon precisely those elements of her nature which are accounted for in the root of her nativity. She revels through the day of her marriage festivities like a true daughter of Venus and Jupiter; and when evening has come, she prepares to go meekly to the bed of her lord. But her father interrupts her passing with threats of death unless she will carry out his command to slay her husband that night. What should this pious, honest young wife do under such circumstances? The fatal knife is produced, from which she shrinks away in terror. Still, because of the fear in her timid heart, she hides the instrument in her robes and promises that her husband shall not live. The night is cold; the destined hour approaches. As she looks upon the face of him whom she must murder, all the tenderness and pity which the stars have bestowed upon her rises up in revolt against the infamous deed; staggering here and there about the room, she is torn by the inner conflict be-

tween fear, lest she should lose her own life, and her
gentle feminine nature which recoils at the sight of a
knife. And, besides, he is her husband; she has plighted
her faith to him. It were better to die than to shame her
wifely purity or to become a traitor to her marriage
vows:

> Now certes, quod she, sin I am his wyf,
> And hath my feith, yit is it bet for me
> For to be deed in wyfly honestee
> Than be a traitour living in my shame
>
> (*LGW.* 2699 ff.).

Weeping upon the face of her sleeping husband, she embraces him; he must escape through the window. After
he has departed in safety, she awaits with a noble calm-
ness the blow which must crush her because of her un-
selfishness. Her angry father sends her away to prison
— where she must die. Chaucer's experiment — if I
may call it so — is complete; he is moved, I think, at
the pathetic spectacle of Hypermnestra's suffering, but
by referring the outcome of the story to the influence of
the stars he has given a semblance of meaning to life
and has transformed an ancient tale into a work of art.
There is little more to be said after Hypermnestra has
been lodged in prison. Consequently the poet ends his
story in the middle of a sentence, which apparently begins to point a moral; but since the tale has been adorned,
he is doubtless artist enough to see that, for once, moral-
ising would be out of place. Presumably, he never continues the writing of the *Legend of Good Women.*
Some time after having finished his story of Hypermnestra, Chaucer sets about translating the pathetic, sad

story of Constance, into which he has introduced — either at the time of composition or later — the motivating influence of the stars.

II

In this connection I do not wish to raise the vexed question of relative dates; my argument is not materially affected by the priority of either of these stories. I am merely treating the simpler case first as though it preceded in time the more complex — as it probably did.[7] Having satisfied himself that the rationalisation of a given story is made possible through the introduction of astrological material, we may suppose, Chaucer proceeds to place an exceedingly intricate and effective horoscope in the *Man of Law's Tale.* The original story is followed more or less closely up to the point where Constance, a devout Christian, is compelled to marry a pagan Sultan; whereupon the poet, intent upon explaining the succeeding misfortunes, breaks out in an apostrophe:

> O firste moeving cruel firmament . . .
> Thy crowding set the heven in swich array
> At the beginning of this fiers viage,
> That cruel Mars hath slayn this mariage.
> Infortunat ascendent tortuous,
> Of which the lord is helples falle, allas!
> Out of his angle in-to the derkest hous.
> O Mars, O Atazir, as in this cas!
> O feble mone, unhappy been thy pas!
> Thou knittest thee ther thou art nat receyved,
> Ther thou were weel, fro thennes artow weyved.
> (*C. T.,* B, 295 ff.)

Professor Skeat's analysis of this passage, is, in the main, correct (V, 150 ff.). He observes that the ascendent, tortuous sign — i.e., the sign just rising above the horizon — is Aries, one of the mansions of Mars. The lord of this sign, Mars, has just passed from an angle into a succeedant house, in this case from Libra into Scorpio, which is his other, darker mansion. Luna, also falling from an angle into a succeedant, is found to be in corporal conjunction with Mars without reception in Scorpio. What Professor Skeat does not observe is that when the horoscope is in Aries — for horoscopes in all other signs the situation would be different — the sign Libra happens to correspond with the seventh house of the horoscope and Scorpio with the eighth (see Plate V). This is a conjunction of Mars and Luna not only in the sign Scorpio but also in the eighth house of the horoscope. In order, then, to understand the full power of such a nativity upon the life and fortunes of Constance, the following data must be interpreted: the horoscope is in Aries; Mars, *casus ab angulo*, is discovered in Scorpio, which occupies the eighth house of the figure; Luna is also cadent, having passed from a favorable sign-angle, Libra-seventh, into an unfavorable sign-succeedant, Scorpio-eighth, where she is in conjunction with Mars * (see Plate VI).

---

* Explanation of these technical terms may aid in making the horoscope clearer. In ancient astrology a figure of the heavens takes the form of a circle with a diameter drawn from left to right, representing the eastern and western horizons, and with another diameter drawn at right angles, representing the meridian. The quadrants thus made are further divided each into three equal parts, forming what is called the "twelve

It is not quite clear whether Chaucer considers this horoscope a " nativity " or an " election." The science of " elections," much cultivated among the ancient and

PLATE **V**

In medio coeli

30° Angle
Succeedant 30°
30° Cadent
Tenth House
Feminine
The house of kings and dignities.
Eleventh House
Masculine
The house of friends and friendship
Twelfth House
Feminine
The house of private enemies and affliction.
Equator
First House
Masculine
The house of life.
Second House
Feminine
The house of fortune.
Third House
Masculine
The house of kindred and journeys.

In oriente
30° Angle

Fourth House
Feminine
The house of treasure and terminations.
Fifth House
Masculine
The house of children and childbirth.
Sixth House
Feminine
The house of servants and sickness.
Equator
Seventh House
Masculine
The house of love and marriage.
Eighth House
Feminine
The house of fear and death.
Ninth House
Masculine
The house of voyages, learning, and religion.

30° Cadent
30° Succeedant
Angle 30°
Cadent 30°
Succeedant 30°
Cadent 30°
Angle 30°

In occidente

Figure of the Houses when the sun rises and sets on the Equator. When he declines the number of degrees in the Houses from horizon to meridian varies.

In imo coeli

houses of the figure." Of these the first, fourth, seventh, and tenth are called " angles "; the four succeeding these — second, fifth, eight, and eleventh — are called " succeedants "; and the four after these — third, sixth, ninth, and twelfth — are called " cadents." Thus every quadrant (beginning from the cardinal points and progressing counter clockwise) has its angle, succeedant, and cadent house (see Plate V). Supposing this figure

mediaeval astrologers, exercises itself with nothing more
than a careful observation of " days " and " hours " and
the motions of stars and planets by which times are
known to be either lucky or unlucky, as they agree or
disagree with the nativities of persons desiring success in
the business they are about to undertake. A nativity, on
the other hand, is a certain configuration of stars at a
person's birth which determines the course of his future
life. At the birth of a child, therefore, the astrologer
may prognosticate success or failure in business, happiness or unhappiness in life, and may foretell with certainty the specific things in which the native will be fortunate or unfortunate. An election — for example, to
determine an auspicious time for beginning a journey
— is useless and signifies nothing unless the root of a
nativity is known and unless the figure erected for the
election corresponds approximately with the horoscope at

---

to be stationary, we find that the twelve signs of the zodiac pass
in succession through all these houses. If, at a given moment,
the sign Aries is just rising in the East, it occupies the first house
of the figure, Taurus the second, and so on, until we come to
Libra, which occupies the seventh house, and to Scorpio, which
occupies the eighth (see Plate VI). Now, as we have seen, the
seventh house is an angle and the eighth a succeedant. Of the
twelve signs of the zodiac each planet (except Luna) has two,
called its " mansions," in which it is particularly powerful, or
dignified. For example, Saturn's night mansion is Capricorn
and his day mansion is Aquarius; Mars's two mansions are Aries
and Scorpio, of which the darker is Scorpio. These signs in
which the planets are said to be dignified are sometimes referred
to as " houses " — as in Chaucer; but in order to distinguish
them from the houses of the figure, I have consistently called
them " mansions." Both Mars and Luna have passed — i.e.,
they are " cadent " — from the seventh to the eighth house, and
so from the sign Libra into Scorpio, the night mansion of Mars.

birth. If the nativity indicates that the child just born will be unfortunate in marriage, it would be useless later to seek an "election" which might indicate a fortunate *time* for marriage; in such case *all* times would

PLATE VI

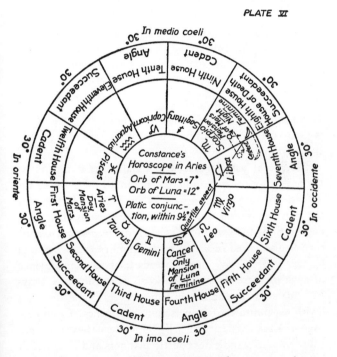

prove unfortunate. We may reasonably suppose, therefore, that the horoscope in question represents the conjunction of stars at Constance's birth; this is the "root of her nativity." Already at the beginning of her life, as any astrologer might have foretold, cruel Mars had slain her marriages — both the first and the second, which were still in the future. Chaucer, indeed, laments the fact that no election [8] was made in preparation for the *journey* to the Sultan's country, pointing out that the root of the nativity is known:

> Of viage is ther noon eleccioun,
> Namely to folk of heigh condicioun,
> Nat when the rote is of a birthe y-knowe?
> Allas! we ben to lewed or to slowe.
>
> (*C. T.*, B, 312)

In an interpretation of Constance's horoscope, therefore, we may refer indiscriminately to both horary and genethliac astrology.

Mediaeval astrologers, who usually draw figures of the heavens representing horoscopes in all the signs of the zodiac, are agreed that a nativity in Aries predestines for the native a rather checkered and precarious life. Indagine finds that when Aries is rising *in oriente*, Capricorn is discovered *in medio coeli*, Libra *in occidente*, and Cancer *in imo coeli*, and proceeds to show the influence of each of these signs: " Capricorn *in medio coeli*," says he, " decrees for the native honors, wealth and the most lavish expenditure of it, personal prominence, (a knowledge of) the mysteries of religion, and subtlety of mind. Libra *in occasu* indicates courtly manners and life, which is approved by few because it is insecure; one is continually raised to high positions and then cast down, now somewhat at the head of affairs now at the tail, sometimes breathed upon by fortune and hilariously acclaimed, then forthwith afflicted by various calamities.

In addition, there is no advantage or benefit without its disadvantage or ill together with other loss or damage; in this case the envy of friends and companions brings to pass the greatest evil, but this loss, whatever it is, is amended by Cancer *in imo coeli.*" [9]   Albumasar gives a broader view to the effect that Aries, rising under certain circumstances, afflicts cities and states with upheavals accompanied by conflicts " with arms, iron instruments, and the like, by murder, devastation, and ruin by fire; scorn and mockery shall light upon men and their actions, there shall be rapid alterations and changes from one condition to another, and deaths shall be greatly multiplied." [10]   And Haly is of the opinion that in matrimonial matters " All three faces of Aries are evil." [11]

Now, for a horoscope in Aries, it must be observed the " significator " is the sign Scorpio, in this instance located in the eighth house of the figure.   In interpreting the Constance nativity, therefore, one must give special attention to the position and status of that sign. For, as Professor Skeat has shown, Scorpio is " called the house of death, of trauaile, of harm, of domage, of strife, of bataille, of guilefulnesse and falsenesse, and of wit." [12]   The casual position of this sign in the eighth house of the nativity produces peculiarly violent and adverse conditions.   With regard to the eighth house Haly says: " This house is the significator of death, murder, strangling by suffocation, the destruction of men by fire and poison, of feebleness, infirmity, and the breaking of bodies by poverty, of great fear, dread, anxiety, and human miseries in this world." [13]   And Indagine,

speaking of the eighth house in an Aries horoscope, observes: " The eighth mansion from the East is that of
Scorpio. This is the house of death, terror, quaking, of
dead men — and of inheritance. If the Sun is posited
in this house, do not start upon a journey nor trust
yourself upon the waters. Wherefore, in this house are
compounded all wars, contentions from unjust causes,
enmities, and the evils of women, especially if these
originate in connection with inheritance." [14] Thus a
malignant fortune prepared for Constance is indicated
by the nature and position of Scorpio.

Moreover, Luna is cadent from an angle, having
passed from the seventh-Libra, where Chaucer says she
was well situated and therefore powerful in exerting a
beneficent influence, into the eighth-Scorpio where she
is not only without reception but in conjunction with
Mars, the lesser infortune. Now any benevolent planet
is weakened and debilitated in passing from an angle
into a succeedant house, or when it is in corporal conjunction with either of the infortunes, Saturn and Mars,
without reception.[15] Among the ten " impediments " of
the Moon to be considered in general prognostications,
Haly notes the following: " Fourth, when she is in corporal conjunction with one of the infortunes. . . .
Seventh, when she is cadent from an angle — for example, falling from the end of Libra into the beginning
of Scorpio — ; and this is worse than any other misfortune of Luna, especially in marriages, in all the relations
of women, and in journeys." [16] The same author remarks elsewhere " De qualitate matrimonij contracti ":
" If you discover Luna in an unfortunate position, such

as cadent from an angle in the eighth or twelfth house, you may say that evil shall come to both the parties contracting matrimony, and that they shall have trials and tribulations according to the nature of the house, of the infortune, and of the sign." [17]   Whereas before Luna was exalted in Libra and in the seventh house — " If indeed she is found in the seventh house, men shall be fortunate in their relations with women " [18] — she has now been weakened by passing into the eighth house and into Scorpio, a mansion of Mars: " If she is located in the eighth house, great mortality shall light upon men, and if she chances to be unfortunately aspected, it shall be worse; and if she should be in either of the mansions of Mars, death shall come to pass through strife and murder." [19]   Further regarding the significance of Luna in Scorpio, Haly affirms: " The location of Luna in all parts of Scorpio is the cause of much anxiety and sorrow, and because of such inadvertence she precipitates great evil upon herself.   Great impediments and hindrances shall be set up for her because of wicked reports and rumors." [20]   And Albumasar is in substantial agreement: " Her location in the middle of Scorpio signifies many conflicts, and plottings, and pestilence, and deaths, battles, and wars coming upon men." [21]   This position of the moon, then, is particularly unfortunate in nativities or in elections for marriage or for a journey.

Not only that, but in Constance's nativity Mars is discovered to be cadent from an angle, situated in his darker mansion, Scorpio, occupying the eighth house of the figure.   This argues definite misfortune, for, says Haly, " if the infortunes are posited in the eighth house, they signify the destruction and death of enemies and manifold captivities," [22] adding with special reference to Mars, the lesser infortune, " If he is placed in the eighth house, he shall be responsible for sudden and horrible death, in accordance with the nature of the sign in which he is located." [23]   And Mars evidences his malignant influence particularly in all the faces of the sign, Scorpio: " In the first face of Scorpio he guards or conserves his powers, applying himself to that which he desires and accomplishing upon his enemies whatever he wishes.   In the second face he is shameless and dishonest, envious and evil in his operations, serving himself with quarrels, brawls, and warfare.   In the third face he delights much in exercising his angry nature upon women, assaulting them by bringing force to bear upon them." [24]   And his power for evil, in this instance, is greatly augmented by virtue of his having fallen from an angle into one of his mansions where he has an essential dignity; " If Mars is in an evil position or if he is evilly affected by being retrograde or by being cadent from an angle," says Haly, " it signifies that he is powerful in planning and producing that which is in accordance with his nature, namely, fears, terrors, anxieties, perturbations of mind, evil thinking, wicked deliberations, and that which follows the execution of such; it signifies also many infirmities, and future afflictions through fire, robbers, or wild animals, journeys unfortunate and dangerous for the stranger wandering out of his native place, and bad blood between sisters and brothers." [25]

When, in addition, a debilitated Luna is found to be

in corporal conjunction with Mars in his own mansion
where his dominion is supreme and undisputed, the resultant influence is disastrous particularly in matrimonial
matters.   Haly is of the opinion that " If Luna is
joined with Mars, you may expect false rumors, lying
reports, and the effusion of blood "; [26] or according to
Goclenius, " Mars elevated above Luna in Scorpio signifies captivities and seditions in many places "; [27] or in the
words of Ganivetus, " It is an unfortunate circumstance
in matrimonial alliances when Luna is joined to either
Mars or Saturn, because there shall be neither peace nor
love between the contracting parties." [28]   Chaucer indicates that, in this conjunction, the resultant influence is
all the more virulent because the " feble " moon is not
" received " by the lord of the ascendant, Mars.   Now
" reception " is a technical astrological term.   A planet is
said to be " in reception " when it passes into one of another planet's essential dignities, e.g., into one of its
mansions.   The planet whose mansion is thus invaded is
called the " dispositor " because it " disposes of " or rules
or governs, or receives the visitor.   Ordinarily when the
dispositor is one of the fortunes, or beneficent planets,
a reception is not without good influence, especially so if
the dispositor of the planet signifying the thing asked
for is himself disposed by the lord of the ascendant, one
of the fortunes. [29]   But when the dispositor is one of the
infortunes, Saturn and Mars, the influence of any planet
" in reception " is vitiated and weakened.   Since, in the
horoscope under discussion, Luna is found to be situated in one of the mansions of Mars, Chaucer does not
mean to say that she is without any reception at all; she

is not *well* received, coming as she does under the influence of the malefic. Now if you are interested in learning the main impediments to happy marriage, says Haly, "Discover the significators and consider which are receiving and which are received; for if the receptor is an infortune or cadent from an angle, the marriage will not be successful after it is made, or at best only half successful. And if the wicked infortunator is the lord of the second or eighth house, you may expect disturbances of the conjugal relations growing out of disagreements concerning the dowery." [30] Since Luna is not well received by the infortune Mars, lord of the eighth house and cadent from an angle, Chaucer may well cry out, as Constance prepares for her nuptials, that "cruel Mars hath slayn this mariage."

But what should be the significance of his exclamation, "O Mars, O Atazir, as in this cas"? This is a dark saying which of necessity must be scanned. So far as I am aware, only one lexicographer has attempted to give anything like an adequate definition of the term *atazir*. M. R. Dozy says: "Atacir is not in the dictionary, but it seems to have been cited from the thirteenth century. It is the Arabian word *al-tâthir*, which signifies *influence*; . . . it is especially the influence which the stars exercise either upon other stars or upon various objects, e.g., on things here below, on the destiny of the individual." [31] Though the precise astrological application of "atazir" was being spiritedly discussed among Arabian wise men long before the thirteenth century, still M. Dozy's general and rather indefinite explanation is, for the most part, correct. What he does not indicate is that any concrete interpretation of the term *atazir* involves a consideration of its relation to *alcocoden* and particularly to *hyleg*, about which, says Haly, " the ancient wise men have vehemently disagreed among themselves, so that in continual and fierce contentions their exceedingly subtle and profound speculations have made disturbance and uproar." [32]   Now *hyleg* is a term used in astrology to denote that position occupied by certain planets or parts of signs, from a consideration of which, in its relation to other planetary influences, exact prognostications regarding the *life or death* of the querent may be made.   It is sometimes called " the point of life." Astrologers have disagreed violently over the number and location of hylegia; but all of them agree, I believe, that there are at least five hylegiacal places.   In order to find the hyleg one must consider the position of the Sun, or of the Moon, or of the precise degree of the ascendent, or the Place of Fortune, or the location of conjunctions.   From either one of these, posited in certain prescribed parts of the horoscope, the hyleg of the nativity may be determined.   For example, Sol in the ninth house, in a masculine sign, and in quartile aspect with any one of his essential dignities, is said to " make hyleg " or may be called " the hyleg." [33]   *Alcocoden* is nothing more than the name applied to the planet having the greatest power in hyleg; [34] enough of *alcocoden*. That which interests us especially in the nativity under discussion is the position of Luna.   " Proceeding further and enquiring after the hyleg," says Haly, " observe Luna, and if you find her posited in an angle or in a succeedant, and in a feminine sign, and in quartile aspect with a feminine sign, and in aspect with any one of her dignities, then you may accept her in that position as the hyleg." [35] Reference to Luna in the Constance-nativity shows that all of these conditions are satisfied: she is in a succeedant house, the eighth, in a feminine sign, Scorpio, and in quartile aspect [36] with the feminine sign, Cancer, which is her only mansion and therefore one of her essential dignities. Luna in this position is the hyleg of the nativity.

Having determined the hyleg in any figure, we are then ready to calculate — and interpret in terms of life and death, health or sickness, prosperity or misfortune — the influences, good or bad, which other planets direct by aspect upon that point. Now the influence resulting from such a calculation of planetary influences exerted upon the hyleg by reference to the aspects of various planets is what astrologers call *atazir*. As Albubather says: "The hyleg signifies the life and death of the native. And *per athazir eius ad aspectum* of the fortunate and unfortunate planets, you may know about the life and death of the native, according to the grace of God." [37] These influences may be either good or bad, depending upon the nature of the planet in aspect, whether a fortune or an infortune: " *Per athazir hyleg ad aspectum* of the fortunate and unfortunate planets, you may determine the times in which good or evil will come to the native, the nature of it, or whether it will come at all or not." [38] For example, if Jupiter is found to be in, say, quartile or oppositional aspect with the hyleg, his influence is uniformly beneficent: " *Per athazir (hyleg per aspectum) Iouis,* you may know that the native will have the friendship of kings and potentates and whatever there is to be had of fortune and beauty." [39] When Mars, one of the infortunes, is in strong aspect with the hyleg, the case of the native is hopeless save for the grace of God: " *Per athazir* (*hyleg per aspectum*) *Martis,* you may prognosticate fornications, marriages, love affairs, and friendships; misfortune or injury to women, conflicts, quarrels, and reverses." [40] In the horoscope of Constance, as we have already seen, Mars is in conjunctional aspect with Luna in the hylegiacal position. This signifies that, in addition to all the other misfortunes which we have predicted above might befall her, she is subject to death unless miraculously protected: " When Luna is the hyleg and the degree of the ascendent in the radix of the nativity is unfortunate and if she is in conjunction with Sol or with one of the infortunes, then the native born at such an unfortunate hour will be in danger of death." [41] The *athazir hyleg per aspectum Martis* hath slain this marriage and precipitated a flood of misfortunes upon the head of Constance.*

* It must be observed that this atazir of the hyleg by reference to the influence of the single planet, Mars, is the least complex imaginable. In a full and complete reckoning of the atazir of the hyleg, the honest astrologer must consider not only the hylegiacal position but also the aspects of *all* other planets, of the tenth house, and of the Place of Fortune. He must observe, moreover, the declinations and relative motions of these planets; their benefic or malefic natures; their situations in good or bad signs; whether their influence is strong or weak, depending upon whether the nativity is diurnal or nocturnal; and whether they are combust, retrograde, or peregrine. He must determine whether the aspects are accurate, or nearly so, and strongly favorable, i.e., semi-sextile, sextile, quintile, trine, and biquintile, or

When the horoscope of Constance is interpreted after this fashion according to the directions of mediaeval astrology, the main incidents of her life as Chaucer lifts them from the chronicle of Trivet are fully explained. This particular addition which the poet has made to the original story is not haphazard and aimless; I believe that it is organic. He is careful to notify the reader at the very beginning of his process of rationalisation that every man's death is written plainly in the heavens:

> For in the sterres, clerer than is glas,
> Is writen, got wot, who-so coude it rede,
> The deeth of every man, withouten drede.

It was so in the case of Pompey, Julius, Hercules, and others; the conflict which raged about the city of Thebes was foreshadowed in the stars. The finite minds of men, however, are so dull that they are unable to read the mysterious messages completely or aright. Else men might have known that, even for the Sultan, his marriage with Constance must bring about misfortune and death; in that great book which men call the heavens it was long ago written with stars that love should prove to be his destruction. And so it happens in the story. As for Constance, her marriages are doomed in advance, by the inexorable laws of the stars having power at her birth, to be accompanied by unhappiness; her jour-

---

unfavorable, i.e., square, semi-square, sesquiquadrate and opposition. And all of these positions and relative motions must be calculated to the minute and second. Chaucer, being an artist and using astrological material for literary purposes, is not concerned with these technicalities.

neys must be attended by suffering; and the baleful influence of Mars directed against Luna, the hyleg, quite clearly makes her death practically inevitable. That she escapes this pre-ordained fate in the midst of calamities is due to the intervention of the grace of God.

When it is remembered that at the birth of Constance Aries was just rising in the East, no one need be surprised that her life is precarious and beset with dangers which, in the ordinary course of human events, would prove fatal. She is continually being raised to positions of eminence and honor and as often cast down. Her marriage to the Lord of Syria is heralded with pomp; but no sooner has she arrived in the pagan country than the wicked Sultaness begins plotting against the happiness and the very life of the young wife. A great feast is prepared, it will be remembered, at which both pagans and Christians are entertained; there is much reveling — but in the end the Christians and all the pagans who are on the point of betraying their faith are murdered and hewn to pieces. Constance alone escapes the vengeance of the Sultaness, to be set adrift in an open boat, carefully provisioned to be sure, but without sails or rudder. It is only after terrible hardships that she arrives upon the shores of England. This once she has escaped the decrees of the stars. Living a devout life in the new country and winning many souls to Christianity, she is entertained by Alla and Hermengild, his wife, with respect and honor. But she may not remain long in peace. A young knight, having conceived an unholy passion for her and having been repulsed, takes his revenge by murdering Hermengild and placing

the bloody knife in the hand of sleeping Constance.
Here again, however, the decree of death pronounced
by the stars is averted at the last moment by a sign from
heaven.

New honors are later showered upon her in the form
of marriage with Alla, and she rejoices afresh in the
birth of a child. But Mars, cadent from an angle,
powerful in Scorpio, and ruling in oppression over Luna,
proves malignant to this marriage also — for a time.
Alla's jealous mother, Donegild, by a skilful interchange
of letters works the downfall of the young wife, who is
torn from her child and again set adrift upon the sea.
In the course of her aimless wanderings she is tortured
by hunger, threatened with the lust of men, beset round
about with pirates, and broken with grief.   Indeed, she
is the afflicted of fortune.   Her marriages, as might
have been expected, are accompanied not only by her
personal sorrows but also by wars and the struggles of
men in arms, by murders and assassinations, and by the
misfortunes of whole peoples.   Scorpio and the eighth
house have taken their toll of the afflicted and the dead;
they with Mars have worked destruction.

No one must suppose, however, that in his astrological beliefs Chaucer is an out-and-out fatalist.   He is
too good a church-man, I suppose, for that.[42]   Being
doubtless familiar with the most advanced astrological
thought of his time, he could scarcely have escaped pon-
dering over the problem of God's relation to the more
or less unalterable influence of the stars upon the lives
of men.   If the laws of astrology are valid and effective,
what part does a Supreme Being play in the universe?

The violent controversy over this matter which raged over Europe for centuries during the Middle Ages [43] must have attracted Chaucer's attention to the subject; he must have been intimately acquainted, I think, with the arguments presented by both sides in the great intellectual conflict. Men believed in astrology; they also had faith in God. In most of the independent passages which he has introduced into the *Man of Law's Tale,* the poet is eager, it seems to me, to make his position unmistakably clear: the stars are undoubtedly powerful in directing human affairs, but they are still subject ultimately to the will of God. While he has not slighted the tragedy of the original story, one cannot help noticing that he has apparently attempted to soften it by insisting upon the power of a Christian faith. As we have seen, Constance might have lost her life at several points in the narrative; according to the laws of astrology her death might ordinarily have been predicted with certainty. Chaucer has indeed permitted the stars to afflict her in many ways, in almost any way — short of death; she *must* escape death. So it is in the original version of the story — which he does not feel inclined to change — and so it may be in real life when God stretches forth His hand among the stars. In addition, therefore, to introducing a horoscope for the purpose of explaining the main incidents of the story, Chaucer now sets about creating other independent passages in order to prove the supremacy of a Divine Power over astral influence.

Thanks to the beneficence of the sign Libra in the East at the birth of Constance, she was endowed with a religious nature and with an insight into religious mysteries; she lives and moves by faith. Why does she alone escape death at the feast given by the Sultaness? It is a miracle, says Chaucer, such as one finds common enough in the pages of Holy Writ and in the legendary lives of the saints.[a] Again, as she is sent out to sea the first time, Constance addresses herself to Christ and submits herself into His hands; it is His power which directs her ship into a safe port.[b] When in despair she is being tried for murder before the court of Alla, alone and without a champion, she remembers that two of God's saints were once similarly oppressed and that by His grace they were rescued;[c] she too is vindicated by the mysterious appearance of an arm from heaven which smites to death her false accuser. And when an impious man comes aboard her ship for the purpose of ravishing her honor, some divine power preserves her chastity; the wicked man falls overboard and is drowned. Nor is this surprising, says Chaucer, for so God gave courage, strength, and protection to David when he went alone against Goliath, and to Judith when she was led to the couch of Holofernes.[d] And the final happiness of Constance, after all her suffering at the hands of a malignant fortune, is presented as a free and pathetic gift of Christ.[e] Chaucer here stands with the best of mediaeval astrologers who recognise, in their darkest prognostications, the fact that certain combinations of stars which

---

[a] See *C. T.*, B, 470–504. This is Chaucer's addition.

[b] *Ibid.*, B, 449–462. Also Chaucer's.

[c] *Ibid.*, B, 631–658. Chaucer's interpolation.

[d] *Ibid.*, B, 925–945. The Author's comment.

[e] *Ibid.*, B, 1037–1043, 1049–1070. Independent passages.

seem to foretell inevitable death are subject to the intervening and arbitrary hand of God. By emphasising this belief Chaucer has made reasonable not only the escapes all along the way of Constance's life but also her final happiness.

After this manner the artist works, it seems to me, when he wishes to rationalise the ready-made incidents of the Constance story and explain some of the elements of a fixed character. Many things in the life of Constance, which may have puzzled the poet and his readers at first, are made clear by reference to the *athazir hyleg per aspectum Martis* and by an insistence upon the intervening hand of God. And all this is accomplished in the independent passages. I cannot understand, therefore, how Professor Skeat's opinion can be any longer accepted as wise when he says, " All of these insertions are, in fact, digressions, and have nothing to do with the story." While I would not willingly have it inferred from the emphasis which I have placed upon these passages that Chaucer is making his story illustrate the workings of astrological principles, still it does seem to me that, without a horoscope showing the influence of the stars and without the recognition of Divine Power, this life of Constance would possess little more unity than Trivet's version. But as we have it the *Man of Law's Tale* seems to be a whole complete within itself, compact in spite of its apparently straggling and unconnected incidents, excellently motivated, possessed of an unusual — in the Middle Ages — unity of character, and therefore a piece of artistic workmanship.

Such a procedure on Chaucer's part should occasion

no surprise; he is in large measure the product of his time. Professor J. L. Lowes has already observed that the Middle Ages seized upon the great stories of the past and, while preserving a core of vital narrative, translated epic machinery and classical mythology into terms of the commonplaces dear to their own heart. They reset the stage and recostumed the actors. "The mediaeval courtly romances of the period were crowded with the marvellous. And the marvellous had built up its own imposing fabric of conventions. And when Benoit and the unknown writers of other classical romances came to their Latin material, they found there a no less imposing paraphernalia of conventional machinery — the wrath of Juno, the wiles of Venus, the missions of Hermes, the instigations of Pallas Athene. But the gods of Greece and Rome had meantime undergone their *Götterdämmerung,* and the elaborate structure built on their interventions had become to the Middle Ages an empty shell. And so when the epics went over into the romances, for mythology were substituted marvels; in place of the interpositions of the gods appears the world of magic — magic robes, magic swords, magic tents, enchanted castles and chambers, *fées* and monsters. . . . The gods have vanished, and instead the land is 'al fulfiled of fayerye.'" [44] Chaucer is of this age, but also somewhat in advance of it. By the introduction of fairy-lore, for example, he has prepared for the climax of the *Marchant's Tale,* which features blind January's recovery of sight just in time to see May's infidelity with the love-lorn Damian, and the skill with which the young wife persuades her aged cuckold hus-

band that all was done for his benefit. Now in one ana-
logue of this incident the blind man's sight is miraculously restored, and the wife explains that his recovery is
due to her contrivance; in another the husband is not
blind, but the tree is supposed to be enchanted and to cause
illusions. But when Chaucer comes to use the story, he
sees that enchanted trees and miraculous recovery of
sight are out of place in a satirical narrative. Consequently, he introduces Claudian's Pluto and Proserpina
transformed after the manner of *Sir Orfeo* into the
King and Queen of Fairyland, and represents them in
sympathy respectively with the injured husband and the
erring wife. Their quarrel is delightfully human.[45]
Pluto, quoting satirical authorities like a mediaeval man
of the world, refers to ten hundred thousand stories he
could tell which present the untruth and infidelity of
women, and resolves to open old January's eyes to young
May's harlotry; Proserpina, recking not a butterfly what
Pluto's authorities write against women, defends the
truth and honor of her sex in general, and determines
to give May a fitting answer when she is discovered at
fault. And so it happens. May enjoys her lover; January's sight is restored by Pluto in time for him to see
— enough; and May is provided with an answer which
delights her duped husband and prepares for continued
stolen sweets. Thus Chaucer has introduced the popular superstitions of his time, a sort of fairy machinery,
in order that the unusual ending of the story may seem
motivated and reasonable to his readers. But so far as
I know Chaucer is the only mediaeval writer who mo-
tivates narrative action by reference to the stars. Still,

since the popular astrology of his age was more scientific and credible than magic, *faerie,* and enchantment of all kinds, I see no reason why he should not have seized upon its principles for the purpose of improving and strengthening the technique of the *Knight's Tale,* the *Legend of Hypermnestra,* and the *Man of Law's Tale.*

CHAPTER EIGHT

MEDIAEVAL DREAM–LORE

Somnia ne cures; nam fallunt somnia plures

AN attempt to sound Chaucer's knowledge of dream-psychology without an appeal to Freud and other modern writers on the subject of dreams may seem to critics a foolhardy procedure calculated to be accompanied at every turn by failure. And to suggest that Chaucer's classification of the various types of dreams together with his perplexed conjectures regarding their causes may not, possibly, have been based entirely upon Macrobius's commentaries on the *Somnium Scipionis* or upon passages from *Le Roman de la Rose,* and that the framework of his dream-poems was not, perhaps, patterned altogether after the Old French *genre,* may appear to be flying wantonly in the face of long-established and therefore respectable fact. But it is comforting to remember that Chaucer knew less about modern psychoanalytical theory regarding dreams than even the present writer, that in trying to fathom the mysteries of a natural phenomenon in which his interest was great and evidently abiding he would not, likely enough, have confined his researches to the commentaries of one or two writers, and that, though he was first and last a literary man and consequently acquainted with all the prevailing types of literary love-visions, he was also broad-minded enough to give more than a passing notice to mediaeval dream-lore in its scientific aspect with the idea in mind, doubtless, of employing it in his art. The purpose of this and the succeeding chapter is to classify dreams and visions according to the medical men, natural and other philosophers, and theologians of the Middle Ages, to show how these classes are named or are represented in the writings of Chaucer, and finally to demonstrate, if possible, how the English poet has brought his knowledge of dream-psychology and the philosophy of sleep effectively to bear upon the creation of two characters in the *Nun's Priest's Tale.*[1]

No one must suppose, of course, that Chaucer's charmingly avowed ignorance of dreams and their sources, as put forth in the introduction to the *House of Fame* (1–55), in any way indicates the actual state of his knowledge; his disarming simplicity and confession of inability to understand are merely assumed for literary purposes. He has almost addled his poor wits, it will be remembered, trying to grasp the significance of certain groups and sub-groups, classes and sub-classes, into which dreams have been divided, and attempting to fathom the true causes from which they spring; but for all that, may God turn every dream to good! For by the cross, says he in effect, it is something to be wondered at, according to his way of thinking, what indeed does cause dreams either in the morning or in the evening, and why some are followed by sure results and others are not. In perplexity he observes that one is sometimes called an " avisioun " and another a " revelacioun," this a " dreem " and that a " sweven," still another a " fantom " and some " oracles," but he does not understand why; let those who know more about these " miracles " than he does solve the problem. For however busily he may work his mind he is still at a loss to determine the exact significance of the " gendres," or to know the time-lengths which ought to be allotted to the various species, or to comprehend why one thing rather than another should be picked out as the cause. For example, some say that " folkes complexiouns make hem dreme of reflexiouns "; others will have it that dreams originate in a certain feebleness of brain caused by abstinence or sickness or prison experience or by some great distress of spirit, or perhaps in the disorganisation of the natural habits of life by too much study, or by melancholy and its attendant fears, or else by the excessive devotion of some, or by too much contemplation, or maybe by the cruel life which lovers lead, hoping and fearing so much that their " impressiouns " appear in "avisiouns." Perhaps, too, the good and bad spirits have power to make men dream at night; or else the Human Soul is of such a nature that it foresees and warns men of coming events, only the flesh cannot fully understand because the warning is glimpsed as through a glass darkly. But Chaucer does not know; he will leave the whole matter to the " grete clerkes " who have treated of this and many another thing. It may be remarked in passing that however definite a significance the poet may have attached to most of these terms, he nowhere else indicates a distinction between " dreem " and " sweven "; apparently he uses them indiscriminately in referring to a certain type of vision which comes to men in sleep.

That skeptic, Pandarus, on the other hand, has no
such respectful consideration for dreams as has Chaucer;
to that dealer in worldly pleasures the whole dream
family is not worth a bean! After Criseyde has been
carried away to the Grecian camp, it will be recalled,
Troilus languishes a sorrowful creature; and when he
slumbers, his dreaming mind is disturbed by the most
dreadful things that could be imagined. Recognising
that his dreams and the shrieking of that fatal bellman,
the owl, may foretell his imminent death, he approaches
Pandarus with the idea of making a nuncupatory will
(*T. C.*, V, 295–320). Whereupon Pandarus laughs to
scorn his " swevenes and al swich fantasye " (V, 358–
78).[2] Away with them, says the comforter; a straw
for the significance of dreams! There is no man living
who can interpret them correctly (360–365). Troilus's
dream proceeds from nothing but his melancholy. Priests
of the temple will tell you that dreams are the " revelaciouns " of the gods, or as likely as not they are nothing but " infernals illusiouns "; physicians affirm that
they proceed from " complexiouns " or from fasting or
gluttony (366–374). Who knows which has the right
of it? Others say that through " impressiouns " — as
when a person has something fast in mind — come
" swich avisiouns "; and still others, forming their opinions from certain books, say that men dream dreams
of a specific character according to the seasons of the
year, and that occasionally " th' effect goth by the
mone " (371–77). But, concludes Pandarus, have no
faith in any dream; they are all false (378). Without emphasising Pandarus's skepticism, assumed doubtless

upon the spur of the moment in order to comfort Troilus, one must not fail to observe that here are three types of dreams not mentioned in Chaucer's modest catalogue, namely, " infernals illusiouns," those caused by the sundry seasons of the year, and those over which the moon has influence.

Now Macrobius considers only visions that come to men in sleep, of which he names five principal species, namely, *somnium, visio, oraculum, insomnium,* and *phantasma* or *visum.*[3] Of these five the first three contain elements of wisdom because they foretell coming events; the last two are foolish and empty of meaning, unworthy of being interpreted because they contain nothing of prophetic value. As to the meaning of these terms Macrobius does not leave us in doubt, though one might wish that his definitions were more precise or that some of his classifications were less elastic. A dream may be recognised as an *oraculum,* says he, " when in sleep there appears a relative or other sacred person, such as a priest or a priestess, or even a god, who openly announces what is or is not to come, what should be done in specified cases and what should be avoided." It is a *visio* " when events come to pass precisely as they appear to the dreamer "; and that is said to be a *somnium* " which conceals with figures and veils with ambiguity the significance of a thing not capable of being understood except by interpretation; though we cannot explain it as it is, still a man with experience in such matters may reveal to us its hidden meaning." Of the *somnium* there are five kinds, *alienum, proprium, commune, publicum,* and *generale,* to which Chaucer probably refers when he speaks of the "gendres" but of which he makes no further use.

Species of dreams without significance, *insomnium* and *phantasma,* are more difficult to understand because their limits are less sharply defined. The *insomnium* is described as follows: "Whatever solicitudes of an oppressed mind, or derangements of body, or whims of fortune may harass or engage the attention of a man in his waking hours, these assail him when he is asleep: disquiet of mind, as if a lover should recognise himself enjoying or being deprived of his delights, or as if one should seem to fear a person threatening him with plots or force — in either case the dreamer seems to encounter or to escape from the semblances or images of what his waking experience has presented to him; discomforts of body, as if a person drunken with wine or distended with a superabundance of food should imagine himself being suffocated by such repletion or pressed upon by a burden, or, on the other hand, as if a hungry and thirsty man should seem to desire food and drink, to seek it, or even to have found it; whims of fortune, as if one should consider himself advanced in office and dignities or driven out in accordance with his waking desires or fears. Though these and similar things, resulting from a man's condition of mind, may disturb the quiet and repose of the sleeper, they fly away and vanish completely with the passing of sleep." This type is called *insomnium* not because it is experienced in sleep — all the species have that in common — "but because only in sleep is the dream-content believed to be as it seems; upon waking one recognises that it has neither value nor significance."

Of the *phantasma* he says: " The *phantasma* or *visum* in truth comes to a man when he is in a certain, as it were, first mist of sleep, somewhat between waking and complete quiet, and when, on the point of beginning to slumber, he considers himself up to this time fully awake. In this state he seems to see crowding in upon him strangely moving or swimming forms, distorted in appearance and out of all natural proportions in size, or he may experience the rushing in of tumultuously whirling, kaleidoscopically changing things, either delightful or disturbing. In this class is the *ephialtes* (or incubus), which, according to popular belief, takes possession of worried and exceedingly sensitive men in moments of passivity or quiescence and burdens them with its weight. Admitting that these two species of dreams are valueless as aids in acquiring a knowledge of the future, we are still provided with instruction concerning the character and possibilities of divination by the other three." Considering further the relation of mind to body in dreaming and how the clairvoyant power of the spirit is often oppressed and, as it were, dimmed by the flesh, Macrobius remarks: " The soul, however, since in sleep it is slightly freed from participating in the bodily functioning, acquires in the meantime the power of superior insight, though never achieving that sharpness of vision which pierces through the covering of things with an absolutely clear view; it does not see with an unobstructed and direct glance, but through a sort of intervening curtain of misty texture, as it were, which darkens or obscures the sight. Still when the body is quiet in sleep, the introspective soul is able in some measure to pierce this veil — which, like horn or ivory reduced to the last degree of thinness, is highly translucent but never perfectly transparent — to the truth beyond."

Critics have seen in these passages from Macrobius the main source of Chaucer's knowledge of dreams. Ten Brink, indeed, considers that the English poet has given in the *House of Fame* a kind of recapitulation of this whole chapter, translating *visio* into " avisioun," *phantasma* into " fantom," *oraculum* once into " revelacioun " and again into " oracle," and possibly *somnium* into " dreme " and *insomnium* into " sweven," though these last two English terms are not sharply differentiated.[4] But, as we shall see later, the Chaucerian terminology is scarcely equivalent to the Latin in the manner indicated by Ten Brink. At any rate, Chaucer does find in Macrobius suggestions for many of his remarks on dreams. Here one meets again the disturbances caused by repletion and inanition, by the disorganisation of the natural habits of life through mental worry, or excessive devotion of lovers, or contemplation, and the conception of the mind's inability to see into the future except with an imperfect vision because of the veil of flesh which obscures the light. But we find nothing in Macrobius corresponding to dreams having their source in complexions of the body, or in natural melancholy, or in the seasons of the year, or in the power of the moon; nothing to indicate that he is acquainted with dreams called " infernals illusious " caused by demons, or with " revelaciouns " proceeding from the influence of good spirits, or with that type of waking vision which comes sometimes to saints, called by Chaucer " avisioun," or with that direct revelation of God called prophecy. Chaucer may be indebted for some of these ideas to the questionings expressed by the author of *Le Roman de la Rose* concerning whether dreams are caused by " diverses complexions," or according to " divers corages," or " des meurs divers et des aages."

> Ou se Diex par tex visions
> Envoie revelacions,
> Ou li malignes esperiz,
> Por metre les gens en pertz (ll. 18708 ff.).

But even so, it will be necessary to consult many other " clerkes," scientists, astrologers, medical men, philosophers, and theologians before the actual dreams recorded by Chaucer can be properly understood and correctly classified. And because scientists are supposed to have superior analytical minds and to possess a clearer style than other men, let us begin with the physicians.

In medical science dream-psychology is inextricably bound up with the philosophy of sleep, which in turn can be explained only by reference to the theory of virtues and complexions. As we have seen already in the discussion of the *Knight's Tale*, the Reasonable Human Soul gets its work done in the body through the mediate functioning of a force called *virtus*. This *virtus* is divided into three general classes: *virtus naturalis*, *virtus spiritualis* or *vitalis*, and *virtus animata* or *animalis*, which, it will be recalled, functions in and through the brain. This *virtus animalis* has two modes of expression, (1) *interior*, having to do with the reason, imagination, and memory, and (2) *exterior*, which is represented in the *sensus,* or *sensibilia,* and in *motus localis,* or voluntary motion, both of which employ the nerves and muscles as instruments.[5]   Above the *virtus naturalis* is the *virtus animalis* which controls, by direction of the sense-activities and through voluntary motion, the judicious heating and cooling of the balanced humours in the body.   Now, psychologically considered, sleep is nothing more than the withdrawal of the *virtus animalis* from its·instruments — i.e., the senses and the muscles upon which depends voluntary motion — into the inner parts, or the return upon itself, so that the *virtus naturalis* may exercise its proper appetitive, retentive, expulsive, and especially digestive functions for the purpose of recreating natural heat, which has been dissipated in the activities of waking moments. Galen and Avicenna, the great Arabian physician, agree in effect: "Sleep is the return to its place of origin of the *spiritus animalis* from acting upon its sensory and motor instruments, which, being relieved from its operation upon them, are quiet except that the *spiritus naturalis* carries on those activities necessary for the sustenance of life and the rehabilitation of the *spiritus vitalis.* Thus in sleep the *virtus vitalis,* withdrawing into the subliminal depths of the interior, aids in the digestion of food and is created anew; the fatigued *virtus animalis* rests during the unconscious period; and the *virtus naturalis* is strengthened in the exercise of its natural functions." [6]   Regarding the immediate cause of sleep, Avicenna further remarks: "The material cause is a sort of vapor, which ascends from the lower members to the brain.   This vapor is an exhalation from digesting foods

and from the bodily humours; when it reaches the limits
of its ascent, it is rendered more dense or less volatile
by the coldness of the brain and receives an added heaviness from other humidities "; [7] and upon the necessity
for sleep: " Sleep always follows the derangement of a
moist complexion, or the cooling and stiffening of the
sensibilia by loss of natural heat, or the vehement dissipa-
tion of the *spiritus animalis* in strenuous exercise or its
withdrawal into itself while food taken into the body
is being digested. Therefore, you may find the necessity for sleep in the restoration of the released virtue,
the digestion of consumed food, and in the rekindling
or regeneration of the tired out body." [8] It is doubtless
to this technical relation between natural sleep and digestion that Chaucer refers when, in the *Squire's Tale*
(*C. T.*, F, 374), he speaks of " The norice of diges-
tioun, the slepe."

Since there is such a delicate adjustment between the
activities of the *virtus animalis* and the *virtus naturalis*,
physicians cannot afford to be ignorant of dreams and
their ways, for, says Galen, " A dream indicates to us
the condition of the body." [9] It is quite apparent that
any disturbance in the normal balance existing in a
healthy person among the bodily humours, blood, phlegm,
choler, and melancholy, is straightway registered in the
mind in the form of dreams; any mental upheaval is
recorded in the Imagination, and the impressions of it
are reproduced in sleep; and when the mind is quiet,
placid, and normally healthy, spirits are said to have the
power of mirroring upon it the images of coming events.
A dream may be defined, in brief, as a sleep-experience

caused by a disturbance in the Imagination; or better, it is a sort of phantasm originating in the movement of sense-images, or figures, or *simulacra* in the Imagination of the dreamer.[10]   One of the most curious facts about a dream is that, in the process of its unfolding, the sleeping man rests under the illusion that he is feeling the actual response of his senses to certain external stimuli, whereas in reality, as we have seen, the *virtus animalis* has withdrawn from its instruments leaving them completely quiescent.   The explanation of this phenomenon is not far to seek; the order of movements necessary in the progress of a dream is simply the reverse of that by which sensations are received and conveyed to the brain. When a man is awake, he receives impressions of the outside world through the *sensus;* the *virtus animalis* conveys these *sensibilia* along the nerves into a kind of mental storehouse of sense-impressions, called the *sensus communis;* and these *sensiteria* move the Imagination, so that the man is able to form or apprehend a definite image of what his senses have experienced.   In sleep, on the other hand, the Imagination is disturbed — perhaps by the after-effects of worry, or by the influence of planetary intelligences, or by the occult energy of good and evil spirits — and moves upon the *sensus communis;* the *sensiteria* act along the nerves and move the particular senses; and the sense-experience following seems to the dreamer as real as if he were awake, though there is actually no external stimulus.   It is quite apparent, therefore, that there can be no dream without images or figures or *simulacra.*   At least, so says " myn autour," Vincent de Beauvais.[11]   It is to this necessary characteristic of dreams that Chaucer doubtless refers when (*House of Fame*, 47) he speaks of the future's being revealed " by figures." We shall see anon, however, that prophecy is a direct revelation from God without intermediary sensory images.

Be that as it may, after careful and scientific study physicians have classified *somnia* according to their causes into three general types, namely, the *somnium naturale, somnium animale*, and *somnium coeleste* or *diuina*.[12] Petrus de Abano calls the first a *somnium naturale* because " it originates in the dominion of bodily complexions and humours "; the second a *somnium animale* because it "springs from the great anxiety and perturbation of the waking mind "; and the third a *somnium coeleste* because " it is brought to pass through impressions made by those celestial minds or intelligences which are said to direct the heavenly bodies in their courses, since they are able to stamp their figures or influences upon the Imagination in accordance with their natures and in proportion to the aptitude or fitness of our minds to receive them; for the human mind is, in its essence and action, far more nearly akin to angelic substances than to bodily sensations." [13] The cause of a dream having been determined, therefore, it is comparatively easy to arrive at some definite conclusion regarding its validity as a harbinger of future events. It may be affirmed with perfect confidence that the *somnium naturale* in what it seems to presage is always and utterly false, and that the *somnium coeleste* is never without some significance which the celestial intelligences wish to impress upon the mind of the sleeper; and even this latter is more credible in the mornings, because at that time the mind, being calm and unoppressed by the humours or by repletions of the body, is in its fittest condition to receive a clear image of the divine impression. And the *somnium animale* " seems to have very little significance, or none at all; it is for the most part an illusion." [14] So the medical men would classify dreams according to their causes and in the light of truth. But since it is palpably impossible to determine with any degree of certainty or accuracy what these causes are in any given instance, dream-psychology cannot be called an exact science; not being subject to practical experiment, it must be classed along with ethics. Still, your observant physician may often find a consideration of dreams helpful in the diagnosis of specific maladies.

There are always to be found certain skeptics like Pandarus, however, who would deny the prophetic import of dreams altogether. But, says Averroes, " To those men who deny the significance of the dream and maintain that it comes merely by chance, I would say that perhaps it is sent for a purpose; all dreams seem to be fallacious only because these ignoramuses cannot distinguish between the false and the true. But to deny dreams, especially clearly authenticated dreams, is to deny consciousness; there is no man living who has not at some time or other experienced a dream which has announced to him something of the future." [15] Still, in the case of Troilus's dream, Pandarus is warranted in scouting the idea of its having any reference to coming events; it is a *somnium naturale* proceeding from melancholia, as Pandarus points out (*T. C.*, V, 360). Some-

times it seems to Troilus asleep that he is alone in some
horrible place; sometimes he is fighting with his enemies
and falls into their hands; and again he seems to be
pitching from some high place into the depths below.
Starting out of his slumber, he feels a quaking dread
about his heart and his body trembles with fear (V, 250
ff.). This is not even a respectable *somnium animale,*
however much the mind of Troilus may have been disturbed over the going of Criseyde. In this case he is
merely oppressed by the fumes rising from too much
melancholy in the blood; he is experiencing a *phantasma,*
or having a nightmare, or being shaken to fear by an
incubus, which — as St. Augustine comments upon the
phantasma of Macrobius — " is nothing more nor less
than a sort of fumosity arising from the stomach or
heart to the brain and there burdening the mind." [16]
It may be observed that such a dream is sometimes popu-
larly interpreted in the Middle Ages as the appearance
of demons in sleep, hence Chaucer's prayer to be delivered " Fro fantom and illusioun " (*Fame,* 493), i.e.,
from horrible apparitions which demons show to sleeping men and from the deceptions which they may practise upon the waking mind. And it is to this idea, widely
current in Chaucer's day, of demons' ability to assume
human forms and lie with mortal women in sleep that
the Wife of Bath refers when she speaks of a certain
limitour's being the only " incubus " in the country-
side (*C. T.,* D, 880).

Among reputable astrologers we find Albohazen Haly
filius Abenragel dividing dreams into three classes: the
first is a " vision sent by the All-High God," the second

is occasioned by planetary influences, and the third proceeds from the humours of the body. He is entirely orthodox in his belief that divine revelations are to be accepted at their face value; and he is equally convinced that dreams caused by humours of the body have no significance whatever. Visions having astral influences as their sources, however, are of two kinds, the false and the true, their vanity or trustworthiness depending upon the power, positions, applications, and aspects of the planets at the time when the vision occurs.[17] He observes further that Sol and Luna must be especially considered in interpreting visions of this class, because " Sol is said to be influential in producing waking visions and Luna in causing dreams in sleep." He then proceeds to illustrate how Luna, variously aspected and posited, is strong in determining whether a dream is false or true, good or bad in its implication. " You must observe among other things," says he in effect, " the position of Luna, especially whether she is discovered in the third or ninth House of the astrological figure. If she be not there, but posited in the ascendent or in any one of the angles, not conjoined with but otherwise aspecting one of the fortunate planets, then this configuration indicates that the vision will be good or pleasant, of beneficent import, and prophetic of happy circumstances to come. If she be not conjoined with but otherwise aspecting an unfortunate planet, the vision will be terrifying and evil in its signification; if she be in conjunction with one of the infortunes, the vision will be pleasing and beautiful but in its purport baneful. But if Luna be aspected by beneficent planets and free from wicked influences, then the vision will be repulsive and foul but of happy signification." [18] It is to this power of Luna that Pandarus doubtless refers when he informs Troilus that in some dreams " th' effect goth by the mone " (*T. C.*, V, 377).

After outlining seven grades of visions ordered according to their relative truth from the lowest, those caused by the complexions, to the highest, prophecy, Arnoldus de Villa Nova classifies them all under two general heads, *natura* and *doctrina*. Natural dreams are those produced by forces which affect the Imagination through the bodily *sensibilia*, such as, for example, the complexions, blood, phlegm, choler, and melancholy, repletion and poor digestion, hunger, nervousness and fear following upon distracting physical and mental experiences. Dreams are also caused by reactions of the body to its environment and by its adaptation to climatic conditions and the various seasons of the year, to the mild temperature of spring and autumn, the heat of summer, and the cold of winter. No such dream presages anything concerning the future.[19] It is interesting to observe how well Arnoldus is supported, in his remarks concerning the influence of seasons upon visions, by Vincent de Beauvais: " Dreams are diversified by the position of the body and in accordance with the seasons; in spring and autumn they are particularly confused, disordered, and false." [20] Here again Pandarus seems to be correct when he informs Troilus that " after tymes of the yeer by kynde, men dreme " (*T. C.*, V, 376), maintaining that all such are meaningless. But to return to the *doctrina* of Arnoldus. Doctrinal dreams are

those resulting from the influences of external forces or
intelligences exerted upon the mind free from base
imaginings and unoppressed by any passions of the senses.
The occult power of planets, signs of the Zodiac, and
Houses are to be placed among such influences. Arnoldus explains that questions concerning specific dreams
are to be referred for interpretation to the twelve
Houses in the figure of a horoscope, and that prognostications of future events may be made by attributing
dreams of a certain character to specified and respective
parts of the body. For example, a vision concerning
family secrets is to be referred to the intestines and for
interpretation to the First House. Dreams about gold
and blood — the one signifies the other — are to be referred to the liver and for interpretation to the Second
House: " The liver is the radix of treasure and of
blood; according to the Hindus blood stands for treasure, because frequently on account of gold, or in the ac-
quisition of it, our blood is squandered." [21] Such a
question of the Second House might run as follows:
" Suppose a person should dream that, on the eve of his
departure for a journey into foreign parts beyond the
sea, he were being let blood in great quantities by one
of his parents or kinsmen. This would indicate that the
dreamer will die soon after and that the other will suc-
ceed to his properties and estates according to the will
of the deceased." [22] It is doubtless of this philosophy
" secundum Indos " that the Wife of Bath is thinking
when she fabricates a dream with which to catch the
worthy clerk Jankin. " I told him," she says, " that I
dreamed about him all night; that he was about to

slay me, and that my bed was full of blood. And yet
I hoped that good would come of it, *For blood bito-
keneth gold, as me was taught*" (*C. T.*, D, 581).

Theologians whom I have consulted are interested primarily in that type of *visio* called revelation, though they
all recognise that *somnia* must receive due consideration. St. Augustine reproduces Macrobius's classification
almost verbatim, though he adds that the *insomnium* is
the result of humours in the blood and the *phantasma* of
fumosity arising from the stomach to oppress the mind.
When he comes to consider *visiones*, he finds that they
are of three genera; namely, the *visio corporale*, which
is received through the natural senses of the body and
in which the heavens, the earth, and all things therein
may be made manifest to the eyes; the *visio spiritale*,
which is the result of spiritual forces impressing themselves upon the Imagination in the likeness of sense-
images; and the *visio intellectuale*, in which divine mysteries, having neither form nor fashion nor any relation
to corporeal images, are directly and intuitively discerned by the Intellect.[23] In other words, the *corporale*
is a vision received through the sense of sight while the
beholder is wide awake and conscious of the *sensibilia;*
the *spiritale*, on the other hand, is a *visio* perceived by
the Imagination only when the *sensibilia* are quiescent,
perhaps in normal sleep or when the body rests from its
passions in a kind of trance deeper than sleep but short
of death, so that the Imagination receives the divine impression clothed in sensory imagery; and the *intellectuale*
is a vision in which the Intellect, quite apart from the
Imagination, where images are recorded and reproduced,

apperceives immediately and intuitively, without thought
or imagery, the secrets of divinity.[24] All of them are
revelations, but the last two are more absolutely true
and significant because they are not subject to the circumstances which affect actual sense-experiences. Now
from another point of view, as Vincent de Beauvais
explains, these revelations may be divided into two
classes: one which is received by the direct apperception
of Divine Will, and another which involves phantasms
or *simulacra*.[25] The first — Augustine's *intellectuale*
— is called *prophecy;* the second — comprising Augustine's *corporale* and *spiritale* — is called a *revelation.*
Again, since revelations represent the impressions made
by external intelligences upon the Imagination through
the aid of images, it must be quite apparent that there
are two species of revelation corresponding to the influences exerted by good and bad spirits. When demons
are responsible for a vision of this sort, it is called an
illusion; when through the instrumentality of angels or
other good spirits the vision is created in the Imagination
of either a waking or a sleeping person, one may call it
simply a *revelation;* and when the vision comes to a
man in a trance, then it is called *ecstasy.*[26]

Though Chaucer is intensely interested in the scientific aspect of dreams as expounded by medical men and
philosophers, it must not be forgotten that he also considers the theologians' presentation of the occult and
supernatural. Following the hagiologist's account,[27] he
records Valerian's waking vision of an old man clothed
in white and holding in his hand a book with golden
letters (*C. T.*, G, 200 ff.), and of the angel with two

crowns of roses and lilies (G, 225 ff.). The Monk
reproduces Belshazzar's vision of an armless hand writing on the wall (*C. T.*, B, 3392), and the Man of
Law relates how a mysterious fist from the air smote
the enemies of Constance (B, 669 ff.). And the Summoner tells of an untidy vision which a certain friar
had while visiting the realms of Satan (*C. T.*, D, 1670
ff.). But it is that delightfully garrulous and versatile
Friar in the *Summoner's Tale* who seems to be most intimately acquainted with the ways of revelation (*C. T.*,
D, 1835 ff.). He has just come for a little visit to
Thomas, it will be remembered, when the good housewife enters to see whether he will have anything to
eat (1835). No, he will have nothing, or at least not
much — just the liver of a capon, a piece of soft bread,
and the head of a roasted pig (1839 ff.); he has been
so busy about vigils and penances that his stomach is destroyed; and, besides, his spirit has its fostering only in
the Bible (1845). It is only after the good woman has
informed him of her child's death within these two
weeks that he launches into his discussion of revelations
and to whom they are made. " Yes," says he without surprise or hesitation, " yes, I saw his death by revelation
at home in our dormitory. It was, I dare say, just about
half an hour after his death that our sacristan and he
who has charge of the infirmary — both true friars for
fifty years — and I saw him in our 'avisioun' carried
to bliss. We arose with many tears trickling down our
cheeks and, thanking Christ for having vouchsafed us
this revelation, sang the *Te Deum*. We mendicants
know more about the mysteries of Christ than common

people; for, you must understand, we live in poverty and abstinence, wedded to fastings and prayers, continence, charity, humbleness, and service, giving ourselves to persecution for righteousness' sake, to weeping, and to cleanness of life, while they live in luxury and in the richness of worldly pleasures. He who expects to have his prayers answered effectually and to be admitted by revelation into God's secrets must fast and be clean, fatten his soul and make his body lean " (1845–1909). Then before his hearers have an opportunity to express their surprise over the wonderful " avisioun " or " revelacioun," he proceeds to classify his own mode of living and the resultant divine experience along with those of the prophets, Moses and Elias (1885–90). Surely this Friar has been reading in the works of theologians, hagiologists, and philosophers, though he is exceedingly presumptuous in ranging himself alongside Moses, the single perfect prophet who, as it were, saw God face to face.[28]

Still he is correct when he postulates as the necessary conditions for the reception of divine revelations a chaste body, a clean mind, and a pure heart. Cornelius Agrippa says: " When a man wishes to receive a celestial vision, his body should be well disposed, his brain unoppressed by fumes or vapor, and his mind free from perturbation; he should abstain from eating and from drinking inebriating draughts; his bedchamber should be cleanly and neat, hallowed and consecrated, and perfumed with incense; his Imagination should be submitted to impressions from celestial intelligences; with the sacred Scriptures before him, he should call upon the name of God with prayer and supplication, and his thoughts should be fixed intently upon that which he desires. If he does this, he will be visited by a revelation of the highest import and have his mind illuminated by truth." [29] Since it appears that the mind is purged by cleanliness, abstinence, penitence, and alms-giving, one might credit such a revelation as the worthy Friar *says* he had when preceded by the regimen of plain living and high thinking which he outlines. But in this particular case, one cannot forget the pig's head and the capon's liver! Chaucer is here having reported a vision or revelation with an exposition of the conditions which make such an experience possible, but he is not interested in the " avisioun " for itself alone as are the theologians. Being an artist, he here makes use of the occult mysteries of sacred revelation in creating the personality and character of the Friar.

This rapid and necessarily incomplete survey of mediaeval thought upon dreams, their origin, classification, and significance, reveals the astonishing ·fact that among philosophers, astrologers, medical men, and theologians there are neither essential differences of opinion nor grounds for controversy. There is only a variety of emphasis. Medical men, naturally enough, are interested primarily in the *somnium naturale* to which they attach significance only as an indication of bodily disturbances, but they are perfectly willing to grant the validity and truth of the *somnium coeleste* and to a small degree of the *somnium animale;* philosophers and astronomers are principally concerned with the psychology of the *somnium animale,* but they readily agree that dreams arising from natural causes are meaningless and that revelations from good spirits are absolutely trustworthy; and theologians, accepting the conclusions of others regarding the *somnium naturale* and the *somnium animale*, devote their attention to the classification and explanation of divinely inspired visions — oracles, revelations, prophecy, ecstasy — which all men claim to be true heralds of coming events. I cannot imagine Chaucer's having been ignorant of these universally accepted conclusions; he might have had access to most of the authors whom I have cited, any one of whom — Vincent de Beauvais, for example — might have given him the general trend of opinion. But it is Chaucer, the man of philosophical mind, who is quick to see the practical and almost insurmountable difficulties in the way of determining precisely the nature of any present dream that has not already been proved true or false by the event. With the vision of last night upon the table, how is one to know whether it is merely a *somnium naturale*, or a *somnium animale*, or a revelation, or an illusion, or a phantom? Here might be grounds for disagreement. And it is Chaucer, the artist, who proceeds to embody in the *Nun's Priest's Tale* such a controversy over the source of a specific dream and to evolve out of it the characters of Chauntecleer and Pertelote.

CHAPTER NINE

CHAUNTECLEER AND PERTELOTE
ON DREAMS

AN attentive observer of that dispute which arises, in the *Nun's Priest's Tale*, between those tantalisingly human barnyard fowls, Chauntecleer and Pertelote, over the large question of dream-origins, is made to feel that their divergence of opinion grows out of a difference in natural temperament. The controversy is precipitated, it will be recalled, by the necessity of determining to what particular class of dreams the cock's fearful experience of last night belongs before an interpretation of its content can be made. The fair " damoysele Pertelote," however courteous, debonair, and companionable she may be, is by nature practical of mind and unimaginative; from the top of her coral comb to the tips of her little azure toes she is a scientist, who has peered into many strange corners of medical lore. That egotist, Chauntecleer, imaginative and pompously self-conscious, would like to pass as a philosopher and a deep student of the occult. As might be expected, when they come to classify a particular dream, each does it in accordance with his temperamental and characteristic way of looking at things. And with the perversity of human disputants — I had almost said of some husbands and wives in disagreement — each presents only one aspect of the question, that which appeals to him and with which congenial study has made him most familiar, and ignores practically all other facts which he may know to be true. Pertelote's contentions are well founded when the dream is a *somnium naturale;* Chauntecleer's claims are undeniable when the vision is a true *somnium coeleste.*

Well, as Chauntecleer sits upon his perch one morning with his wives about him, he begins suddenly to groan in his throat as one who is sorely oppressed by some horrible dream. When Pertelote hears him roar, she is aghast. " O dear heart," says she, " what ails you to groan in this manner? For shame, what a sleeper! " And poor Chauntecleer, at last awake and free from his dream, replies: " By God, madam, I dreamed just now that I was in such trouble that my heart is still terribly frightened. May God interpret my dream aright and keep my body out of prison! It seemed to me that, as I roamed up and down in our yard, I saw a fearful beast something like a dog that attempted to accomplish my death. His color was between yellow and red; his tail and both his ears were tipped with black; his snout was small, and he had two glowing eyes. Because of his aspect I am still almost dead with fright. And this, doubtless, was the cause of my groaning." Pertelote, in some measure the mediaeval woman, is grievously disappointed at this pitiful spectacle of a strong and, to her, heroic cock torn by so base a thing as fear. " Alas and wellaway," she cries, " fie upon you, chicken-hearted! Now have you lost all my heart and all my love; I cannot love a coward, by my faith. For whatever women may say, we all admire and desire husbands who are hardy, wise, and brave, neither a boaster nor one who is afraid of every little thing. How dare you say in the presence of your love that anything can cause you to fear! Have you, who wear a beard, no man's heart? And worst of all, can you be afraid of a mere dream, which is nothing but vanity?

> Swevenes engendren of replecciouns,
> And oft of fume, and of complecciouns,
> Whan humours been to habundant in a wight.
> Certes this dreem, which ye han met to-night,
> Cometh of the grete superfluitee
> Of youre rede *colera*, pardee,
> Which causeth folk to dreden in here dremes
> Of arwes, and of fyr with rede lemes,
> Of grete bestes, that they wol hem byte,
> Of contek, and of whelpes grete and lyte;
> Right as the humour of malencolye
> Causeth ful many a man, in sleep, to crye,
> For fere of blake beres, or boles blake,
> Or elles, blake develes wole hem take.
> Of othere humours coude I telle also,
> That werken many a man in sleep ful wo;
> But I wol passe as lightly as I can.

Then quoting the saying from Cato, *somnia ne cures* — being careful not to mention the other half of what must have been a proverb, *nam fallunt somnia plures* — she advises him to take certain laxatives lest he come down with a tertian fever (*C. T.*, B, 4100–4125).

From all indications it might appear that Pertelote's diagnosis of Chauntecleer's case is about correct; and

certainly her presentation of the effects of red and black
choler upon the dreaming mind is without fault. It
will be seen that she seizes upon the cock's intense fear
as a sign of a superabundance of humours in the blood,
and in this conclusion she is supported by the best medical opinion. Avicenna, for example, remarks upon the
infallible symptoms of melancholia: "The principal
signs of melancholia in the blood are these: fear without cause, swiftness to anger, and trembling; when the
humour is strongly established, dread, defective judgment, uneasiness of mind, a kind of apprehension on account of things which are or are not, and for the most
part anxiety over that which is not ordinarily feared.
Some live in apprehension of robbers, some fear that
the earth will open and swallow them, and others that
wolves may break in upon them. Sometimes they are
terrified at that which comes within the sphere of their
activity; at other times they imagine themselves being
crowned kings, or transformed into wolves, or into demons, or birds, or even into artificial instruments or implements." [1]

Chauntecleer's physical condition has not brought him
quite to this sad pass, to be sure, but his fears and his
dream of a frightful beast are strongly indicative of mal-
adjustment of humours in his system. Up until the
moment when his dream is shown by the final outcome
to be a prophetic vision, one is inclined to agree with
Pertelote's diagnosis, especially so since she is amply supported by the best medical and other authority in her association of Chauntecleer's type of dream with the various complexions. According to Avicenna, for example,

one sign of too much choler is a " dream in which one
sees fires, and yellow banners, many other things yellow which are not naturally so, the fervent heat of the
bath, or of the sun, and such like," and of *cholera nigra*,
" dreams in which terror is produced from the darkness,
by tortures, and by the appearance of black things.² He
is supported by Galen, who declares: " If anyone should
see a fire in his dreams, he is troubled by too much yellow bile; if he should see smoke, or a misty darkness,
or profound shadows, then by black bile "; ³ Rhazes is
of the opinion that " when anyone frequently sees fires
and lightning and strife in his dreams, red cholera
abounds in the blood, but when he beholds many things
tinged with a swarthy color and when he experiences
terror and fear, these things signify the working of black
cholera "; ⁴ Arnoldus de Villa Nova agrees that " if
much red cholera is in the blood, one will dream of
fires, falling stars, and the flashing of lightning; but
excessive black cholera causes dreams in which appear
terrible monsters, apparitions, incubi, and such "; ⁵ Albohazen Haly affirms likewise that the choleric man
dreams of fires, and the melancholic man of dark places
and that he is being suffocated or oppressed by night-
mares; ⁶ and Petrus de Abano associates red cholera with
visions of " red, fiery things, flights, disputes, madness,"
and black cholera with dreams of " black terrifying appearances, lamentations, misfortunes, places of death, and
such like." ⁷ The enthusiastic Pertelote knows many
more wonders about the effects of humours upon dreams
— such as, for example, no doubt, that a super-abun-
dance of blood produces " dreams in which a man beholds

red objects, or much blood flowing from his body, or seems to be swimming in blood," and that excessive phlegm causes " dreams in which are seen water, rivers, snow and rain, and cold weather " [8] — but she will let that pass (4127 ff.). She must hasten on to prescribe a remedy for the malady which she has diagnosed with apparent accuracy and in much detail.

Chauntecleer's affection as indicated by his fear and the dream must be rigorously attacked before it has had time to develop into something more dangerous; and Pertelote's proposed method of procedure is worthy of the wisest medical men. This busy little housewife, in real concern for the health of her lord and husband — and perhaps eager to show him that, for once, in spite of her femininity she is not so ignorant and incapable as might be supposed — counsels that forthwith and immediately steps be taken to purge this choler and melancholy (431–436). Because there is no apothecary in that town, she herself will teach him the properties of all the herbs in their yard which are by nature useful in purging humours, both above and below. " Beware," she warns, " that the sun in his ascension does not find you still replete with hot humours — you are very choleric of complexion — lest you be afflicted with a tertian fever or an ague, which may prove your destruction." For a day or two at first he shall have digestives of worms before he takes his laxatives of *laurus, centauria, fumaria, elleborus, euphorbium, rhamus,* and *hedera helix.* He must

Pekke hem up right as they growe, and ete hem in.
(*C. T.,* B, 4140–57.)

Evidently Pertelote has been reading after the physicians. They all understand that it is not safe to administer purgatives or laxatives for hot humours until after " digestives," i.e., medicines for absorbing or dissipating melancholy and choler, have been given for some time. Richard Saunders, in *The Astrological Judgment and Practice of Physic,* requires several pages upon which to record the best digestives of these humours — though, of course, he has nothing to say about " digestyves of wormes "! And the little hen is wise in her selection of simples. Dioscorides — Chaucer's " Deiscorides " (*C. T.*, A, 430) — says of *laurus nobilis* ("lauriol") that " when taken in water it sits heavy on the stomach and incites vomiting "; of *centauria,* " It expels bilious and heavy humours through the bowels "; of *fumaria* or *fumus terre* (" fumetere "), " This herb consumed in food induces bilious urine "; of black *elleborus* ("ellebor "), " It purges through the lower tracts both phlegm and choleric humours, when given by itself or with scarmonia; it is good for epileptics, mad men, and for those afflicted with melancholia and nervousness "; of *euphorbium* (" catapuce "), " It is a continuous irritant having power to dissipate the suffusion of noxious humours "; of *rhamus* (" gaytres beryis "), " When placed in the doors and windows the branches of this herb are said to repel the evil influences of magicians "; and of *hedera helix* (" erbe yve "), " All species of ivy are acrid, astringent, and particularly effective in cases of nervousness." [9] Surely after Chauntecleer has taken any small part of this prescription to purge him above and below, he will be in dire need of the *hedera helix.* But it is only by such an heroic course of action that fevers and agues may be avoided.

Pertelote is, moreover, quite right again when she informs her dear husband that the corruption of red and black choler in the blood causes intermittent fevers and rigors. Having decided that red choler especially is at the bottom of Chauntecleer's trouble (4118), she arrives at the logical and scientific conclusion that his fever will be tertian. Avicenna would pronounce her deductions correct. He observes that there are in general two species of fevers, *febres aegritudines* and *febres accidentes,* with the latter of which he would identify the *febris putredinis.*[10] (We are not concerned with the *febris apostematis,* which is also classified under *accidentis.*) Now this *febris putredinis* is so named because it results from a corruption of the four humours of the body, giving rise, in consequence, to four different kinds of fevers, namely, *tertiana, quartana, quotidiana,* and *continua* (which must not be confused with the *febres accidentes,* all continuous). " The corruption of cholera produces the *tertiana;* the corruption of melancholia, the *quartana;* of phlegm, the *quotidiana;* and the corruption of blood, the *continua.*"[11] Of these we are interested only in the *tertiana,* which may be the result of *cholera pura* or *non pura,* i.e., unmixed or mixed with other humours. Of the *tertiana* type, therefore, there are at least three kinds, *tertiana continua, tertiana periodica,* and *causon* (or *febris ardens*).[12] The *periodica,* being the result of corrupted *cholera pura,* is mild and easily controlled; but the other two, since before the patient can recover from one attack another paroxysm is upon him, are more violent and usually accompanied by agues. It is possibly to one of these that Pertelote refers, most likely to the *causon,* because as we have seen in Chauntecleer's case red choler is supposed to be mixed with black choler, or melancholia. Avicenna describes the symptoms of an attack: " A paroxysm of tertian fever begins with a kind of goose-flesh sensation as if the skin were being pricked with the point of a hot needle; then a sudden chill descends upon the patient attended by rigors, each one of which becomes harder than that before. And during the first three days of the fever's course these rigors are strongest and most vahement." [13] One may expect the progress of the malady to run as follows: " First there is felt the prickling sensation mentioned above, then the chill and the rigor; afterwards the rigor moderates and the chill abates, and fever begins; this state continues for awhile; and after that the fever gradually diminishes until it disappears altogether." [14] Indeed, if Chauntecleer's dream were caused by the corruption of red and black choler in the blood — and Pertelote seems to have made out an excellent case — it would be foolish for him to carry his hot humours into the sunshine.

Against Pertelote's presentation of scientifically accurate facts and sound medical theory, Chauntecleer has nothing to oppose but his colossal conceit and a few stories gleaned from old authorities. His manly self-love must have writhed under the lash of his little wife's outspoken contempt for his fears at so paltry a thing as a dream caused by choler. Still, assuming a lordly air of con-

descension — as no doubt befits a husband when confronted by unanswerable arguments — the cock proceeds
to shift the basis of the discussion from fact to authority.
" Madam," says he, " I have great respect for your
knowledge. But as for this Cato with his *somnia ne
cures*, let me inform you that many men of vastly more
authority than ever Cato was have held the reverse of his
opinion and have found by experience that dreams are
significant as presagers of future joy and tribulation."
(4160–70).

> Ther nedeth make of this noon argument;
> The verray preve sheweth it in dede (4172).

As a matter of fact, never having thought independently
for himself, Chauntecleer has no conception of what
rightly constitutes a proof. For all his show of scholarly
learning and for all his evident desire to pass as a widely
read and deep student of the occult, he has never investi-
gated the philosophy or the psychology of dreams. His
puerile mind is capable of grasping only the thread of a
marvellous story, trusting blindly and with childlike simplicity to the correctness of interpretations offered by
authorities. He impresses his audience with the narra-
tion of two stories from " oon of the gretteste auctours
that men rede " — being careful not to mention Cicero
as the author, probably because he does not know — in
which certain events perceived in dreams come true precisely as visualised in sleep (4175–4294). He is copious
in detail and points with pedantic pride to the exact book
and chapter where one of the stories may be found, but
he has no way of determining whether such dreams —

which belong to the type *somnium animale* — are to be considered more credible than the true revelations which he mentions later. With blithe unconsciousness of any fundamental difference, he lumps them all together. He has read and enjoyed immensely the fulfilled " avisioun " of St. Kenelm — he was the son of Kenulphus, King of Mercia, be it known! — and in the Old Testament the dream of Daniel (4319) and of Joseph (4320) and of the King of Egypt (4323), all of which proved to be significant. He recalls that Croesus — who was the King of Lydia — was warned in a dream that he should be hanged (4328), and that Andromache — she was Hector's wife — saw in a vision precisely how her husband should be slain at the hands of Achilles (4330). The testimony of Macrobius as to the validity of dreams is presented (4314), though complete silence is observed regarding this same Macrobius's *insomnium* and *phantasma*. At any rate, before the overwhelmed little hen can speak what may be in her mind — one may suspect that she smiles behind her wing — her erudite husband proceeds to close the argument to his complete satisfaction with a bit of flattery and with the assurance that, since events have followed upon the dreams of these other great men, his own " avisioun " will surely be fulfilled in adversity (4341). Besides, he sets no store by these laxatives; they are venomous and nauseous; he defies the whole prescription (4345).

It is entirely characteristic of Chauntecleer to classify his dream as an " avisioun." Common, ordinary men may experience such dreams as the *somnium naturale,* or the *insomnium* or the *phantasma,* but most of the ful-

filled dreams recorded by the authorities have been authentic *visiones*, or divine revelations granted to famous men,
illustrious warriors, mighty kings of nations, prophets,
seers. Why should the cock be considered — in his own
estimation — less worthy than these to receive an " avisioun "?   Still, the fact remains, as Antonius Gaizo observes regarding the dreams recorded by Valerius Maximus, that " those visions which may be called celestial are
most rare, and are not granted except to great men.   But
because such are sometimes significant no one ought,
therefore, to identify himself with that class of men who
persuade themselves that they should put faith in their
own *somnia naturalia* or *animalia*." [15]   Granting, however, the authenticity of Chauntecleer's " avisioun," one
need experience no surprise at his impudent disregard of
its apparent warning.   In the full joy of conscious
strength he flies from the beams as usual, thinking no
doubt that, though these other great ones might have been
controlled by the fate revealed in dreams, one so powerful and favored as he is may surely escape.   That is
Chauntecleer!

Evidently the mind of this self-satisfied personage has
never attacked the problem of " necessity " in its relation to foreknowledge as revealed in the *somnium coeleste*.   Consequently, since the cock has made so poor a
showing as a philosopher and theologian, the Nun's Priest
feels called upon to broach the subject at least in direct
connection with Chauntecleer's " avisioun."   " Alas,"
says he in mock-heroic vein,

> O Chauntecleer, accursed be that morwe
> That thou into the yerd flough fro the bemes!
> Thou were ful wel y-warned by thy dremes,

That thilke day was perilous to thee,
But what god forwoot mot nedes be,
After the opinioun of certeyn clerkis.
            (*C. T.,* B, 4420 ff.).

He cannot settle the question, upon which there has been altercation by an hundred thousand men, as to whether God's foreknowledge of coming events constrains a man by " simple necessitee " or whether the power of choice residing in human free-will may alter such constraint into " necessitee condicionel." Happily this writer is also spared the task of solving the problem; Augustine, and Professor Carlton Brown, and Boethius, and Professor J. S. P. Tatlock, and Bishop Bradwardine, and Professor H. R. Patch have already " bulted it to the bren." [16] It may be noted in passing, however, that in showing how Grosseteste solves the general problem of foreknowledge and free-will through the postulation of two kinds of necessity, *antecedentis* (" simple necessitee ") and *contingentia* (" necessitee condicionel "), Bradwardine applies the same method to the relation of necessity to foreknowledge as made patent in *revelations.* " In the same way," he concludes, " may be solved the problem of free will in relation to the foreknowledge of the prophet. For the whole question of why these seem to be mutually contradictory, so that they cannot exist at the same time, is none other than that one is contingent and possible whichever way you look at it, and the other is absolutely necessary and seems not to allow of any contingency in that which follows. A thing that is foreknown is possible from any point of view. The foreknowledge of a thing, when it actually is, cannot be otherwise than it is. Hence it is necessary that knowledge be perfected by that which follows, even though that which is to follow is for the time being contingent. Thus contingent necessity, as has been said, does not seem to permit antecedent necessity, but to contradict it." [17] One may conclude, therefore, that if Chauntecleer had ever taken the trouble to learn the distinction between simple and conditional necessity and if his mind had been less obsessed with the idea of his own importance, the fulfilment of even so true an " avisioun " as his might have been averted by the mere expedient of remaining upon the beams.

In the *Nun's Priest's Tale* Chaucer has given an excellent demonstration of how the true artist may use scientific and philosophical material in the development of his characters. Nearly half the space compassed by the story is devoted to the controversy over dreams, but by the end of it the reader is fairly well acquainted with Chauntecleer and Pertelote and is ready to accept the ensuing action in which they play their parts. While the discussion is staged, of course, for the sole purpose of developing these characters, still it *seems* as if the divergence of opinion arises naturally out of a fundamental difference in temperament. Hence the reader forgets for the time being that Chaucer is perhaps deliberately manufacturing a situation peopled by creatures of his imagination, and suffers himself to rest under the illusion that he is beholding the expression of personality in action as in real life. And the creation and maintenance of this illusion, I take it, is art.

II

The Dream-Poems

Chaucer's dream-poems, the *Parliament of Fowls,
Book of the Duchess, House of Fame,* and the Prologue
to the *Legend of Good Women,* are, as dreams, perplexing in the extreme. Since most of them were written
at a time when the poet's mind was still absorbing poorly
assimilated knowledge largely for its own sake and was
more or less passively plastic to the multifarious influences that thronged upon him, they seem to lack that
discriminating selection of material in the interest of
original and direct artistic purposes which characterises
his later work. Professor Sypherd has shown that in
these poems the form, setting, and devices for heighten-
ing interest are determined in some measure by the literary *genre* of the Old French love-vision, but that for
all the poet's indebtedness he is by no means a mere
imitator.[18] Professor Kittredge observes that Chaucer's
predecessors, adopting the fiction of a dream as a literary device for introducing the reader into a kind of
fairyland, nowhere attempt to reproduce the actual phenomena of dreams, but that the English poet, on the
other hand, while employing the same fiction is also
careful that the unfolding of his visions shall be in accordance with real dream-psychology.[19] I should like
to suggest — but without any too great conviction —
that Chaucer secures this effect through the process of
deliberately choosing in composition a specific type of
the *somnium* into which his material is to be formed,
then indicating in the introduction and elsewhere the

nature of this particular type and the psychology of its manifestations, and finally creating the poem as nearly as possible in accordance with the laws of this psychology. This must not be taken to mean that he is in any way using the story-content of his poem to illustrate the scientific development of a dream; on the contrary, he is employing just enough dream psychology of a specific character to give verisimilitude to the story, in which he is primarily interested. The *somnium naturale*, on account of its evanescent quality, offers but little for exploitation; the *somnium coeleste*, because its sources are entirely occult and its operations highly theoretical, cannot be used except at an obvious disadvantage. But the *somnium animale*, with its complex and readily comprehensible psychology, is just the form upon which the poet may most conveniently build his poem.

Chaucer wishes his reader to understand, I think, that the *Parliament of Fowls* is primarily a *somnium animale*. In the Proem he seems to announce that out of old books, which it is his custom to read with diligence, is about to come something new in the way of dream-lore:

And out of olde bokes, in good feith,
Cometh al this newe science that men lere (24).

On this particular occasion he has picked up a book containing such delightful matter that he peruses it all day long. It is Tullius Cicero's *Somnium Scipionis*, which tells of how Africanus the Younger saw his father in a marvellous vision and which treats in seven chapters of heaven and earth and of the souls that dwell therein.

Indeed, the volume is so strange that he must give an
outline of it (34–85). But the coming of darkness
bereaves him of his book for lack of light, and he prepares himself for bed, somewhat discontented, full of
thought and " besy hevinesse " (86–91). Exceedingly
weary from the day's labor, his spirit takes its rest in
sleep. And, behold, in his dream this same Africanus,
arrayed precisely as he was when Scipio saw him, comes
and stands by his bed's side. What is still more wonderful, Africanus speaks to him: " Thou hast done well
in reading my old and tattered book, of which Macrobius
thought highly, and now I shall somewhat requite thy
labor." Chaucer cannot say whether his having wearied
his mind with reading the *Somnium Scipionis* is responsible or not for the vision, but that explanation seems
likely enough. For, says he quoting from Claudian,[20]

> The wery hunter, slepinge in his bed,
> To wode ayein his minde goth anoon;
> The juge dremeth how his plees ben sped;
> The carter dremeth how his cartes goon;
> The riche, of gold; the knight fight with his foon,
> The seke met he drinketh of the tonne;
> The lover met he hath his lady wonne (99–109).

Yet lest someone should doubt the significance of his
somnium animale, he proceeds to give it a touch of the
somnium coeleste by addressing a prayer for help to
Venus; for, after all, Venus is ultimately responsible for
this love-vision (113–119). But it is Africanus who
leads him in the dream before two gates in a park,
pushes him through the gateway of the " sweven "

(154), and keeping fast hold of his hand, pilots him through the remainder of the adventure (169). The guide does not appear again and there is very little dream-psychology in the narrative proper, but the realistic setting and the poet's elaboration of the nature of a definite dream-type create that illusion of truth to fact under which the reader's mind rests throughout the succeeding incidents.

Both the *Book of the Duchess* and the Prologue to the *Legend of Good Women* belong to the same type. They are, however, more artistic than the *Parliament of Fowls* because in them the poet has developed the stories themselves in accordance with psychological laws of the *somnium animale*; they have many characteristics of actual dreams. In the Proem to the *Duchess* Chaucer is so powerfully disturbed in mind by some present sorrow that sleep has forsaken him these many days. " I have great wonder," says he, " how I may live so many days and nights without sleep. My mind is so full of useless thoughts that I care not how the world goes or comes; joy, sorrow, or whatever it may be, all are alike to me, for I have no feeling in anything. And well you know it is against nature to live in this wise, for all earthly creatures cannot endure any long time without sleep. Thus melancholy and the dread I have of dying, sleeplessness, and heaviness of heart have slain that alacrity of spirit I was wont to have. If you ask me whence comes this restlessness, I cannot truly say; but I guess, indeed, that it springs from that sickness I have suffered these eight years — and my healing is never the nearer because there is only one physician who could aid me —

but let that pass! " (1–40). To help drive the night away he picks up an ancient volume and reads the sad story of Seys and Alcione (45–220), in the course of which he learns for the first time of a god who can make men sleep. It is very strange that he has never heard of Morpheus; he had known only one God (230–240). Still lest he die, he playfully promises to this Morpheus, or to his goddess Juno — or to anybody else who can give him rest — the best feather-bed imaginable if only his prayer for sleep may be granted. Immediately such a drowsiness takes hold upon him that presently he falls upon his book asleep. The dream which comes to him is so wonderful and sweet that no man has the wit to read it aright; not even Joseph, who explained Pharaoh's dreams, nor Macrobius, who wrote all the " avisioun " of Africanus, could have interpreted this marvellous " sweven " (270–290). Here Chaucer is indicating that the dream-content which follows grows in large measure out of his conscious perturbation of spirit and sorrow of heart. As Professor Tupper remarks, " The stimuli of the dream in the *Book of the Duchess* were not only such explicit causes as the poet's melancholy and the Ovidian tale of bereavement, but a graver implicit reason, the ' rooted sorrow ' of Blanche's death which fills all his recent memory." [21] And Professor Kittredge has already shown with admirable skill how well the psychology of actual dreams is exemplified throughout the story,[22] adding, however, that the " childlike Dreamer, who never reasons, but only feels and gets impressions, who never knows what anything means until he is told in the plainest language is not Geoffrey

Chaucer, the humorist and man of the world. He is a creature of the imagination." [23] Likewise in the Prologue to the *Legend of Good Women* Chaucer's sensory impressions which come to him in the daisied fields are in some sort reproduced in the dream which follows. Professor Tupper, finding that " men have failed to read aright the *Legend* Prologue because they have overlooked the close relation of the phantasies of the vision to their exciting sources," presents an excellent study upon the subject, the purpose of which is to " trace the translation of the waking thoughts of the poet's day into the picture writing of the next night, to examine the speedy conversion of the actual ideas, latent dream-material, into dream-content." [24]

Chaucer's *House of Fame,* on the other hand, is a pure *somnium coeleste.* After a discussion of dreams in general — which we have reviewed already — he tells how on the tenth of December there came to him the most wonderful vision surely that man ever had. It is the only one of the dream-poems worthy to take rank along with the " avisioun " of Chauntecleer or with that of Croesus (105) and other great receivers of revelations:

> Now herkeneth, every maner man,
> That English understonde can,
> And listeth of my dreem to lere;
> For now at erste shul ye here
> So selly an avisioun,
> That Isaye, ne Scipioun,
> Ne king Nabugodonosor,
> Pharo, Turnus, ne Elcanor,
> Ne mette swich a dreem as this! (507–517)

Like Saint Paul he is caught up, as it were into the Seventh Heaven — whether in the body or in the spirit, he knows not; but God, thou knowest! (980) — and his progress through the skies is marshalled by Jove's own messenger, the Eagle. Fearing, however, that demons may be practising their occult powers upon him, he quiets his mind with a little prayer directed to Christ to save him " fro fantom and illusioun " (492). Surely his is a divine revelation! But having ranked it so and in consequence having forfeited the privilege of using the psychology of the *somnium animale*, which has stood him in such good stead, he is forced to fall back upon frequent invocations to the gods to help him secure its being accepted as true. May Morpheus, in whose power stands every dream (66–80), and Apollo, the god of wisdom and light, guide him in telling his " avisioun " so that men hearing it will believe (1090–5). And if anyone, out of malice or hostility, shall treat this work lightly or attack it in any way, may the curse of evil dreams and worse fulfilments come upon him (80–107).

After this manner, it seems to me, Chaucer makes use of the various classes of dreams in the composition of his love-visions. By indicating in the introduction and elsewhere to what particular type the poem is to belong and by thus creating a kind of framework, he is able to model the material of his visions according to certain psychological laws. But as an artist he is quick to see that for the purpose of serving as a background for a dream-poem the *somnium naturale* is unsuitable because it is without significance. He finds that the *somnium coeleste* can be used only within very narrow limits because its sources and manifestations are hardest to understand. But the *somnium animale* is made of the stuff of human experience; it represents the resurging in sleep of the dreamer's waking thoughts, desires, joys, and sorrows. Consequently Chaucer's best dream-poems are those which exemplify the psychology of the *somnium animale.*

CHAPTER TEN

DESTINY IN *TROILUS AND CRISEYDE*

CHAUCER's *Troilus and Criseyde* is a tragedy, strongly deterministic in tone, the action of which is presided over by a complex and inescapable destiny. Professor Kittredge has already given an excellent exposition of the fate which hangs over the chief characters and over the doomed city of Troy, and has analyzed the sources of the feeling that we are "looking on at a tragedy that we are powerless to check or to avert." [1] And Professor Root, remarking upon the high seriousness and the moral import of Chaucer's poem, says:

> He has called *Troilus* a tragedy; and it is a tragedy
> in the medieval sense of the term—the story of a
> man cast down by adverse fortune from great pros-
> perity and high estate into misery and wretchedness.
> The five books into which he has disposed his story
> suggest the five acts of the tragic drama. There is,
> moreover, a quite tragic insistence on the idea of
> destiny. [2]

It seems to me probable, however, that the destiny in this poem is perhaps more hugely spread than has been hitherto conceived and that the tragedy of it is far in advance of the usual mediaeval idea. It is the aim of this study, therefore, to attempt an exposition of one mediaeval conception of fate or destiny—the sources and nature of

its power, its various manifestations, its relations to providence, fortune, chance, and human free-will—and to
indicate its vital and complex functioning in Chaucer's
Troilus.

Undoubtedly Chaucer's idea of destiny is derived primarily from the *Consolation of Philosophy*, though he may
draw occasionally upon the conceptions of other writers.
That part of Boethius's philosophical system pertinent to
the *Troilus* is comparatively simple, schematized, mechanical, and rigid. In general it deals with God's simplicity
or one-ness in relation to the heterogeneity and multifariousness of His creations; in particular it treats of questions
concerning the nature of Providence, the orders of destiny,
the processes of fortune, the significance of so-called
chance or accident, and the relation of all these to human
free-will. How does God, infinitely removed, intervene in
the affairs of men dwelling upon this mundane sphere?
This God, stable, indivisible, and benevolent, transmits the
power of His will through successive stages of action, each
one of which, as it is discovered to be further and further
away from the unchangeable source, shows more and
more diversity, change, and alteration than the one before.
First, standing outside and aloof upon the tower of His
one-ness, God plans in His divine reason a universe as a
complete and final whole, an entirely unified conception
so infinite that it embraces every possible part—the creation of all things, the progressions of changing nature,
all forms, causes, movements that have been or can be.
This ordinance, assembled and unified in the divine
thought, is called Providence.[3] Secondly, in order that

this conception may be realized in all its diverse particulars, God in His Providence delegates executive powers to a blind force called Destiny, which administers in detail whatever has been planned. But because Destiny is somewhat removed from the absolutely stable center of divine intelligence, it necessarily becomes split up and divided into many manifestations; Providence is One, but He administers through Destiny in many manners and at various times that which as a whole He has ordained. Destiny is, therefore, the disposition and ordinance inherent in movable things by which Providence knits all things together in their respective orders. Thus whether Destiny be exercised by divine spirits (servants of Providence), or by some soul (*anima mundi*), or by all Nature serving God, or by the celestial movings of stars, or by virtue of angels, or by the machinations of devils, by any of these or by all of them together, the destinal ordinance is woven and accomplished.[4]

Thirdly, this Destiny so divided and distributed sends its influences outward and still further away from the stable center until they move upon still another blind and capricious force called Fortune, whose function it is (being personified as a sort of goddess) to rule over the checkered careers of human beings in this world. And because this plane of activity is the farthest possible removed from the one-ness characteristic of God, the chief qualities of Fortune are mutability, change, instability, and irrationality. In other words, whatever comes to a man in this precarious existence—for example, birth, riches, power, happiness, grief, sorrow, reverses, friendship, love, death, anything and everything—is the immediate gift of Fortune. This unsympathetic, erratic force which continually whirls human beings from good to bad, from poverty to riches, or from eminence to destruction, cares no more for one man than for another; its activities *seem* in their infinite capriciousness and diversity to be entirely illogical and chaotic.[5]

But they only *seem* so to those who are ignorant or themselves blinded by success or adversity. For Fortune has two aspects: namely, (a) that "common" Fortune, which represents all common experiences of humanity, and (b) that more personal fortune, according to which an individual may be born at a given time and place, grow up in this or that environment, love one person in particular, and die in youth or middle age by war or flood or poison. Thus any individual experience is likely to be the complex result of the combined influence of two or more destinal forces. Fortune as "common" comes from the moving of Nature-as-destiny. Or in more poetic terms, God binds together the diverse elements of His creation and maintains their proper status by the universal bond of Love; planets move in prescribed courses without faltering, seasons follow in regular order, neither day nor night encroaches upon the other, the sea remains within its bounds, men's lives progress in general from birth and youth to age and death, and men and women are joined in the sacrament of marriage—all this because God has bound them with the chain of Love.[6] But Fortune in its more personal bearings may be the result also of other destinal forces such as, for example, that of the erratic stars. It is Fortune in this latter aspect that is sometimes spoken of as chance or "hap" or "aventure of fortune" or accident.[7] But if accident be taken to mean that which comes to pass without cause or design, there is really no such thing. What through ignorance is called chance is nothing more than an occurrence whose causes are not understood. When, say, a man finds a pot of gold in a field, no one should say that this chances without a cause. The causes for this and for everything else, though perhaps not perceived by finite men, stretch back in an unbroken order through Destiny to the divine plan in God's mind. For all things are inescapably bound together and unified in the ordinance of Providence. It is only because men are short-sighted that they rail at the mutability of Fortune or the cruelty of Destiny or even at Providence itself. But the philosopher whose thought is stayed upon the stability of God may rise in some measure above the vicissitudes of Fortune. The relation between human free-will and the Destiny prepared in the Providence of God we shall discuss anon.

Now of all the destinal forces manifesting themselves in the affairs of men—"whether exercised by divine spirits (servants of Providence), or by some soul, or by Nature serving God, or by the celestial movings of stars, or by virtue of Angels or by the machinations of devils, by any of these or by all of them together"—that which seems usually to appeal most strongly to Chaucer as artist is the celestial moving of the erratic stars. The personal fortunes of Palamon and Arcite in the *Knight's Tale* are presided over by the planets Saturn and Mars.[8] Again, in the

Merchant's Tale the narrator is in light mood undecided what combination of destinal forces brings May to bestow her love upon Damian: "Whether it was by destiny or chance, by the influence (of spirits), or by nature, or by the power of a constellation thus-or-so placed in the heavens that it was a favorable time for presenting a love-letter to a woman to get her love, I cannot say; let that great God above, who knows that no act is causeless, judge the matter." [9] The destiny governing the Wife of Bath resides in a conjunction of Mars and Venus in Taurus; [10] it is evident that the destinal forces hanging over Hypermnestra in the *Legend of Good Women* are associated with the movements of Venus, Jupiter, and Saturn, [11] and that Constance's fortunes in the *Man of Law's Tale* are in large measure subject to the power of Mars and Luna cadent from an angle in Scorpio and the eighth house. [12] These more or less capricious and uniquely personal fortunes are caused by the destinal forces emanating from the erratic stars or planets as they move through the heavens.

The "common" fortunes of men—birth, growth, love, reproduction, death, and so on—are, as we have said, under the control of Nature, which serves God in the capacity of Destiny. We must now observe that, according to some mediaeval thinkers, this Nature is the product of the regular movements of the fixed stars. Aristotle says:

> The motion of the heavens, to which all change on earth is due, is two-fold, and has a twofold effect upon sublunary matter. The perfect diurnal motion

of the fixed stars from east to west constitutes the
principle of permanence and growth; whereas the
motion of the planets, running their annual courses
at irregular paces from west to east athwart the
diurnal motion of the fixed stars, constitutes the principle of earthly change.[13]

But it is the Arabian, Albumasar, who develops the
theory more fully:

> All that is born and dies on earth depends upon the
> motions of the constellations and of the stars. . . Now
> the seven wandering planets march along the zodiac
> more swiftly than do the constellations, often chang-
> ing from direct to retrograde. They are, therefore,
> better adapted than the upper spheres to produce the
> effects and the motions of the things of this world.
> To the sphere of the constellations is assigned a gen-
> eral rule; whereas to the wandering stars belongs
> the care over the details of earthly life. . . The more
> rapidly a planet moves, and the stranger the course
> it follows, the more powerful will be its influence on
> things below. The motion of the moon is swifter than
> that of any other planet; it has, accordingly, more to
> do than any other in regulating mundane affairs.
> The fixed stars govern what is stable in the world, or
> what suffers gradual change. The celestial sphere
> of the fixed stars encircles the earth with a perpetual
> motion; the stars never alter their pace, and main-
> tain invariably their relative distances from the earth.
> The seven planets, on the contrary, move more rap-
> idly and with diverse motions, each running its own
> variable course. . . As the motions of these wander-
> ing stars are never interrupted, so the generations

and alterations of earthly things never have an end. Only by observing the great diversity of planetary motions can one comprehend the unnumbered varieties of change in this world.[14]

Thus, we may safely conclude, the regular progressions of Nature—the successions of the seasons, birth, growth, death—and consequently the common fortunes of men are ultimately attributable to the motion of the fixed stars.[15]

That Boethius shows familiarity with some such theory as this seems evident. As Professor Thorndike remarks of the *Consolation of Philosophy*:

> The heavenly bodies are apparently ever present in Boethius' thought in this work, and especially in the poetical interludes he keeps mentioning Phoebus, the moon, the universe, the sky, and the starry constellations.[16]

In Book IV, Meter VI, Boethius seems to imply that the destinal power of the Chain of Love is inherent first and primarily in the movement of the sphere of the constellations and that its influence is projected thence outward and farther away from God, the stable center, into certain movements of the Sun and Moon and into the natural order of things upon the earth:

> If thou, being wise, wilt judge in thy thought the laws of the high Thunderer, behold the heights of the sovereign heaven. There the stars, by the rightful alliance of things, keep their old peace. The Sun, moved by his ruddy fire, does not disturb the cold sphere of the Moon. Nor the star that is called the

Bear, that runs his course about the sovereign height of the world, nor the star Ursa is ever washed in the deep western sea, nor desires to dip his flames in the water of the ocean, though he may see other stars plunged into the sea. And Hesperus the star foretells the coming of night, and Lucifer brings again the clear day. Thus Love creates concord in the everlasting courses, and thus is conflict put out of the country of the stars. This concord controls in a uniform manner the elements, so that the moist things striving with the dry things yield place at times; and the cold things join themselves by faith to the hot things. . . By the same causes the flowery year yields sweet savours in the first summer-season warming; the hot summer dries up the corn; the autumn comes again, heavy with apples; and the heavy rain washes the winter. This concord brings forth and nourishes everything that has life in the world; and this same concord, destroying, hides, snatches away, and overwhelms under the last death all things that are born.

Thus the power of Love, communicated by God first to the constellations of the eighth sphere, is transmitted through the more regular movements of the planets (especially the Sun and Moon) and through the elements so that it becomes finally in this mundane sphere Destiny-as-nature, which produces the common fortunes of men.

With this exposition of the destinal forces in mind, let us return to a study of Chaucer's *Troilus and Criseyde*. It must be observed at once that in this tragedy the poet has not been able, or perhaps has been unwilling, to define the limits of the destiny back of the story's action

with such precision and accuracy as he has employed elsewhere.[17] He insists time and again, as we shall see, that
the common fortunes of Troilus and Criseyde are caused
by Nature-as-destiny and hence by God, who is the
author of Nature; he suggests as often that the special,
individual fortunes of the protagonists are directed by the
destinal power inherent in the movements of the erratic
stars. But he nowhere postulates a more definite system
of destinal forces. Still one is made to feel—by means of
reference to this or that planet, by striking suggestions of
destructive influences hanging over the doomed city of
Troy, and by mysterious intimations of tragedy announced
by dreams, oracles, and divinations—that the days of
Troy are numbered and that the cloud of fate hovering
over Troilus and Criseyde will presently overwhelm them
in the general disaster.

For example, in the beginning of Book I, Chaucer
states, with his usual swift artistry, that the story deals
primarily with the double sorrow of Troilus, who loved
Criseyde and who was in the end forsaken by her. But,
like a true tragedian, he conceives the brilliant idea of
throwing the lamentable history of the two lovers against
the dark background of the Trojan war, which has already progressed nearly ten bloody years and which is
on the point of ending with the fall of the great city.
Apollo's unappeasable enmity is about to strike; and in
some sense the movements of the stars are bound up with
the city's imminent destruction. For Calchas, celebrated
astrologer, magician, and augurer, receives announce-
ments from a variety of sources all agreeing that mysteri-

ous powers are about to meet in one line for the doom of Troy. Apollo speaks to him through an oracle, saying that the Greeks will shortly be victorious; "by calculynge," i.e., by astrological observation, he finds the same message written among the stars; and "by sort," i.e., by the casting of lots, or by the chance opening of sacred books, or perhaps by augury from the flights of birds, his conclusions are further confirmed. Then since his native city must fall, Calchas departs from it, and seeks sanctuary among the enemy Greeks (I, 64–83). But in the meantime fighting continues for a season, bringing successes now to one side, now to the other; Fortune turns her wheel, and each in succession is whirled aloft to victory and afterwards under to defeat (I, 134 ff.). Since it is not apposite, however, to tell the whole process of the city's destruction, the author directs the reader to Homer, Dares, and Dictys (I, 141 ff.). Thus, at the very beginning of the story, Chaucer has suggested the lively pageantry of a romantic war and has sketched back of this narrative of chivalry and love the destinal forces which produce the city's downfall. And when the protagonists appear upon the scene, one senses that a doom is already prepared for them. This method of precipitating tragic characters into a situation already overshadowed by a gloomy fatality is characteristic of Shakespeare in his greatest tragedies.[18]

Troilus is introduced scoffing at love and deriding lovers, but Nature-as-destiny is preparing his inevitable subjugation to her laws. When he sees a knight or squire feasting his eyes upon a lady and sighing, he smiles con-

temptuously upon such folly. But the angry god of love
prepares to pluck the fine feathers of this peacock. At
this juncture, Chaucer introduces a long, independent
passage in which he philosophizes upon the power of Love
(Nature-as-destiny) that is presently to subdue the proud
heart of Troilus. It is the nature of man and, therefore,
his destiny to love. Since love binds all things together
and no man may escape the law of Nature, let no man
refuse to be bound by Love (I, 214–66). So Chaucer
initiates the love-story with the announcement of one
source of the destinal power which is to direct the life and
actions of Troilus; the Boethian principle of Love, which
binds together all parts of God's creation, is invoked to
explain why the proud Trojan is made to love at all.[19]

Having fallen in love with Criseyde, Troilus himself
seems to recognize that Nature-as-destiny is in large
measure responsible for his experience, which is in a sense
common to all men. But since his code enjoins absolute
secrecy and since she can know nothing of his passion as
yet, he is constrained to lament the fate which has decreed
that his particular fortune should be to love Criseyde, and
not perhaps some other woman. This is the fool who
laughed at love's pains; now he, too, is caught in the
snare and gnaws his own chain (I, 507–09). If this
were known (he thinks) no doubt his friends would
jeer and say:

> O thou, woeful Troilus, since thou must of neces-
> sity love through thy destiny, would to God that
> thou hadst centered thy affections upon one who
> might know of thy woe, even though she should

lack pity. But thy lady is as cold toward thee as frost under the winter moon, and thou art fordone as is snow in fire (I, 519–25).

He does not understand the destinal origin of this individual fortune which has come upon him; consequently when Pandarus comes and offers to medicine his complaint, he rails at Fortune and refuses aid (I, 835–40). And now to comfort him Pandarus, following Boethius, postulates that Fortune is not to be greatly blamed, because she is in some measure common to all men. If she should stop turning her wheel for a single moment, she would cease to be Fortune. Troilus should take this comfort to his soul: if the joys given by Fortune must pass away, so also must the sorrows—for her wheel cannot stop turning. Who knows but that, out of her very mutability, she may be preparing happiness for the woeful lover? (I, 840–54).[20] At any rate, Troilus should not be ashamed to love Criseyde; nothing but good comes of loving well and in worthy place. He ought not to call this hap or chance but rather grace, i.e., a special mercy of whatever destinal or divine forces there are (I, 895 ff.). Pandarus himself will entreat Criseyde for his friend with hope of success, for wise men say that there was never yet man or woman who was unapt to suffer heat of love, either celestial or natural; it would become her much more to love and cherish a worthy knight like Troilus (I, 975–86). Here Chaucer is showing that the mysterious movings of Nature in the capacity of destiny have conquered the proud heart of Troilus and may influence the decision of Criseyde. But as to why either lover, as an individual, should choose the other and not somebody else, he has nothing to say as yet.

In Book II, however, one is made to feel that the wandering or erratic stars, especially Venus and Luna, exert a powerful influence upon the personal fortunes of Troilus and Criseyde. For example, before Pandarus sets out to woo his niece for Troilus, he deems it necessary to set up a figure of the heavens in order to learn whether the Moon is favorable to such a journey; and having determined that the election is favorable, he proceeds with confidence (II, 74 ff.). We are not told in precisely what position he finds Luna, nor how she is aspected by other planets, but he shows himself wise in astrological lore in assuming that Luna especially must be consulted when one starts upon a journey of any sort and particularly upon a journey for the purpose of acquiring love or friendship. Albohazen Haly says:

> For an election to determine the best time for beginning a journey Luna should be crescent in light, free from the influence of the infortunes, and not in the second, or eighth, or sixth, or the twelfth house of the figure; she should be in good aspect with the fortunes; Mercury should not be combust and should be free from the infortunes; the lord of the ascendant should not be combust or unfortunately placed, but in good position; and a fortune should be found in the ascendant or in any one of the angles. Such an election signifies health of the body, promptness, and joy in the journey. . . And if you are not able to have all of this, place Luna aspecting the ascendant and the lord of the ascendant,

and both should be free from the infortunes. And if Luna should be in corporal conjunction or in trine or sextile aspect with Jupiter or Venus, you have the best possible situation. . . . When Luna is separated by a degree from conjunctions with Sol and is in trine or sextile aspect with Saturn, and afterwards comes into aspect with any fortune, it signifies that whatever is undertaken at that time will be completed, be durable, and will bring joy. And if your going forth is to a woman, apply Luna to Venus situated in a masculine sign.[21]

Pandarus, no doubt, applies Luna to Venus, since he is going forth to Criseyde; indeed, a consideration of the relationship between these two planets seems to be necessary if he is to secure her love and favor for his friend. For as Haly says:

In order to elicit or secure love and friendship it is agreed that Luna should be favorable, and likewise the eleventh house and the lord of the eleventh house, and that both should be received by Venus in trine aspect. And if the reception is in her house or exaltation, it will be better.[22]

At any rate, assured of the benevolent aspect of the heavens, Pandarus sallies forth jauntily.

Criseyde's knowledge of God, Providence, and Destiny is apparently slight, but she is acquainted in some measure with the eccentricities of Fortune. Consequently, when Pandarus comes to her with an appeal on behalf of Troilus, his message is couched in terms which she can readily understand. He arouses her curiosity at first by referring

mysteriously to a "fair adventure" (II, 224) which has
befallen her, and urges her to seize upon it. She has
lightly found good fortune, and she must accept it lest it
should abate (II, 281–91). Troilus loves her and, if fortune wills it so, must hasten to die unless she will requite
his love (II, 335 ff.). "Alas! for woe," says she playing
slyly, "I should have thought that, if it had been my misfortune to love him or Achilles or Hector or any other
man, you would have had no mercy on me." (II, 415–
19). But Pandarus assuages her assumed perturbation
by recounting Troilus's eloquence in bewailing his woe
to Love. Here, strangely enough, the god of love is made
to have the power and momentarily to take the place of
the Boethian God, who in his Providence directs through
Destiny the fortunes of every man. "O god," says Troilus, "who at thy disposition leadest the end of every
man, by just Providence, accept my confession and send
me such penance as seems good." (II, 526–30). In the
meantime, while Pandarus and Criseyde talk, Troilus
comes riding by on his return from battle, and she sees
him as he is, a romantic and attractive figure. Why
should he have come at this precisely psychological moment? It is destiny, fate, necessity, says Chaucer,

> For which, men say, may nought disturbed be
> That shal bityden of necessitee (II, 621).

We are not yet informed what the source of this necessity is. But it is suggested that Nature-as-destiny is responsible for Criseyde's beginning to pity the woe of Troilus (II, 1373–75); and after that, her first inclination

toward love is deepened into real passion partly by contemplating his manhood and pain, and through his good service to her.

But here Chaucer emphasizes that, in the development of Criseyde's budding love for Troilus, the destinal influence of the planet Venus is, if not the most potent of the destinal forces, at least powerfully contributory. It is suggested, in the first place, that Venus was not entirely unfavorable ("nas nat al a fo") to Troilus in his nativity (II, 684). If this may be interpreted to mean that this planet was the ruling influence at his birth, we can account in some measure for his character in general and for his personal attractiveness to women in particular. As I have shown elsewhere,[23] it is the province of Venus to bestow upon her children beautiful and elegantly formed bodies, together with characters inclined to luxuriousness and passionate love but withal honorable and upright. Though voluptuous and temperamental by nature, the children of Venus possess a fine sense of duty, a ready faith, great refinement, good breeding, delicacy of feeling, and kindliness of heart. They easily become leaders and perform whatever they undertake with facility. They are given to games, to laughter, to joyous living, rejoicing in the companionship of friends and relying upon others to the point of being often deceived. So Troilus is described. He is said to be so well grown in stature and to be of such complete proportion that Nature might not amend it; he is young, fresh, strong, hardy as a lion, and in every situation true as steel. He is so endowed with good qualities that there are few like him in the world (V,

826–33). And Criseyde loves him finally, in part, for his innate honesty and trustworthiness, for his wisdom in making love, for his secrecy, and for his honor in affairs of the heart. His every act indicates that he is a child of Venus.

Moreover, at the precise moment when Troilus seeks the full love of Criseyde, Venus is said to be so well situated in the heavens that she aids materially in furthering the amatory cause. This naturally benefic planet is favorably located in the seventh house of the heavens,[24] having other planets disposed in such good aspect to her that she helps poor Troilus to escape his woe (II, 680 ff.). Since we are not told specifically how the other planets stand in relation to Venus, it is impossible to interpret fully the astrological situation. But Chaucer is correct when he suggests that, in elections to determine a favorable time for securing the love of a woman, Venus should be located in the seventh house of the heavens. To this house are referred all questions concerning love, marriage, the quarrels of lovers, pleasure, passion, and desire.[25] As Professor Root well says:

> For any question concerning love, the astrologer inquires what planets are at the moment in the seventh house, which "gives judgment of marriage and all manner of love-questions." A malefic planet —Saturn or Mars—in the seventh house causes ill fortune in love. But Venus is a benefic planet, and especially concerned with affairs of love. Venus in the seventh house marks a very propitious hour.[26]

In this instance Chaucer is careful to indicate that, at the critical moment when Criseyde (urged at first by

Nature-as-destiny) is on the point of making up her mind to love the individual, Troilus, the wandering planets in favorable combinations exert their destinal power and aid in producing the special fortunes of the characters.

It is in Book III, however, where Troilus finally secures and enjoys the love of Criseyde, that Chaucer shows most effectively the combined and intricately working forces of destiny. He has apparently confused the influence of the planets, sometimes with that of the pagan gods and goddesses of the same names and sometimes with the power of the Boethian bond of Love. But here is in reality no confusion; the mythological dress is a poetical device, and with a clear mind the poet has demonstrated how the destinal urge emanating from the erratic stars combines and intermingles with that having its source in Nature-as-destiny. In order to make this idea immediately emphatic he removes Troilo's song (based on Boethius, 2, m 8) from its natural position in Boccaccio's *Filostrato* to the beginning of Book III and raises it to the dignity of a Proem.[27]

Here Venus in several aspects is praised as the source of all love and unity in the world. As Professor Root has it:

> In this passage, Venus is addressed sometimes as the pagan goddess, sometimes as the planet with astrological influence. She is the power of Love, both in its earthly aspect as sexual attraction, and in its platonic aspect as the unifying principle of the universe.[28]

It is the favorable light of the planet Venus, the Sun's

friend, which adorns the third heaven[29] and which, always ready to repair into gentle hearts, is in part the cause of that wholesome joy accompanying the advent of love. It is Venus, the symbol of unifying Love, whose might is felt in earth and sea, in heaven and in hell; all created things feel at times her eternal and all-pervasive influence. God loves and will refuse nothing to love; and in this world no creature has worth or may endure without it. The planet Venus appeases the wrath of the infortune, Mars; Venus, the symbol of unity, overcomes the tendency of created things to fly asunder and to destroy themselves in conflict. Venus—in both her philosophical and astrological aspects—holds realm and house together; she is the true cause of friendship; she knows all the hidden qualities of things—i.e., "the disposition and ordinance inherent in movable things," which, according to Boethius, is destiny—at which people wonder so, when they cannot understand why this woman loves that man, or why another loves elsewhere, or why this fish and not that comes into the weir. She has established an inescapable law in the universe (III, 1–36). Consequently, we may conclude that Venus in both her aspects is largely responsible for the consummation of Troilus's love.

But the other planets are also in general accord with her. When Criseyde visits Pandarus on the fatal night and is on the point of returning home without having seen Troilus, her Fortune ruled over by a combination of planets compels her to remain. "But, O Fortune, executrix of fates," says Chaucer of this critical moment, "O influence of these high heavens, it is truth that, under

God, you are our shepherds, though to us beasts the causes are hidden. Criseyde started home, but by the god's will it was executed other than she desired. For the bent Moon joined with Saturn and Jupiter in Cancer brought such a deluge of rain that she was compelled to remain" (III, 617–25).[30] Moreover, just before Criseyde is made to come to Troilus, the apprehensive lover appeals for assistance to every planet except Saturn. It must be recalled that Venus exerted a favorable influence in his nativity. Consequently, he prays that, if Venus the happy planet had bad aspects of Mars or Saturn or if she were combust at his birth, she may ask her father Jupiter, a powerfully benefic planet, to turn aside these evil influences (II, 715–21). In this situation he is particularly wise in asking to be relieved of the possible bad aspects of Mars and Saturn, for as Albubather says:

> When Venus and Mars, without the good influence of Jupiter, are *in medio coeli* or in the East, the native will be a fornicator and of evil reputation. . . When Venus in a diurnal nativity is located in her mansion and Mars influences her from his mansion, the native will be given to harlotries; when Venus is posited in the mansion of Mars or Mars in the mansion of Venus, the native will be a manifest fornicator and without modesty. When Venus and Mars are joined in either quartile or oppositional aspect, or if Mars and Venus are in a masculine sign, or if Venus is in the mansion or term of Mars, the native will commit wicked and base fornication and will be given to sodomy.[31]

The same author gives other instances of the unfavorable position of Venus:

> When Venus is located in Pisces and Mars aspects her from his exaltation, the native will be given to much fornication and from it shall procure his death. . . When Venus and Saturn are unfortunately joined in the tenth house and peregrene, the native will be impotent.[32]

And Ptolemaeus points out the dangers in even more sweeping terms:

> If Venus is combust and in any one of the angles, and without beneficent aspect of Jupiter, the native will commit many secret acts contrary to nature, and especially so if Venus is found in any of the incontinent signs.[33]

Well may the gentle-minded Troilus, going in honor to enjoy his love for the first time, pray to be delivered from the dishonorable and unnatural acts which Venus, if she were under the evil influence of Saturn or Mars or if she were combust at his birth, might impose upon him.

Moreover, lest any loop-hole should be neglected through which malefic influences may be streamed upon him in this situation, Troilus is careful to supplicate all the planets with the single exception of Saturn. Astrologically speaking, Saturn is the cold and dry planet, the malignant infortune, sending violent death by inundation and storms of pestilential winds, fomenting conflicts of all kinds, dealing destruction by poison, in prison, and by means of disease. He is never favorable under any circumstances, and that is why Troilus asks to be delivered from his bad aspects (III, 716) and why his help is not solicited.[34] Mars is the lesser infortune and as such may, in certain situations, exert a powerful influence for evil; but when he is favorably located and beneficiently aspected, he may aid materially in the consummation of happy love-relations. For example, considering a certain question referred to the seventh house, "In iacendo cum mulieribus," Albohazen Haly says:

> When you wish to lie with a woman, observe those signs which take delight in such business; namely, Aries, Capricorn, Leo, and Libra, because these signs signify great power in this act and because they are never inactive. And if Luna is joined to Venus and Mars, it will be better; because Venus signifies the joy which the participants have mutually and delightful relations, and Mars signifies much sperm.[35]

Therefore, Troilus hopes that Venus was in his nativity free from Mars's unfavorable influence (III, 716) and goes on to pray that, in this election for securing Criseyde's love, the lesser infortune with the "blody cope" may help or at least not hinder Pandarus's plans (III, 724 ff.). The other planets, being for the most part benevolent, are appealed to in their astrological order (III, 721–31). As Professor Root admirably sums up the matter:

> Troilus prays first to Venus, as goddess of love, and as an astrological influence, favorable unless she was "combust or let" at his birth. He asks her to intercede with her father, Jupiter (who is astrologi-

cally benefic),[36] to turn aside any evil planetary influence. Troilus next appeals to the gods who are
identified with the several planets: Jupiter, Mars,
Apollo (the Sun), Mercury, Diana (the Moon).
They are named in the order of their distance from
the Earth according to the old astronomy. Venus,
whose place is between the Sun and Mercury, has
already been invoked at the beginning of the prayer.
Saturn, most distant from the Earth, is not invoked,
since his influence is inalterably malefic, and since
there is no Ovidian myth which relates any Saturnine
amour.[37]

Finally, Troilus appeals again to whatever destinal forces
there may be, using this time the symbol of the pagan
Fates:

O fatal sustren, which, er any clooth
Me shapen was, my destene me sponne,
So helpeth to this werk that is bi-gonne (III, 734–36).

Apparently the lover's intelligent prayers are answered
in some detail. At any rate, when Troilus finds that
success has crowned his efforts and Criseyde lies in his
arms, he renders thanks to precisely those destinal forces
upon which he called for aid. He expresses fervent gratitude to "the blisful goddes sevene" (III, 1202), that is
to say, gratitude to the benefic planets no doubt for their
active and favorable interference in his behalf and to the
malignant infortunes for their apathy or indifference. He
acknowledges especially that Venus, "the wel-willy
planete" (III, 1257), has had an important part in
bringing the lovely lady to his arms. If Venus were
indeed combust at his birth or if she did have bad aspects

of Mars or Saturn, as he feared at one time might have been the case, then the good Jupiter has apparently heard his prayer and has indeed neutralized the harm which such planetary combinations might have worked upon his love. Chaucer is very careful to state that this relation between Troilus and Criseyde is no madness or folly; here is no wicked love which might lead to base actions (III, 1373–94). The love of Troilus and Criseyde, watched over and guided by the kindly planets, has taken no taint from the possible bad aspects of the infortunes. The practice of it only "souneth in-to gentlenesse." (III, 1414).

But Troilus does not forget in the first flush of his happiness to praise also Nature-as-destiny. When he holds Criseyde in his arms for the first time, he acclaims that benign Love, the holy bond of all things, through whose grace he, the former rebel against love's laws, has been raised to a place of boundless contentment (III, 1261–74). And after he has enjoyed the companionship of Criseyde for a season, he is accustomed to descant to Pandarus upon the perfections of his love, and to sing a joyous hymn in praise of that mysterious power which holds them together.

> It is Love that establishes laws in the high heavens, in the earth, and in the hearts of men and women, so that all things obey their respective natures. Without Love all Nature would be in chaos and human life useless. May God, who is the author of Nature, bind with the power of Love all human hearts so that no man may escape (III, 1740–71).[38]

So Troilus pays his final respects to the great power which

has been instrumental in giving him the consummation of his desires.

We must observe in passing, however, that the hymn to Love sung by Troilus at this juncture is not found in manuscripts supposed to represent the first draft of the poem. Professor Root says:

> At this point in *Filostrato*, Troilo sings to Love a hymn (3. 74–9) which is based in part on this Metre of Boethius. These stanzas of *Filostrato* Chaucer has used as a Proem (lines 1–38) to his third book. Having so used them, it was necessary to find new material for the song of Troilus; and Chaucer turned back to the passage in Boethius from which Boccaccio had received his inspiration. . . It would seem that the poet did not in the first draft provide a song for Troilus to sing.[39]

In that case, why should Chaucer feel it expedient to return to his original manuscript and add this particular song for Troilus? Our analysis of the destinal forces back of the third book supplies the answer to this question: he wanted to give climactic emphasis to the conception of Nature-as-destiny, with which the book begins and which underlies the progress and consummation of the love affair. Fearing that his readers might possibly miss the technical significance of the Proem and of Troilus's earlier song (III, 1254–74) he returned and inserted, near the end of the book and at the point where the lovers are most supremely happy, this full-throated song which reiterates and confirms the inescapable power of Love. In this way he has to some degree palliated what may have seemed to his age a rather immoral situation; and he has bestowed dignity upon ephemeral human relationships by linking them up with the processes of cosmic forces. Having so established his purpose, he does not refer again to Nature-as-destiny.

Then comes the turning point of the story's action. It is in Book IV that we have the reversal of personal Fortune out of which grows the tragedy of Troilus and Criseyde. Up to this time the lovers have been for the most part increasingly happy and successful; Nature-as-destiny had decreed their passion and destinal forces residing in the erratic stars have determined in large measure the conditions, times, and places which figure in their joyous coming together. But, well-away the while, says Chaucer remembering Boethius, for all too short a season endures such joy, thanks to Fortune! She seems most favorable when she is just on the point of beguiling. From Troilus she turns aside and hides her bright face, and takes no heed of him; she casts him completely out of his lady's grace, and sets Diomede on her wheel. The poet himself feels compelled now to write with quaking pen the story of how Criseyde forsook Troilus, or at least how she was unkind; may the Furies and cruel Mars help him (IV, 1–28).

And at this inauspicious moment, when Fortune seems to withdraw her favor from the protagonist, Chaucer the artist emphasizes again the imminent doom of Troy. Through the first three books we are likely to forget the ominous warnings concerning the city's coming destruction, seeing that Troilus and Criseyde are apparently the

darlings of Fortune and feeling that destiny itself sub-
scribes to them; the tragic qualm which we experienced
at the beginning of the story has been allayed to some
extent by the growing sense that cosmic forces are arrayed
on the lovers' side. But now the old gray Calchas, who
fled from Troy long ago because he knew it must fall,
begins his croakings again. He demands of the Greeks
that his daughter, Criseyde, be exchanged among other
prisoners of war in order that she may escape the general
holocaust. He tells the Greeks:

> On peril of my life, I do not lie, Apollo has taught
> it to me faithfully; I have also known it to be true
> by astrological observation, by the casting of lots, and
> also by augury; and I prophesy that the time is close
> at hand when Troy shall be reduced to dead ashes!
> For certainly Apollo and Neptune, who built the
> walls of Troy, are so angry with the city that they
> shall bring it to confusion out of spite for King
> Laomedon. He would not pay their wages; there-
> fore, the town of Troy shall be set on fire (IV,
> 113–126).

The ancient enmity of the incensed gods still hangs
over the city, and we hear closer and more pronounced
rumblings, as it were, of the Fate which is soon to be
unloosed upon it. How shall Troilus survive when he
is caught in the maelstrom of such colossal forces?

When he learns that Criseyde must depart from Troy,
Troilus is at first thrown into a panic. In his progressive
happiness he has been able to discern, back of his common
and individual fortune, the destinal powers moving under

the direction of God. But now he is so blinded by grief and so unphilosophical that he can understand nothing beyond the waywardness of Fortune. Conceiving of her as a pagan goddess, he laments pathetically:

> O Fortune, why hast thou taken away Criseyde without a reason? I have honored thee above all the gods; I am too insignificant to have incurred thy enmity. If Criseyde had been left, I would have scorned thy gifts. It is thy nature to bereave a creature of his dearest possession, and in that way to prove thy changeable violence. All is lost! (IV, 260–86).

He does not understand why the lord of Love, who knows his heart and the travail he has undergone for Criseyde, can permit this separation, since it was Love in the first place who brought him and Criseyde into his grace and sealed their hearts (IV, 288–94). Whatever else he may do while suffering this life of torment and cruel pain, he will always complain this "infortune or this dis-aventure" which has come upon him (IV, 295–98). And he prays that, after his soul has fled from his heart, these lovers who are now set high upon the wheel of Fortune in good "aventure" may find their loves as true as steel (IV, 323–29).

The sympathetic Pandarus also weeps out his observations upon the fickleness of Fortune. "Who would have thought," says he, "that in so short a time Fortune would have so overthrown our joy! For in this world there is no creature who ever saw stranger ruin than this, through 'cas or aventure.' But such is the way of this

world. Therefore, I thus conclude: no one may consider
what Fortune sends to be his own peculiar possession;
her gifts are in common to all men" (IV, 384–92). He
holds out to Troilus the consolation, however, that Fortune supports the hardy man in his undertakings and
abandons wretches who exhibit cowardice (IV, 600–2).
But Troilus is a fatalist and can derive no comfort from
such an idea; a dire necessity has been imposed upon him
from without, and nothing he can do will have the least
effect in altering it. And when upon his last painful visit
to Criseyde she falls into a swoon so deep that he thinks
her dead, he rails at both God and Fortune:

> O cruel Jove and you, adverse Fortune, you have
> falsely slain Criseyde; and since you can do no worse
> to me, fie upon your power and upon your contra-
> dictory works! You shall never win over me in
> this cowardly manner; no death shall separate me
> from my lady. For since you have slain her thus,
> I shall also die (IV, 1192–1200).

Though Criseyde also senses a kind of fatality back
of her parting from Troilus, still she is self-reliant and
is willing to oppose her woman's cleverness and wit against
whatever may be the decrees of Fortune. She once
attributes her present misfortunes to the fact that she
must have been born under a cursed constellation (IV,
745). But she is philosophically shortsighted and is apparently ignorant of the relations of Destiny to God and
Fortune; or her conception of Fate (if she has one) is
so dim and limited that she does not realize the futility
of human struggles against what God ultimately has
planned. Or perhaps she is so superficial in her thinking

and so conventional that she actually places no faith in
her father's prognostications regarding the doom of Troy;
or maybe her feminine childishness is responsible for the
supposition that, in hoodwinking her father into believing
his own prophecies false, she may be averting the city's
destruction altogether. At any rate, she is undoubtedly
the clever woman planning an immediate return to her
lover, provided she may be able to secure her father's
permission. Desire of gold will so blind his soul that she
will be able to do anything she pleases with him; for
neither Apollo, nor his clerk's laws, nor his astrological
prognostications shall avail him three haws! And if
Calchas attempts to prove by divination that she lies, she
will pluck him by the sleeve and assure him that he has
not well understood the gods; for the gods speak in am-
biguities and, of a truth, they tell twenty lies. She will
insist to him that dread first created the gods and that
his coward heart made him interpret amiss the gods' text,
that time when he fled for fear out of Delphi after having
received the oracle concerning Troy's fall (IV, 1395–
1411). She attempts to comfort Troilus further with
the idea that the man who pays no attention to Fortune
is lord of her; for she subdues nobody but the wretch
(IV, 1586–89). Troilus may expect her return within
ten days. But Chaucer makes us feel already the irony
of the situation: a weak woman ignorantly contemning
Fortune and either disregarding the decrees of Destiny
that have gone forth concerning herself and Troilus or
opposing to them her puny strength. As Professor George
Lyman Kittredge wisely remarks: "She soon discovers that
she has matched her woman's wit, not against her

dotard father merely, but against the doom of Troy." [40]

After this manner Chaucer must have represented, in the original draft of the poem, the destinal forces working back of the fourth book. But when he came finally to revise his text, he apparently found that the general effect produced was not precisely, or at least not completely, what he had intended. Consequently, at the intense moment when reversal of fortune strikes the protagonist, he chose to introduce Troilus's now celebrated soliloquy on the relation of God's foreknowledge to man's free-will (IV, 955–1085). And that the insertion of the passage satisfied permanently whatever purpose he may have had seems to be attested by the fact that he never withdrew it.[41]

Perhaps no passage in Chaucer's works has received quite such universal condemnation as has Troilus's monolog on predestination. Professor Lounsbury, for example, says:

> It is the grossest instance of the failure on the part of Chaucer to comply with the requirements of his art. . . . The passage is a versification of the argument on the subject of God's foreknowledge and man's free-will that is contained in the fifth book of the treatise of Boethius. It utterly interferes with the movement of the story. It is tacked to it by the flimsiest of fastenings. . . . The bad taste exhibited by the poet in such passages will be conceded by all. His most fervent admirers would be readiest to admit the justice of this censure.[42]

Ward thinks the matter is "pedantically put, perhaps, and

as it were dragged in violently by means of a truncated quotation from Boethius." [43] T. R. Price says: "The passage is the chief artistic blemish." [44] Professor Manly is of the opinion that the poet "did not restrain within proper limits the ideas brought up by association (note the famous passage on predestination in the *Troilus*)." [45] Professor Root defends the passage to a certain extent: "Prolonged beyond its due proportion it may be; but it is no more a digression than are the soliloquies of Hamlet. It is thoroughly in accord with the character of Troilus as Chaucer conceived him." [46] And Professor Kittredge concludes: "Doubtless the passage is inartistic and maladjusted; but it is certainly not, as some have called it, a digression. On the contrary, it is, in substance, as pertinent as any of Hamlet's soliloquies." [47]

As to Chaucer's probable purpose in writing and introducing the passage, scholars are still in disagreement. For instance, some will have it that the soliloquy "has a special interest in showing us the settled determinism of Chaucer's philosophical conception of human life"; [48] others are of the opinion that he uses Boethius "for a moral tone to emphasize the stages of the action." [49] Ten Brink says: "It is his tragic intensiveness that leads the poet into such depths, and makes him express ideas in sonorous verses, which agitated deeply the most eminent minds of his age, ideas which touch strongly on the doctrine of predestination." [50] Professor Patch states tentatively: "Interested in a certain conception of philosophy, he may have seized an occasion to preach. After the story itself had grown cold for him, he picked up his manuscript and saw in one of the most intense scenes of the tragedy a splendid opportunity to point a moral." [51] But he later seems to come to the conclusion that the passage is neither too long nor inappropriate since it reveals the character of Troilus as Chaucer conceived him and illustrates the subtle humor for which the poet is celebrated.[52] And at the end of years of study Professor Root says:

> The ideas of Boethius are taken over not merely as poetical elaborations of Chaucer's theme; they are sum and substance of the deeper significance which he sees in the story of the tragic love of Troilus, a story which transacts itself in a world of which Destiny is the ineluctable master, and in which Fortune, the principle of deceitful mutability, is forever turning into bitter vanity the hopes of man, and even the happiness which he seems to have achieved.[53] . . . The addition of the soliloquy on free choice . . . enhances appreciably the serious and philosophical tone with which the poet has overcast his story. Presumably that was the effect he desired to attain.[54]

Misconceptions concerning the function of this passage originate, it seems to me, in a misunderstanding of Chaucer's artistic methods. The supposition that the argument on predestination is too long or that it interrupts the action of the story may imply that in this case a pedantic poet has dumped an unassimilated knowledge of Boethius into the smooth flow of a simple narrative of human affairs. We must observe, however, that Chaucer is not writing a simple story; he is evidently giving a very complex account of the intricate relations between the happy or miserable human being and the destinal forces which rule the universe. Again, the idea that he is here pointing a moral or giving expression to his own personal beliefs suggests that he is at times primarily a philosopher. If this be true, the passage is an almost perfect expression of a philosophical point of view, but it has no place whatever in the story. It seems more reasonable to assume that Chaucer is primarily the literary artist, particularly in an objective and dramatic work like the *Troilus*, using philosophical material wherever necessary to secure an artistic effect presumably aimed at. And finally, the more or less light tone of the first three books has influenced some critics in concluding that he lacks high seriousness in his representations of human life and that his "all-pervasive humor" may imply a want of artistic earnestness. But such assumptions are apparently without adequate foundations. Let us put out of our minds for a moment the idea that, in Troilus's argument about predestination, Chaucer is trying to express his own settled determinism or that he is being facetious or that he is carried away by dramatic intensity or that he is betrayed into a digression for whatever purpose. And let us assume for once that he is primarily the objective artist, deliberately putting back of the story's action *for purely dramatic effect* the conception of Destiny which actually finds expression there. In that case, we shall doubtless find the passage in question dramatically appropriate and of such tremendous importance that it emerges as the pivotal point upon which turns the destinal action of the story.

from chaucer's point of view

Emphasis cannot be too strong when placed upon the fact that in *Troilus and Criseyde* an absolutely inescapable necessity governs the progress of the story. The Boethian God may be discerned back of every incident working out the plans of Providence through His ministers, Destiny and Fortune. All Nature-as-destiny (serving God) makes it inevitable, as we have seen, that Troilus should love; and the destinal powers of the erratic stars, in conjunction possibly with other forces, impose upon him the doom of loving Criseyde. Both Chaucer and the protagonist insist time and again that the lovers coming together precisely as they do is unavoidable. And so long as God in his Providence gives Troilus what of his own free will he would choose, the happy lover is vastly contented with the plan upon which the universe is run; he even praises the inevitability which places upon him the necessity of loving and being loved. But just so soon as it becomes apparent to him that reversals of fortune are also included in the divine plan, he revolts, ironically and humanly enough, against precisely those forces which before he praised so fervently. Criseyde is to be taken from him, and his first reaction to adversity is naturally a grief-stricken cry against the immediate cause of it, Fortune!

But it is not the nature of Troilus to rest content with childish railings at Fortune. That he should be blinded for a moment by sorrow is dramatically appropriate, but that he should remain insensible of the higher destinal forces which have shaped his life from the beginning is inconceivable. Consequently, when Chaucer came to revise his poem, he must have recognized the inconsistency in his representation of Troilus's character at this point and must have realized that this most critical reversal of fortune was not properly motivated by reference to the fatality which informs the remainder of the tragedy. In the revised text, therefore, Troilus's naturally philosophical mind is represented as reasserting itself and as urging him to push to their logical conclusions the Boethian principles which he has espoused all along. In the depths of despair he retires into a temple where he prays to the pitying gods for the privilege of dying and communes with himself upon the relations between God's fore-knowledge and man's free-will. But he is perfectly honest with himself and uniformly consistent in his attitudes toward Destiny or Fate. Just as before his love for Criseyde was considered inevitable, so now in adversity he recognizes that "all that comes to a man, comes by necessity"; and just as his happiness was the inescapable product of destinal forces, so now he acknowledges that to be lost is also his destiny (IV, 958–59). For he seems to be sure that the foresight of divine Providence saw from the beginning of the world that he must forego Criseyde, since God without doubt sees all things and disposes them, through His ordinance and according to their merits, as they shall come by predestination (IV, 960–66). But, after all, the Boethian conception of God's relation to his universe is grim and forbidding when Providence is seen to involve human suffering as well as happiness. And Troilus now experiences a quite human revulsion of feeling against the whole scheme of things when it appears to include his loss of Criseyde; there must be something wrong either with his philosophy or with God's plan. At least, his whole argument represents a powerfully dramatic struggle in his mind to find some way out of the web of fate which seems to have been woven for him. His emotional upheaval urges him to review all the arguments at his command with the idea of determining whether there may not be some logical escape from his long-engrafted conviction that Destiny rules the world and the fortunes of men; there are some great clerks who postulate an inescapable Destiny, but there are others who hold that there is no such thing because man has been given the power of free-choice and is capable, therefore, of directing his own life (IV, 967–73). If he can only convince himself that the latter point of view is true, then the energies of his apathetic body and mind may be released for effective action.

His arguments, however, lead him to one inevitable conclusion. Since as some clerks say, God fore-sees everything and since He may not be deceived, then everything must transpire precisely as He has foreseen it; if from all eternity He has known our thought and our deed, then we have no free choice (IV, 974–80). For if God's foresight is perfect, then we can have only such thoughts and deeds as he has foreseen; and if the contrary were possible, then we should have to ascribe to God imperfect knowledge, which is heresy (IV, 981–94). There are other clerks, however, who assert that God's prescience does not cause the happening of events but that He foresees them because they are to happen. In that case, we have merely changed the order of causes without having altered the quality of necessity imposed upon everything that occurs; for it seems to Troilus that, whether God's foreknowledge is the cause or not, whatever He foresees, be it fair or foul, must come to pass by necessity (IV, 995–1023). For example, if a man sits in a chair, he sits by necessity; if we see him sitting, then the truth of our seeing is also determined by necessity (IV, 1023–43). In like manner, God's foreknowledge of coming events is governed by necessity; and that which He foresees must transpire of necessity (IV, 1045–56). Troilus is not greatly concerned with the necessity which compels God to foresee; he is interested mainly in the inevitability of events which happen to men and in the impossibility of free-choice. Consequently, he states his original conclusion finally and for the fourth time: God necessarily foresees all things that come to pass; and whatever He foresees may not be escaped in any manner (IV, 1075–78). In other words, Troilus in his happiness is a fatalist; and in his grief, even after he has gone over thoroughly the grounds upon which he bases his philosophy, he is still consistently the fatalist. He does not here raise the question of God's justice in thus imposing a dire necessity upon the lives of both good and bad men, who have not a chance of escape; nor does he emphasize his own merits or demerits.[55] Still, in spite of his firm conviction that events transpire precisely as ordained, he is tragically human enough to pray to Almighty Jove that He may have pity upon his sorrow and slay him or return Criseyde and deliver him from this distress (IV, 1079–82). But we are made to feel that Jove is not moved by the prayers of men; governed Himself by necessity, He has planned in his Providence a universe, his destinal decrees have gone forth and cannot be recalled; and the Fortune of Troilus, conceived from the foundation of the world, must be executed with inevitable precision.

That Chaucer fused such a fatalistic philosophy into the structure of his tragedy and that he did it with calculating deliberation cannot, it seems to me, be doubted. It is now well known that, in the passage under discussion, he put into the mouth of his dramatic character, Troilus, a paraphrase of precisely those deterministic arguments which Boethius represents himself as addressing to Lady Philosophy in the *Consolation of Philosophy*.[56] The poet undoubtedly knew the later reply of Philosophy to Boethius, in which man's free-will is reconciled with the necessity residing in God's foreknowledge.

> She resolves the conflict by declaring that necessity is of two sorts: simple necessity, which cannot be avoided, and conditional necessity. The necessity which derives from God's foreknowledge is of the second sort. *If* God foreknows that a man will do a certain thing, he will necessarily do it; but the man's action is free, and is not constrained by God's foreknowledge of the choice that he will freely make.[57]

Moreover, Chaucer was evidently acquainted with the solutions of the problem offered by Augustine, Bradwardine, and other thinkers of the time.[58] As Professor Patch admirably concludes:

The Church Fathers held to the faith in divine predestination of human affairs, but they reconciled it with human free-will none the less. Those who held independent views on these points would be considered heretical and, like the Lollards, would be marked extraordinary. If Chaucer introduced such alien doctrines into the moral of his poem, he must have been deliberate in the fact and must have been conscious that he was thereby making his work conspicuously revolutionary.[59]

Precisely so! We must observe, however, that Chaucer was apparently not writing philosophy; he was not in the *Troilus* interested personally in the problem of pre-destination and, therefore, offered no solutions such as he might have evolved had he been writing philosophy. He was probably orthodox in his own beliefs; but in the drama proper I can find no indication of his personal views. But he was, for his time, undoubtedly an extremely intrepid artist who conceived that the action of a great tragedy should be under the direction of a stern necessity and that the doom of a struggling protagonist should be inevitable. Admirers of Sophocles and Shakespeare would scarcely criticize this principle of tragic composition. The speech of Troilus on predestination is the most powerful element of the poem in the confirming of that fatality which governs the tragic action; it makes clear that the ultimate power behind the destinal forces inherent in movable things is the arbitrary will of God, whose plans for the universe do not include human free-choice. Representing merely a fragment of the Boethian discussion, it serves to warn the intelligent reader emphatically that solutions of the protagonist's tragic problems have been deliberately ignored for dramatic purposes. The whole speech is in character and is dramatically appropriate; and since its philosophical import is in conformity with the settled determinism which the enlightened artist has fused into his tragedy throughout, its length seems to be nicely proportionate to the great sweep of the poem's action.

Accordingly, Book V represents the final consummation of the fate prepared for Troy and its inhabitants. At the beginning of the book we are warned that the fatal destiny, which Jove has at His disposal and which He turns over for execution to the three angry sisters, the Parcas, approaches swiftly; Criseyde must of necessity leave the city, therefore, and Troilus must remain in pain until Lachesis no longer spins his thread of life (V, 1-7). Fortune intends to glaze the hood of the lover more thoroughly still (V, 467) and to trick him in the end (V, 1134).

After Criseyde has departed for the Greek camp, Troilus is inconsolable. In his frenzy he now curses Jove, whose Providence he has praised before, and Venus— together with her servants, Cupid, Ceres, and Bacchus —whose power has been instrumental in bringing the lovers together; he curses his birth, himself, his fate, all Nature—indeed, every creature save only his lady (V, 205-10). When he slumbers, his dreaming mind is disturbed by the most dreadful things that could be imagined. Sometimes it seems to him asleep that he is alone in some horrible place; sometimes he is fighting with his enemies and falls into their hands; and again he seems to be pitching from some high place into the depths below. Starting out of his slumber, he feels a quaking dread about his heart, and his body trembles with fear (V, 250–60). Pandarus attempts to comfort him with the opinion that dreams have no significance, or at least that no man knows how to interpret them aright (V, 360–77); indeed, as I have indicated elsewhere,[60] this sort of dream does not bear the marks of even a respectable *somnium animale*, however much the mind of Troilus may have been disturbed over the going of Criseyde. In this case he is merely oppressed by the fumes arising from too much melancholy in the blood; he is experiencing a *phantasma*, or having a nightmare, or being shaken to fear by an incubus. Still, he himself is convinced that these dreams and the shrieking of that fatal bellman, the owl, undoubtedly foretell his approaching death (V, 316–20). And Troilus's qualm in the presence of these supposed harbingers of coming events communicates itself to the sympathetic reader, who is also made to feel that the protagonist has not long to live.

This feeling is deepened and confirmed when it transpires that a subsequent dream is an authentic *somnium coeleste*, sent by that divine Intelligence which has control over his destiny. After Criseyde does not return upon the appointed tenth day, Troilus complains his fate and desires death. And one day he dreams that, while walking through a forest, he beholds a boar with great tusks asleep in the sun, and by his side lies the bright Criseyde, folding him in her arms and kissing him again and again (V, 1238–41). Now Troilus's faith in his lady is shaken at last; he believes that the blissful gods, through their great might, have shown him in his dreams that Criseyde has satisfied her heart elsewhere (V, 1247–52). In spite of Pandarus's comforting interpretation (V, 1275 ff.), he is still convinced that Jove in his Providence has shown him, through the figure of a boar seen in his dream, the significance of Criseyde's untruth and his own misfortune (V, 1445–49). But in order to be absolutely sure of it, he calls upon the sibyl, Cassandra, for an interpretation.

Cassandra's elaborate exposition of the vision, introduced independently by Chaucer,[61] proves conclusively that Troilus's surmise about the divine origin of this warning is correct. The prophetess begins with a smile to recount how Fortune overcame many lords in ancient times. She tells him how, once upon a time, Diana was angry with the Greeks because they would do no sacrifice upon her altars and how she sent a great boar to destroy their corn and vines; how a beautiful maiden came to look upon the destroyer, and Meleager, lord of that country, became so enamoured of her that he manfully slew the boar and sent its head to her for a present; how from Meleager descended Tydeus, who made war upon the strong city of Thebes and performed many wonderful deeds of valor; and finally, how from Tydeus descended Diomede. And concluding her narrative—which is based largely upon the *Thebais* of Statius—[62] Cassandra gives her interpretation to Troilus: "This boar which you have seen in a dream betokens Diomede, the son of Tydeus, descended from Meleager who made the boar to bleed;

and wheresoever your lady may be, Diomede has her heart and she has his. Weep, therefore; for without doubt this Diomede is in, and you are out." (V, 1457–1519). Though Troilus at first refuses to believe the accursed Cassandra (V, 1520 ff.), he is presently confronted with indisputable evidence of his lady's perfidy (V, 1660–95). And being convinced, he is again forced to the inevitable conclusion that in sundry forms the gods foreshow in dreams the coming of both joy and sorrow; at least this dream, sent by the gods and interpreted rightly by Cassandra, has come true to the letter (V, 1710–15). In this manner Chaucer strengthens our impression that the destiny prepared for Troilus is inescapable.

Moreover, the linking of Troilus's doom with the destruction of Troy is finally further emphasized with splendid effect. Diomede wins the love of Criseyde in part through the argument that Troy must inevitably fall.

> The folk of Troy are in prison, and not one of them shall escape. Such revenge shall be taken upon them for the ravishing of Helen that men shall always fear to do the like again. Calchas exchanged Antenor for Criseyde because he knew that the city should be destroyed. She must let Troy and Trojans pass from her heart (V, 833–917).

It must be remembered, moreover, that Cassandra's account of the battles waged about the city of Thebes and her report of the fatalities which overtook eminent lords of ancient times, serve as a fitting background against which to cast the waning fortunes of Troy. She tells

Troilus how Archimoris was buried, how Amphiorax
was swallowed up in the earth, and how Tydeus was
slain; how Ypomedon was drowned, and Campanëus
was blasted by a stroke of lightning; how Eteocles and
Polynices slew one another before the walls of Thebes,
and how Thebes was itself finally destroyed by fire (V,
1485–1510). So Fortune overthrew the lords of old (V,
1460). And now this same Fortune, who has immediate
rule over the transmutation of things in this world as it is
committed to her through the Providence and disposition
of high Jove, who regulates the passing of realms from the
hands of one people into those of another or determines the
destruction of nations—this same Fortune now begins
to pull away the bright feathers of Troy from day to
day until its inhabitants are bare of weal (V, 1540–47).
Among other dire misfortunes, now approaches the end
of that period of life assigned to the great hero, Hector:
Fate purposes the unbodying of his soul and shapes the
means by which it is to be driven forth. Against this
Fate his struggles are in vain; he goes into battle and is
slain (V, 1548–54). There remains only the final
catastrophe; read Dares for an account of the last battles
(V, 1771).

Into this maelstrom of battle between two mighty
peoples Troilus rushes seeking death. Since Criseyde has
given her heart to Diomede, there is nothing further for
him to do in this world except to take vengeance upon
his enemies. The gods have warned him in dreams that
his end is already decreed, but he goes out struggling
admirably. He slays his thousands, raging cruelly through

the Greek hosts. But most he seeks for Diomede, with whom he fights many bloody battles. Fortune has determined, however, that neither of these enemies shall die by the other's hand (V, 1763 ff.). For in the last great battle Troilus is slain by the fierce Achilles. And this eventuality, the poet is careful to state, is brought about by the will of the gods (V, 1805–86). Such is the inescapable doom of a protagonist whose common and individual fortunes have been, in the Providence of God, directed in part by Nature-as-destiny and partly by that destiny inherent in the movements of erratic stars.

We must observe in passing, however, that there is a third destinal force, postulated by Boethius, which Chaucer has not forgotten in presenting the spectacle of Troilus caught in a web of fate. Among the other agencies to which God turns over the execution of His plan, Boethius mentions *anima mundi*, which Chaucer understands to mean "some soul." [63] That is to say, there is in this mundane sphere a destinal power exerted through the influence of one soul upon another in ordinary human relationships. In a certain mediate sense, moreover, the character of an individual himself constitutes one of the "movable things" to which cleave the disposition and ordinance of destiny. For a character, with the stamp of Nature and of the stars upon it at birth, is itself responsible in large measure for whatever fortune it suffers. But Boethius maintains that it is possible for a man to dominate his fortunes and to transcend the necessity of his destiny in proportion as he cleaves to the steadfastness of the thought of God. [64] And Thomas Aquinas is of the opinion that, since a man's will and intellect are not corporeal, they do not directly come under the compelling influence of the stars, but that, since will and intellect are connected with the body, they may indirectly be influenced through the passions, which are subject to the stars. Says he:

> The majority of men, in fact, are governed by their passions, which are dependent upon bodily appetites; in these the influence of the stars is clearly felt. Few indeed are the wise who are capable of resisting their animal instincts. Astrologers, consequently, are able to foretell the truth in the majority of cases, especially when they undertake general predictions. In particular predictions, they do not attain certainty, for nothing prevents a man from resisting the dictates of his lower faculties. Wherefore the astrologers themselves are wont to say that "the wise man rules the stars," forasmuch, namely, as he rules his own passions.[65]

Therefore, the man who does not exercise his free-will in the control and direction of his emotions, finds himself presently without free-choice in the guidance of his actions when the power of the stars descends upon him or when he comes in contact with the destinal force inherent in other people's influence.

His creator has been at considerable pains to make Troilus such a man. Though Troilus possesses a philosophical attitude of mind, his thinking is limited and incomplete where his emotions are concerned; indeed, he never entertains the conception that a man may transcend destiny by virtue of controlling his passions. Consequently, near the beginning of the story he is so harassed and perplexed by the driving power of his overwhelming love that he likens himself to a man caught upon the sea in a rudderless boat and tossed to and fro by conflicting winds (I, 415 ff.). So he is throughout the drama. He is a great warrior and a pure-minded lover, but his emotional and sentimental nature leaves him the sport of every human influence brought to bear upon him. The consummation of his love is brought about largely through the influence and machinations of Pandarus; he comes to his tragic end partly through the persuasions and treachery of Criseyde. The whole action of the story *seems* to evolve so logically from the interplay of character upon character that Professor Price is moved to conclude:

> Only by force of human will, by ardor of human passion, by cleverness of human contrivance and persuasion, is any character to be led, or to be driven, under the influence of some other character, to its own inevitable action.[66]

But Professor Price is betrayed by appearance into such an overstatement of the truth. As we have seen, Chaucer has linked his drama of human passions with the destinal power of the stars and of Nature, and has created his tragedy of human experiences against a mysterious background of divine foreordination.

Thus Chaucer's conception of tragedy as exemplified in the *Troilus* transcends the conventional mediaeval idea of what a tragedy ought to be. Dante writes: "Tragedy in its beginning is admirable and quiet, in its ending or catastrophe foul and horrible." [67] Chaucer himself glosses his translation of Boethius: "Tragedie is to seyn, a ditee of a prosperitee for a tyme, that endeth in wrechednesse." [68] And the Monk prefaces his series of 'tragedies' with the remark:

> Tragedie is to seyn a certeyn storie,
> As old bokes maken us memorie,
> Of him that stood in greet prosperitee
> And is y-fallen out of heigh degree
> Into miserie, and endeth wrecchedly
>
> (*C.T.*, B, 3163 ff.).

Now, because Chaucer has defined tragedy in the mediaeval sense and has exemplified it in the *Monk's Tale,* most critics seem to reason after this fashion: Chaucer evidently understands the mediaeval conception of tragedy; he has called *Troilus* a tragedy (V, 1786); therefore, *Troilus* must be a tragedy in the mediaeval sense. [69] Such a conclusion is a *non sequitur*. Though *Troilus* (and almost any other great tragedy, for that matter) may in a measure be brought within the limits of the mediaeval definition, still it ultimately shatters the old form and, in the hands of a genius, flowers into an original and independent creation which embodies a sublimity comparable to that of ancient Greek tragedy and a dissection of the human heart which presages modern drama.

For one thing, the *Troilus* is artistically far in advance of other mediaeval "tragedies" because it is essentially dramatic. As Professor Price well says:

> Chaucer, in this poem, is dramatic, not because he allows action to dominate or run riot in his work,

but because he deduces action, with a profound psychological skill, from the working of emotion. . . . He is dramatic, because with intense realism of effect, he has made each spoken word of each character, and each action of each character . . . spring as inevitable necessity . . . from the soul of the character that he has imagined. And, in the highest sense of all, Chaucer in this poem is dramatic, because, in tracing the emotional life of his chief characters, he has led that play of passion to its final expression in definite action. . . . And so, in this great poem, we have, as nowhere else in our literature, the evolution of literary form from narrative to drama.[70]

Moreover, the five books, into which the fifty scenes of the story are cast, suggest the five acts of the modern drama.[71] In addition to being dramatic in quality, the poem represents a powerful conflict between the protagonist, Troilus,[72] and such forces of character, circumstances, and destiny as are arrayed against him; and conflict has come to be recognized as the main essential of all tragedy. No one can help seeing that, externally, the dramatic action of this story is concerned with Troilus's earlier struggle to consummate his happiness in love and with his later efforts to recapture and maintain it. The turning point of this struggle comes in the dramatic scene where Chaucer represents the grief of the lovers at the prospect of separation (IV, 1128–1701).[73] Internally, however, the main tragic conflict is between Troilus and the mysterious destinal powers overshadowing him. He may be classed among those other essentially noble protagonists whose "blindness of heart" brings them to destruction; his tragic fault lies in the fact that his

passions leave him unable to exercise his free-will in trans-
cending the destinal decrees promulgated by Nature and
the stars. He fights at first against the destinal powers
that would give him Criseyde for a season; he struggles
against the forces which would finally take her away from
him. And the climax of this conflict comes in the soliloquy
on predestination and free-will (IV, 960–1085), at the
point where Troilus signally fails to rationalize his true
relationship to the necessity of destiny. Here the passion-
blinded protagonist, as we have already seen, makes his
last stand against the powers which have decreed his
destruction. Having made up his mind to a settled determinism, he rushes forth pitifully enough to the doom
prepared by destiny. The tragedy of Chaucer's *Troilus*
may be defined, therefore, as the representation in a
dramatic story of an essentially noble protagonist of heroic
proportions who is brought into conflict with circumstances and with the destinal powers—character, Nature,
and the stars—and who, because his passions overshadow
and becloud his reason and judgment, is brought into
subjection to adverse destiny and finally to his destruction.

This dramatic narrative, founded ultimately upon a
mediaeval philosophy, occupies a sort of middle ground
artistically between the ancient Greek tragedy and the
modern tragedy of Shakespeare. It is wholly like neither,
yet it participates spiritually in the characteristics of both.
In Greek tragedy, on the one hand, we sense a mysterious
and unalterable Fate or Necessity back of human action,
imposing its judgments arbitrarily from without upon men
and women whose criminal actions, intentional or other-

wise, have brought them into conflict with these destinal powers. In Shakespearean tragedy, on the other hand, while one may dimly glimpse a shadowy fatality connected with a mysterious moral order, the principal destiny which rules the fortunes of men is the fatality of character. In other words, in Greek tragedy the emphasis is put upon the mystery of those powers which force men to destruction; in Shakespeare the emphasis is laid upon the fact that a man is the architect of his own fortunes.[74] Now Chaucer, in the *Troilus*, has placed approximately equal stress upon the external and internal sources of human happiness and misery. No one can help perceiving that Troilus's fortunes are in large measure the result of the action and inter-action of character upon character—which, it must always be remembered, is itself one aspect of destiny. But it is one of the glories of Chaucer's tragic art that he should have dignified his drama of human experiences by linking them up with those more mysterious and awe-inspiring forces of destiny which govern both men and the universe. No purely psychological work can ever have such a powerfully tragic effect as does the tragedy in which human actions are made to have cause-and-effect relationships with whatever external forces there are in the world. Deploring the limitations of the modern psychological drama, Maurice Maeterlinck says:

> From time to time in the past a true genius . . . succeeded in writing a play with that profound background, that mist about the summit, that feeling of the infinite here and there which . . . permitted us to

mingle our images of it while we spoke, and seemed
necessary in order that the dramatic work might flow
by, brimming to the banks, and attain its ideal . . .
the third character, enigmatic, invisible, but everywhere present, which we might call the sublime
character, and which is perhaps no other than the
unconscious though powerful and undeniable concept
of the poet's idea of the universe, and which gives
the play a far greater reach, a certain aspiration for
existence after the death of other things, and makes
us return to it without ever exhausting its possibilities
of beauty.[75]

Such a genius is Chaucer, and he has gained such an
effect in the *Troilus* by creating back of his tragedy the
mystery which shrouds the activities of Nature, and the
stars.[76] And this deterministic tragedy is entirely complete
when Troilus is brought to his death by an inescapable
destiny (V, 1806).

What follows in the Epilog to the completed drama
(V, 1807–69) is dramatically a sorry performance. From
one point of view one may lament the fact that an enlightened artist, who has held himself with admirable
courage to the composition of a stirring tragedy, should
have in the end deemed it expedient to drop into the role
of an extraordinary moralist, pointing out to his contemporaries that earthly joy is but false felicity. Here in
the Epilog the poet, without having given the slightest
hint of warning, suddenly denies and contradicts everything that has gone before in the poem. The love-affair
of Troilus and Criseyde, which he has presented with

gusto and which we have watched with sympathy develop
into a tragedy, is now condemned as worldly vanity: such
is the end of Troilus's false love and desire, and such is
the end of all this world's frailty (V, 1828–34).[77] He
expresses the pious wish that all young people may repair
home from such vanities and cast their countenances up
to that true God in whose image they are made, for this
world is but a fair which, like a flower, soon passes away.
May they set their love upon that Christ who died for
our souls upon the cross, arose, and sits in heaven above;
He will play false to no man whose heart is fixed wholly
upon Him. Since love to Christ is best, what need is there
to seek a false love? (V, 1835–41). Moreover, having
taken great pains to throw about his story a pagan cloak
and, as it were, to tinge it with a pagan coloring, Chaucer
now condemns the ancient pagan rites attendant upon
the worship of such unvailing gods as Jove, Mars, and
Apollo; behold Troilus, whose end is the finish of those
who put faith in such "rascaille" (V, 1849–55).[78] And
all this is in denial of those figures in the story who, as
gods, have not a vestige of power over the fortunes of the
protagonist; the names of the pagan gods, as we have
seen, are employed merely as a literary device to sym-
bolize the real destinal forces back of the drama. In the
next place, the dedication of the poem is illogical and in
bad taste, or at least inappropriate. Having written deliberately what must have seemed to his age an immoral
poem, Chaucer proceeds to dedicate it to the "moral
Gower," who would have disapproved heartily of the
whole action; having fused into his drama an entirely

deterministic philosophy, he has the temerity to dedicate
it in part to the "philosophical Strode," whose adherence
to the "school of the middle" would have made him
abhor Troilus's attitude toward predestination (V, 1856–
59).[79] And finally, the poet closes his worldly poem with
a fervent prayer to the Trinity for protection against
invisible foes and for divine mercy. As Professor Tatlock
well says:

> We must not regard this ending as merely throw-
> ing back an ironical light over what precedes, so
> that we should read the story a second time with
> quickened understanding. The feeling in the Epilog
> is in no way foreshadowed at the beginning or else-
> where; it does not illuminate or modify; it contra-
> dicts. The heart-felt worldly tale is interpreted in
> an unworldly sense. He tells the story in one mood
> and ends in another.[80]

But Chaucer is not yet content with that nest of con-
tradictions, the Epilog; having finished his sermon, he
must needs return to his manuscript and insert the three
stanzas (V, 1807–27) which represent the flight of
Troilus's spirit through the heavens to the realm of true
felicity.[81] This Troilus, who—according to the Epilog—
has served false gods to his destruction and has concerned
himself with the gratification of this wretched world's
appetites, now sails serenely to an apparently Christian
bliss.[82] This Troilus, who—as implied in the Epilog—did
not set his heart's love upon Christ but upon the vanity of
this world, is rewarded with perfect felicity in heaven. And
this Troilus, looking down from his coign of vantage above,
laughs at those who weep for his death and condemns all

human experiences motivated by blind desire, which is evanescent, realizing at last that every man should set his heart upon heaven and not upon worldly things. I cannot imagine a more dramatically inappropriate end for a great tragic protagonist than this or a more illogical solution of the philosophical problem involving the relationship between the false felicity of this world and the perfect felicity hereafter. Fortunately, however, this Troilus is in no sense to be identified with that Troilus of the tragedy proper who suffers for love, struggles against an inescapable destiny, and dies like a hero.

One may deplore, therefore, the tendency of certain critics to interpret the action of the whole story in the light of this entirely contradictory Epilog, with the result that the tragic quality of the poem is blurred and the supreme artistry of it vitiated. Professor Root, for example, commenting upon the moral that earthly joy is but false felicity, says: "The modern reader who dissents from this moral may disregard it, if he will, and find the story but little injured for his taste by its concluding stanzas. Yet it is no mere tacked-on moral. It is implicit in the whole poem." [83] And basing his criticism apparently upon the assumption that the passage representing Troilus's flight to heaven constitutes an integral part of the unified work, Professor Root concludes: "And yet the story does not make on us a really tragic effect. It is rather a tragic story handled in the spirit of high comedy. Chaucer has not treated his theme with *tragic* intensity. Great tragedy leaves us with the sense of irreparable loss, of a hurt for which there is no healing. Hamlet dies with the unforgettably tragic words: 'The rest is silence.' The last we hear from Troilus is a peal of celestial laughter." [84] It should be observed, however, that no modern reader is justified in either approving or rejecting the Epilog to *Troilus* because the moral of it happens to flatter or disagree with his taste in morals. The main point is that the passing of Troilus's more or less pagan spirit through the heavens toward a Christian realm of perfect felicity destroys the tragedy of this drama with as much effectiveness as would have been the case in *Hamlet* had Shakespeare, following the pious suggestion of a conventional Horatio, actually represented Hamlet's spirit's being ·sung to its rest by flights of angels. Fortunately, however, the Epilog is not a part of the whole and is detachable at will, and one need not of necessity consider it at all in an interpretation of the drama.

In fact, the line of cleavage between the two productions is so abruptly and sharply drawn that it may fairly be said to represent the complete separation of the pure artist from the religious man. Considered by itself, the Epilog is a poem of great beauty, lyrical in quality, the spirit of which is exalted by the undoubted sincerity and religious fervor of its author. And the drama proper, considered in its own right, is the most effective tragedy written in mediaeval times. It is to Chaucer's everlasting glory that in the composition of this work of art he should have suppressed his private beliefs (as indicated in the Epilog) and that, in an age when man and artist were not readily separable, he should have been courageous enough to exercise his artistic faculties alone in the creation of *Troilus*.

CHAPTER ELEVEN

ARCITE'S INTELLECT

WHEN in a preceding chapter I attempted to diagnose the malady which produces Arcite's death in the *Knight's Tale*, I neglected to take account of the dualism which obtains in mediaeval philosophy between the human body and the rational soul. I was concerned primarily with an explanation of how the virtue expulsive, or animal, was unable to cleanse that virtue called natural from the venom which causes the hero's physical death.[1] I should like now to consider the nature and powers of the great lover's passing soul.

When Arcite has been given up by his physicians and when he is just on the point of death, he says to Emily: "My lady, the woeful spirit in my heart may not declare to you any small measure of the sorrow which I experience; but I bequeath to you the service of my ghost, to you above every creature, since I may no longer live." Then, with a pathetic lament over the passing of life, he turns her over to Palamon. And, as Chaucer reports:

And with that word his speche faille gan,
And from his feet up to his brest was come
The cold of deeth, that hadde him overcome.
And yet more-over, in his armes two
The vital strengthe is lost, and al ago.
Only the intellect, with-outen more,
That dwelled in his herte syk and sore,

Gan faillen, when the herte felte deeth,
Dusked his eyen two, and failled breeth.
But on his lady yet caste he his yë;
His laste word was, 'mercy Emelye!'
His spirit chaunged hous, and wente ther,
As I cam never, I can nat tellen wher.
Therfor I stinte, I nam no divinistre;
Of soules finde I nat in this registre,
Ne me ne list thilke opiniouns to telle
Of hem, though that they wryten wher they dwelle.
Arcite is cold, ther Mars his soule gye.[2]

In this short description of the passing of Arcite's soul, Chaucer has gingerly touched upon a matter about which church fathers and philosophers and scholastics had full busily beset their wits for centuries before 1386. Heaven forbid that I should attempt to reduce to order the welter of conflicting opinions about the human soul, which were defended before Chaucer's time, or to trace the history of the mediaeval ideas concerning its essence, activities, and faculties. But I should like to indicate the possible relation between the "woeful spirit" in Arcite's heart and the "ghost" which he bequeaths to Emily; to determine the precise nature of that function of the reasonable soul called "intellect," which still dwells in his heart after the vital spirits[3] have left his arms and other limbs; to define the "spirit" which changes house and the "souls" of which the poet says he finds no register in this story; and to suggest why Chaucer declines to follow the progress of the released spirit into its other house.

In a general discussion of the soul it seems well to

ignore those early philosophers who conceived of it as divisible into parts: Plato, for example, into two parts; Zeno, into three; Panaetius, into five or six; Soronus, into seven; Chryssipus, into eight; the Stoics, into twelve; and Posidonius, into as many as seventeen.[4] Since mediaeval psychology derives largely from Aristotle, let us begin with him. Aristotle defines the soul as the first act of an organized body,[5] by virtue of which it lives,[6] moves,[7] and understands or thinks.[8] Since the soul is a certain act and the essential Form of that which possesses the possibility of such an act,[9] since it is the cause and the principle of a living organism,[10] it cannot be separated from the body.[11] He conceives of the soul's activities as being arranged in a hierarchical series of three grades or strata,[12] each one of which furnishes material for the formative activities of the next higher. The *nutritive* or *vegetative soul* performs the functions of nutrition and generation;[13] the *sensitive soul* is the active Form of the body by virtue of which it lives, has senses,[14] appetite,[15] and motion;[16] and the *rational soul*, which includes the other two, is that by which the individual conceives universals and through which he attains immortality.[17] The rational soul, however, is actually divided into two parts: the *nous pathetikos* and the *nous poietikos*.[18] The *nous pathetikos* is the unifying Form of the materials presented by imagination, memory, sensation, and will;[19] the *nous poietikos* is the unifying principle of all the other syntheses,[20] the Form of Forms.[21] The *nous pathetikos*, therefore, is mortal like the sensitive and vegetative souls which it includes, and passes away at the death of the individual.

Only the *nous poietikos*, the pure reason, attains immortality.[22] "It alone cannot be explained as a function
of the body; nay, it is essentially different and separable
from it. The active intellect is not a capacity, but an actual
being; it is not a product of nature, a result of the development of the soul, like sensibility, imagination, and
memory; it is not a product, an effect, or a creature at
all, but an absolute principle, that existed before the soul
as well as before the body, and was united with it mechanically. This separate intellect is absolutely immaterial,
impassive, imperishable, and eternal; without it the perishable and passive intellect cannot think."[23] It "comes
from without" and is not a part of the individual by any
organic tie.[24] Just what it is would be hard to say;
logically it ought to be God,[25] or perhaps it is "pure reason
considered as a unity in its nature and principles, common
to all individuals."[26]

Aristotle's views on the soul are thus given in some
detail because his division into vegetative, sensitive, and
reasonable soul passes over into the Middle Ages, though
it must be observed that the best mediaeval thinkers consider these, not as stages or strata of psychic activity, but
as faculties of a single, indivisible, and immortal soul. I
have already discussed the activities of Arcite's soul in its
vegetative and sensitive capacity.[27] These faculties need
delay us no longer, except to note that, though memory,
reason, and imagination are the inward faculties of the
sensitive soul, they also play an important part in the
activities of the pure reasonable soul. By the subsuming of
these functions under the rational soul, the Middle Ages

postulate a personal immortality for the individual where Aristotle, by attributing them to the perishable *nous pathetikos*, seems to deny it. But we are interested primarily in the rational soul.

For mediaeval thinkers the rational soul may be conceived as possessing two principal faculties, *intellectus*, or understanding, and *voluntas*, or will; and out of a defense of one or the other as the more important emerge two schools of scholastic philosophy, determinism and indeterminism.[28] But we are concerned here neither with that problem nor with the activities of *voluntas*. Our attention is directed to *intellectus*, its nature, its two-fold function, and its destiny. It may be remarked in passing that Aristotle's *nous pathetikos* and *nous poietikos* become identified in some sense with what mediaeval philosophers call *intellectus possibilis* and *intellectus agens*. Interpretations of these latter functions of the reasonable soul seem to be about as varied as individual points of view.

Now, Tertullian defines the soul as a conscious entity, "sprung from the breath of God, immortal, possessing body, having form, simple in its substance, intelligent in its own nature, free in its determinations, rational, endued with an instinct of presentiment, evolved out of one (archetypal soul)." [29] One faculty of this soul may be called mind (*animus*);[30] but quite above this is another "directing faculty, with which the purpose of God may agree; in other words, a supreme principle of intelligence and vitality," [31] which rules the activities of all the other faculties and which may be identified with *intellectus*. In the *Confessions* St. Augustine concludes his discussion of the three functional souls: "And thus, by degrees, I passed from bodies to the soul, which makes use of the senses of the body to perceive; and thence to its inward faculty, to which the bodily senses represent outward things, and up to which reach the capabilities of beasts; and thence, again, I passed on to the reasoning faculty, unto which whatever is received from the senses of the body is referred to be judged, which also, finding itself to be variable in me, raised up to its own intelligence, and from habit drew away my thoughts, withdrawing itself from crowds of contradictory phantasms; that so it might find out that light by which it is besprinkled, when, without all doubting, it cried out, 'that the unchangeable was to be preferred before the changeable;' whence it also knew that unchangeable, which, unless it had in some way known, it could have had no sure ground for preferring it to the changeable. And thus, with the flash of a trembling glance, it arrived at that which is." [32] And the faculty with which he sees immediately into the truth of God is *intellectus*. Just as the eye is the only part of the body which is sensitive to light, so *intellectus* is the supreme faculty of the soul which is capable of receiving and interpreting the Light from God. [33] And Duns Scotus, in his criticism of the *De anima* of Aristotle, concludes that *intellectus* is the essential Form of the human being, which enables him to perceive universals and to handle the materials of reason, which makes it possible for him to reflect upon and to judge his own acts, and by virtue of which he is accounted human. [34]

As to the relation between *intellectus possibilis* and *in-*

tellectus agens several points of view may be recorded. Aristotle, as we have seen, supposes that they are two separate things, differing in essence the one from the other; and this, says Duns Scotus, is according to the Scriptures which postulate that God himself is *intellectus agens*, the creative activity (Aristotle's *nous poietikos*) which illumines the *intellectus possibilis*.[35] Most of the Arabian philosophers agree with Aristotle that *intellectus agens* is a separate substance; and Avicenna identifies it with those Intelligences which guide the movements of the stars and which govern our minds, streaming ideas into them.[36] Others deny the existence of *intellectus agens* altogether. But more probable, says Duns Scotus, is the supposition that *intellectus possibilis* and *intellectus agens* are not to be distinguished in essence; they merely differ in office or function, because *intellectus*, as it initiates the act of understanding, is called *agens*, and in its receiving capacity is designated as *possibilis*. Or according to Augustine they are two powers of *intellectus*, the one superior and necessary, the other inferior and contingent.[37] As Burton sums up the matter: "The *agent* is that which is called the *wit* of man, acumen or subtlety, *sharpness* of invention, when he doth invent of himself without a teacher, or learns anew, which abstracts those intelligible species from the phantasy, and transfers them to the passive understanding, *because there is nothing in the understanding, which was not first in the sense.* That which the imagination hath taken from the sense, this *agent* judgeth of, whether it be true or false; and being so judged he commits it to the *passible* to be kept. The *agent* is a doctor or teacher, the *passive* a scholar; and his office is to keep and farther judge of such things as are committed to his charge: as a bare and raised table at first capable of all forms and notions." [38]

Now what of Arcite's intellect? It may be identified in some sense, I think, with what Aristotle calls the *nous poietikos* (i.e., the immortal part of the individual); or, since Chaucer does not know Aristotle, with the supreme principle of intelligence and vitality of Tertullian; or with the faculty of the reasonable soul which St. Augustine calls the "eye of the soul" and which enables the individual to behold spiritual realities without the intermediate help of phantasms; or, more probably, with that *intellectus* of the scholastic philosophers which has within itself an active and a passive function, enabling the individual to perceive universals. In any case, we may say that Arcite's intellect is that supreme faculty or power or essence of the rational soul of a man which, containing within itself the complete materials of the individual's experience and serving as the eye of the soul in the perception of universal truth, is capable of a personal immortality when separated from its instrument, the body.

As to the location of the reasonable soul in the body there is great difference of opinion among mediaeval thinkers. Some suppose that it resides in the crown of the head, others that it is enclosed in the head; some say that it reposes in the brain, or around the bases of the brain, or in the membranes of it, or in the space between the eyebrows. Others are of the opinion that it floats along the blood and informs the humors.[39] Roger Bacon supposes that it is everywhere in the body, in every single part, as Form or unifying principle;[40] and Duns Scotus affirms that the rational soul, as a total essence, is in every part of the body alike, but as an integral whole, it is found in none.[41] But Chaucer says that Arcite's intellect, or spirit, is lodged in his heart.[42] In this opinion he is supported by the church fathers, though not by the best scholastic philosophers. Jerome locates the rational soul in the heart, reprehending Plato for placing it in the head, and adduces in support of his position Matt. 15:19, "Out of the heart proceed evil thoughts."[43] Tertullian agrees and calls upon the witnessing authority of Protagoras, Apollodorus, Chryssipus, and the Egyptians.[44] Augustine, trying to explain how the Word of God passes into the spirits of man, says in illustration: "My intellect (*intellectus*) remaining in my heart passes out to you, though it does not leave me. Nevertheless, when intellect is in my heart and I wish to send it into yours, I seek to do so by means of, as it were, a vehicle of sound; I make a sound and, as it were, impose, reach forth, send out, and cause you to know my intellect, but do not part with it or dismiss it."[45] And Bartholomaeus Anglicus, quoting from Laladuis, says: "Just as the spider sits in the middle of the web and feels every movement of it, so the soul, abiding in the middle of the heart without spreading itself, gives life to all the body and governs the movements of all the limbs."[46] Thus when Chaucer locates Arcite's intellect in the heart, he is not thinking of the sensitive soul, which Albertus Magnus and others would seat in like position, nor of the irascible soul, which Plato places in the heart;[47] he is following trustworthy authority of his time in establishing the supreme and immortal eye of the soul in the most vital part of the body.

Moreover, when Chaucer says that "His spyrit chaungede hous," making "spirit" synonymous with "intellect," he is at least echoing the lively controversy waged by the early church fathers over the celebrated "trichotomy of man," body, soul, and spirit. When for example, St. Paul in I Thess. V, 23 speaks of our "spirit, soul, and body being preserved to the coming of our Lord Jesus Christ," he is giving expression to what we have come to call the Biblical view of psychology, according to which, in general, "the soul is that passionate and affectionate nature which is common to us and to inferior creatures, while the spirit is the higher intellectual nature which is peculiar to man. . . . The soul being liable to the emotions of pleasure and pain . . . the spirit is the seat of the will . . . and of consciousness."[48] In discussing the wide and narrow sense of the word *spirit*, St. Augustine says: "The questions we might consider are: whether, when mention is made of the soul, the spirit is also implied in such a way that the two comprise the soul, the spirit being, as it were, some part of it . . . whether, in fact, under the designation *soul*, the whole is so designated from only a part; or else, whether the two together make up the spirit, that which is properly called the soul being a part thereof; whether, in fact, the whole is not called from only a part, when the term *spirit* is used in such a wide sense as to comprehend the soul also."[49] Thus in this "dominant thought of mediaeval religious metaphysics,"[50] where the division of man into body, soul, and spirit masquerades under a variety of expressions,[51] the soul, which is identified with the physiological principle of vitality,[52] is conceived as a mean between two extremes: on the one hand matter, on the other hand spirit, which is the psychological principle of creative energy and personal consciousness.[53] "These, however," says Augustine, "are but subtle distinctions, and ignorance about them is certainly attended with no great danger." [54] But that Chaucer shows some familiarity with them, either through his own reading or through their having passed into the language, cannot be doubted. He seems to identify, and correctly, Arcite's intellect, which is the supreme essence of the rational soul according to one school of philosophers, with his spirit, which is the immortal and conscious member in the trichotomy of man, body, soul, and spirit. It is the spirit of Arcite which changes house.

When Chaucer affirms that Arcite's spirit changes house, he is not by any means speaking euphemistically, as some have thought;[55] he is here again touching upon the live question as to whether, after death, the human soul is corporeal or incorporeal. He is apparently postulating that, Arcite's physical body having been left behind, his spirit immediately houses itself in another body of some description. He is thus definitely taking one side in a mighty controversy. Origen, for example, concludes "that we must believe our conditions at some future time to be incorporeal; and if this is admitted, and all are said to be subject to Christ, this (incorporeity) must necessarily be bestowed upon all to whom this subjection to

Christ extends; since all who are subject to Christ will be in the end subject to God the Father, to whom Christ is said to deliver up his kingdom; and thus it appears that then also the need of bodies will cease. And if it ceases, bodily matter returns to nothing, as formerly it also did not exist." He is very careful, however, to give the alternative "that when, notwithstanding all things have become subject to Christ, and through Christ to God (with whom they formed also one spirit in respect of spirits being rational natures), then the bodily substance itself also being united to most pure and excellent spirits, and being changed into an ethereal condition in proportion to the quality or merits of those who assume it (according to the apostle's word, 'We also shall be changed') will shine forth in splendour." [56] And St. Augustine concludes flatly: "That the soul cannot exist in absolute separation from a body of some kind is proved in my opinion by the fact that to exist without a body belongs to God alone." [57] Chaucer no doubt follows the Augustinian tradition.

But as to the ultimate destiny of Arcite's immortal part, Chaucer professes himself to be ignorant. "His spirit changed house," says he, "and went to a place where I never was, I cannot tell where. Therefore, I stop; I am no diviner. I do not find anything about souls in this record; nor do I wish to reproduce the opinions of them, though they have written about where they dwell. Arcite is cold; may Mars guide his soul." Remarking upon this perplexing passage, Professor Tatlock says: "In this undoubtedly flippant refusal of the eternal blazon to ears of flesh and blood, there may well be nothing but flippancy;

Chaucer did not know and undoubtedly had never been there. A somewhat light tone is characteristic of the poem. But more than this, he may be rejecting impatiently Boccaccio's lengthy and frigid description of Arcite's aviation through celestial spheres; or (Dryden's interpretation in his *Palamon and Arcite*) he may be doubtful as to the eternal destiny of such a virtuous pagan as Arcite." [58]

These interpretations have virtue in them, but one must not suppose that Chaucer's knowledge of the soul's eternal destiny is confined to the opinion of Boccaccio in the *Teseide*. He has evidently gleaned information upon so important a question from every available source. He draws continually upon classical, pagan conceptions of the lower world and the Elysian Fields; Claudian and Virgil are his familiars, and he is thoroughly conversant with the idea of Cicero that good souls at death rise to a realm of bliss above the ninth sphere and that evil souls must whirl about the earth in pain for ages.[59] He has entertained the conception of "eternal recurrence" or cycles of creation,[60] and he may well have known the further development of the idea according to which the individual reappears at stated intervals to live his life over again precisely as he did before.[61] He is acquainted with the *Divine Comedy* of Dante with its rounds of Hell, Purgatory, and Paradise prepared for good and bad souls, shows indications of having read the church fathers in connection with his Bible, and has absorbed the popular, conventional ideas regarding Purgatory (and possibly Paradise)[62] which were current everywhere in the Middle Ages.[63] He might easily have found in Tertullian a discussion of the transmigration of souls;[64] or, being interested in demonology, he might have espoused the popular tradition "that those souls which have succeeded in freeing themselves from all union with the flesh become guardian demons and help those of their fellows whom they can reach." [65] But, says he, I do not wish to review at this time the opinions of those who have written about the soul's destiny after death. Arcite indeed, always romantic and for the moment mediaeval, is permitted to bequeath the service of his ghost to Emily since he may no longer live in the flesh; he seems to be comforted, as death approaches, by the thought that he may still through love serve and help her in the capacity of guardian spirit.[66] But the poet himself has no further need of this conception.

It is perfectly clear to me that Chaucer's refusal to follow the flight of Arcite's spirit into another house is based on artistic and philosophical grounds. Nobody can fail to observe that most accounts of the after life of the immortal soul are associated with moral or ethical considerations; the good or pious go to Heaven or Paradise or to the Elysian Fields or to some other place of supreme happiness; the wicked are condemned to Hell or Purgatory or Hades or to some other place of punishment. But nowhere in the *Knight's Tale* is Chaucer greatly concerned with the moral or religious aspect of the situation; this is a romantic and pagan story, representing the good and bad fortunes of two lovers who strive for the hand of one woman. Both Palamon and Arcite are honorable, virtuous, and upright, to be sure; and Arcite, like a good pagan, sacrifices at the shrine of Mars. But the question as to whether either is saint or sinner is not raised, nor is the evenhanded justice of whatever gods there be considered at all—except when Palamon fails to see the ultimate source of all fortune and destiny (A, 1303 ff.). There is indeed a destiny prepared for each, but it is in no sense connected with virtuous action or with wicked character; here is no suggestion of a system of balanced rewards or of a commensurate punishment. In other words, Arcite does not win Emily in the first place because of any superior claim to virtue, nor does he lose his life in the end on account of any moral turpitude. Since the question of spiritual values is not raised in this story, therefore, Chaucer the artist sees that it would be artistically incongruous to postulate any definite resting-place for the released spirit of Arcite. Here is one soul that cannot be consistently relegated to either a pagan Hades or Elysian Fields or to a Christian paradise or Purgatory.[67] Hence the author seems to beg the whole question, merely adding that the soul on its way to a new house is guided by Mars, who has been the protector of Arcite during his life.

But Chaucer only *seems* to beg the question; in reality he has solved the problem of Arcite's ultimate existence, not according to any religious system, but according to the philosophical eschatology of Boethius. I have already shown elsewhere[68] how, for technical purposes, he has made use of the motivating power of the stars in the action of the story, how he has analyzed the destinal forces which produce the fortunes of Palamon and Arcite into the impulses of Nature (on the one hand) and the influence of the planets (on the other), and how, under the direction of Boethius, he has solved the problem of these variegated fortunes in their relation to destiny by referring them to God, who is the unified source of all things. I have shown specifically that Arcite comes to his death through the machinations of the malefic planet, Saturn, and that this destiny was prepared for him from the beginning in the Providence of God. As Theseus concludes the whole matter near the end of the story: "When the first Mover in the cause above made the fair chain of Love, high was his intent and great was the result. He knew why and what his purpose was. For with that fair chain of Love he constrained the fire, the air, the land, and the water within certain bounds so that they may not escape. This same Prince and Mover has established in this wretched world certain days and duration to all that is created, beyond which span of time they may not pass, though it may be shortened. Then by this order men may well understand that this Mover is stable and eternal. Well may men know, unless one be a fool, that every part of creation is derived from the whole (in God's mind); for Nature has not taken its beginning from any part of a thing, but from that which is stable and perfect, descending thence until it is corruptible. And therefore, of his wise Providence he has so fixed his ordinance that species of things and progressions (of birth, life, death) shall continue by successions and not be eternal." Thus Arcite's death, like that of every other man, is but an incident in the progressions of Nature; it belongs to the common fortune of all corruptible things. And whatever may have been the destinal cause of his more personal fortunes, that too many be included in the Providence of God. "Who brings all this about but Jupiter—(i.e., God)? He is Prince and cause of all things, converting everything back to its proper source from which it was first derived." (*C. T.* A, 2987–3038). In this passage Theseus is paraphrasing Boethius's great meter on Celestial Love, the harmonizing principle through which God governs his universe, ending: "This powerful Love is common to all things, which for desire of good move back to the springs from whence they first came. No worldly thing can have a continuance unless Love bring it back again unto the cause which first the essence gave," to which Chaucer adds, "that is to say, to God." [69] Thus in the *Knight's Tale* Chaucer has deliberately declined to become embroiled in any theological controversy over the place where souls find a habitation after death and has refused to be entangled in scholastic dialectic. He has rather chosen to solve the problem of his hero's after-existence by employing the philosophy of Boethius. In short, Arcite's spirit, having served its preordained purpose in the physical body, now follows its destiny in returning to the source from which it originally came, to God. [70]

NOTES

CHAPTER I

1. W. W. Skeat, *Oxford Chaucer, C. T.*, A, 410–444.

2. Skeat, V, 40–42; E. E. Morris, " The Physician in Chaucer," *An English Miscellany*, pp. 338 ff.; Hinckley, *Notes on Chaucer*, pp. 31–36; Hammond, *A Bibliographical Manual*.

3. Quoted from H. P. Cholmeley, *John of Gaddesden and the Rosa Medicine*, pp. 93–94. See Isidore Hispalensis, *Opera*, ed. Migne, *Patr. Lat.*, CXCIX, and the same author's further discussion of the division of medicine into *metodica, empirica*, and *logica* in *Liber Etymologiarum*, Venetiis, 1483, lib. iv, cap. 4, fol. 20r.

4. Joannes Salisburiensis, *Polycraticus*, ed. Migne, *Patr. Lat.*, CXCIX, lib. ii, cap. 29, col. 475; cf. Cholmeley, *op. cit.*, pp. 96–97 for translation. See John Flint South, *The Craft of Surgery*, London, 1886, p. 7.

5. Joannes de Burgundia, *De pestilentia liber*, Sloane MS. 3449, fol. 6; quoted from Cholmeley, *op. cit.*, pp. 72–73. Traill, *Social England*, I, thinks that possibly John of Burgundy may have been the model for Chaucer's Doctor. Cf. Barclay's arraignment " Of folysshe Fesycyans and vnlerned that onely followe paractyke knowynge nought of the speculacyon of theyr faculte," *The Ship of Fools*, ed. Jamieson, I, 260–4.

6. *Astronomia Hypocratis de infirmitatibus*, Lugduni, 1508, p. 1.

7. *Liber Rasis de secretis in medicina qui liber Aphorismorum appellatur*, in *Opera parua Abubetri filij Zacharie filij Arasi*, Lugduni, 1511, fol. 243. This Rhazes — Chaucer's ' Razis ' (*C. T.*, A, 431) — is Muhammad ibn Zakariya (Abu Bakr), *Al-Razi*, who was born near the middle of the ninth century, studied in Baghdad, and who died A.D. 932. In the work cited above, fols. 239–244, he deals fully with the secret influences of the stars in various illnesses. For further opinions of wise men upon the supremacy of the heavens over earthly things, see Professor Lynn Thorndike's excellent work, *A History of Magic and Experimental Science*: Arnoldus de Villanova, II, 855;

Roger Bacon, II, 670; Raymond Lull, II, 871; Petrus de Abano, II, 890; Cecco d'Ascoli, II, 957, etc. Professor Thorndike's book has been invaluable to me in the preparation of this chapter; and though my material was collected before its appearance, I have not hesitated to use freely his expositions and translations of passages which I have at hand.

8. This sketch is taken largely from Roger Bacon, *Opus Majus*, ed. Bridges, I. 377–382. Cf. Thorndike, II, 670–1.

9. Bacon, *op. cit.*, I, 380. I have used in some measure Thorndike's phraseology, II, 670.

10. *Ibid.*, I, 381–382. Thorndike, II, 670.

11. Skeat, V, 32, 40–1; *Secreta Secretorum*, ed. Steele, EETS. E.S., 74, pp. 65 ff.; Constantinus Africanus, *Opera*, Basileae, 1536, pp. 1 ff.; *Liber Ptolomei quattuor tractatum, cum Centiloquio eiusdem Ptolomei & commento haly*, Venetiis, 1484, Verb. LVI; or any full work on medicine from the Middle Ages.

12. Since most mediaeval medical treatises are divided into Theory and Practice (see for example, Haly filius Abbas, *Liber totius medicine necessaria continens*, Lugduni, 1523), the punctuation of this passage should probably be as I have it.

13. The contents of this paragraph are taken from *Astronomia Hypocratis de infirmitatibus*, Lugduni, 1508, probably spurious. Thorndike says of Galen's *Prognostication of Diseases by Astrology*, "This treatise is the same as that ascribed in many manuscripts to Hippocrates," I, 179. Cf. Galen, *De diebus decretoriis*, Paris, 1663, "On the Influence of the Moon," caps. I–VI, "On the Truth of Astrological Medicine," caps. XII–XIII; Hermes Trismegistus, *Iatromathematica*, in Virdung (J), J. Hasfurti *de cognoscendis et medendis . . . moribus ex corporum coelestium positione libri iiii*, 1584 (see translation into English by Iohn Haruey, 1583); Bacon, I, 383–4.

14. Quoted from Bacon, I, 383. See Ptolemaeus (with Haly's commentary), *op. cit.*, Verb. LVI.

15. Bacon, I, 384.

16. *Ibid.*, I, 383; Skeat, V, 382, to *C. T.*, F, 352.

17. Bacon, I, 382; Thorndike, I, 670; Skeat, V, 86, 97.

18. For a full discussion of the diseases attributed respectively to the planets, see Baptista Porta, *Physiognomoniae coelestis libri sex*, Rothomagi, 1650, pp. 18, 21, 25, 28, 35, 50, 55, 59.

19. For a full discussion of *febris putredinis* with its four divisions, *tertiana, quartana, quotidiana*, and *continua*, caused re-

spectively by the corruption of the humours, cholera, melancholia, phlegm, and blood in the system, see my study in *Englishche Studien*, LVIII, reproduced in Chapter IX.

20. For a full account of Mars in this position, see my article in *Jour. Eng. Germc. Philol.*, XXII, revised in Chapter VII.

21. The patient may be called at the third hour before sunrise, the " hour " of Saturn, but let us hope that his constitution will bear him up until the first hour before sun-up.

22. See the pseudo-Hippocrates, *op. cit.*, " Luna in Ariete."

23. For an explanation of the relative importance of angle, succeedant, cadent, see Chapter VII, p. 172, note.

24. Mars is thus bereft of his malice, as Chaucer might say, " by the oppression of houses " (*LGW.*, 2590); Skeat, III, 348.

25. For the beneficent influence of Jupiter in nativities and elections and his opposition to Saturn, see Chapter VI, p. 127.

26. For an account of the digesters and purgers of cholera and melancholia, together with the conforters of phlegm, see Richard Saunders, *The Astrological Judgment and Practice of Physic*, London, 1677, pp. 87–93; Arnoldus de Villa Nova, *Opera omnia*, Basileae, 1524, p. 363.

27. Quoted from Thebit ibn Corat, *De Tribus Imaginibus Magicis*, Francoforti, 1559, sig. A1. For further information on images, see Thorndike, II, 164 ff., 177, 220, 257, 327, 350, 588, 610, 673, 802, 835; Wedel, *The Mediaeval Attitude toward Astrology*, pp. 69, 74, 150.

28. See Chaucer's *H. F.*, 1265 ff., where he speaks of clerks who are able to make images in certain ascendents and who are able by the exercise of such natural magic to make a man whole or sick. He implies that an ascendent may be " fortuned " or " infortuned." See Hinckley, *op. cit.*, p. 32.

29. Skeat, V, 40.

30. Bacon, *Opus Majus*, ed. Bridges, I, 395: Thorndike, II, 673 ff.

31. Bacon, *Opera quaedam hactenus inedita*, ed. Brewer, p. 527.

32. Quoted from Bacon, ed. Bridges, I, 384. The full name of this great philosopher-scientist is Thābit ibn Kurrah ibn Marwan ibn Karayā ibn Ibrāhim ibn Marinos ibn Salamanos (Abu Al Hasan), *Al-Harrani*. He was born A.D. 836 at Harran in Mesopotamia, and died A.D. 901. See Bacon, ed. Bridges, I, 394.

33. *Op. cit.* For an account of Thebit and his work on images, see Thorndike, I, 663.

34. See his *Tractatus Sigillorum,* in Arnaldi Villanovani *Summi philosophi et medici excellentissimi,* Lugduni, 1586, Praxis medicinalis, pp. 30–32. Thorndike discusses this tract (II, 858) and translates Arnold's directions for engraving a seal in Aries.

35. *Op. cit.,* sig. B4.

36. Since there is no suggestion that Chaucer's Doctor employs images made by black magic, I have not gone into that subject. But see Thorndike, II, under "Image" and "Incantation."

37. I have taken this passage almost bodily from Thorndike's excellent exposition, II, 665.

38. Constantini Africani Medici ad Filium *De incantationibus & adiurationibus Epistola,* in *Opera,* Basileae, 1536, pp. 317–18.

39. Arnoldus de Villa Nova, *op. cit.,* p. 30; Thorndike, II, 858.

40. Since Saturn is located in Sagittarius and has his power bereft him by Jupiter posited in oppositional aspect in Gemini, and since Saturn does not aspect Luna, it is not necessary to place on the image either Saturn or Jupiter. The house of death — the eighth now occupied by Scorpio — has no unfortunate planet in it or aspecting it; indeed, the lord of the house of death, in this instance Mars (whose darker mansion is Scorpio), is unfortunately placed, as we have seen and as has been already noted on the image.

41. See Bacon, ed. Bridges, I, 381–382. He quotes and illustrates from the *Centiloquium* of Ptolemaeus with the Haly commentary (*op. cit.,* Verb. LVI); cf. Thorndike, II, 855 ff.

42. For the nature of plants and the influence of Luna in the compounding of medicines, see John of Burgundy, *op. cit.,* p. 72; Arnoldus de Villa Nova, *Tractatus de virtutibus herbarum,* Venetiis, 1499; Pedanii Dioscoridis Anazarbei *De materia medica libri quinque,* ed. Springel in *Opera quae extant,* I; Thorndike, II (see Index "Pharmacy").

43. For discussions upon the diet proper for each month of the year, see *Tractatus Ioannis de Zantuliete barbantini de dietis totius anni,* Lugduni, 1508. See also the *Opera omnia* (Lugduni 1515) of Ishak ibn Sulaiman, Al-Isra'ili, "Liber dietarum vniuersalium," fols. xj–cj, "Liber dietarum particularium," fols.

cij–clvy.   Thorndike gives (II, 502–507) interesting extracts from Petrus Hispanus's Commentaries upon Isaac.

44. It does not seem necessary to discuss here further the fifteen celebrated physicians whose works are said to come within the Doctor's course of reading. See Hinckley, *op. cit.*, p. 33; Skeat, V, 31; Lounsbury, *Studies in Chaucer*, II, 393; Morris, *op. cit.*, p. 340. But since none of these commentators seems able to identify Chaucer's " Haly," it might be well at this juncture to distinguish between the writers to whom the poet may have referred (*C. T.*, A, 431). Haly Abbas, whose full name is 'Ali ibn 'Al-Abbas, was a Persian physician called Al-Majusi or Majus, who died A.D. 994 (Cholmeley, *op. cit.*, p. 185); Hali filius Rodbon, whose Arabian name is 'Ali ben Ridhwan ben 'Ali ben Ja 'Far, was born in Ghizeh about A.D. 980; he was famous during the Middle Ages for his commentary on the *Tegni* of Galen (Cholmeley, p. 167). Albohazen Haly filius Abenragel, whose full name is 'Ali ibn Abí Al-Rajjál (Abú Hasan), was a famous Arabian astrologer, born at Cordova, who lived toward the beginning of the eleventh century (see Michaud, *Biographie Universelle*); I shall have occasion to quote from him anon. He must not be confused with either Albohazen or Albohali. Albohazen, respectively Alhazen, Alhacen, Alocen, named in full Hasan ibn Al-Haitam (Abu 'Alí Al), *Al-Basu*, was born in Cairo A.D. 1038. He was especially known as the author of a work on optics, cf. Risnerus, editor, *Opticae Thesaurus Alhazeni Arabis libri septem*, 1572, and Bauer, *Die Psychologie Alhazens auf Grund von Alhazens Optik* (*Beitr. Gesch. der Philos. des Mittelal.*, Bd. 10, H. 5). He is mentioned by Chaucer, who calls him " Alocen," in connection with certain " queynte mirours " and perspectives (*C. T.*, F, 232). The Albohaly who sometimes figures in mediaeval literature is none other than Avicenna. See MS. Royal 12. G. VI in the British Museum, *Albohaly Avicennae Canon Medicinae*, etc. Chaucer's " Haly " may be identified with Haly filius Rodbon, Skeat says, V, 42 (but see his query in the *Academy*, March 2, 1889); or with Haly Abbas as Hinckley suggests, *op. cit.*, p. 33; certainly *not* with Alhazen, as Morris has it, *op. cit.*, p. 340.

45 Quoted from John Flint South, *The Craft of Surgery*, p. 7.

46. *Polycraticus*, ed. Migne, *op. cit.*, CXIX, lib. ii, cap. xxix, 475; trans. Cholmeley, *op. cit.*, p. 95.

47. Ahasveri Fritschi *Medicus peccans, sive Tractatus de*

peccatis medicorum, Norimbergae, 1684, Conclusio V, p. 27. See also Conclusio VIII, pp. 33–37.

48. See *The Laws of Physicians, Surgeons, and Apothecaries,* London, 1767, beginning with Henry the Eighth's "Act for Appointing Physicians and Surgeons," 1511. South says, "In 1215 the ecclesiastics were debarred by order of Pope Innocent III from undertaking any operation involving the shedding of blood. . . . By two subsequent decrees, the one issued by Pope Boniface the Eighth at the close of the thirteenth century and the second by Pope Clement the Fifth about the beginning of the fourteenth century, surgery was formally separated from physic, and the priests were absolutely forbidden to practice the art," *op. cit.,* p. 12. In Chaucer's day the Doctor of Physic was much superior in dignity and authority to the Doctor of Surgery. For regulations governing the School of Salernum, see H. E. Handerson, *The School of Salernum,* pp. 43–44, and Cholmeley, *op. cit.,* p. 106.

49. Cf. *The Vision of William concerning Piers the Plowman,* ed. Skeat, C, IX, 291–297; *The Testament of Cressid,* ed. Skeat, VIII, 240–253; Wright's *Political Songs* (Camden Soc.), p. 333.

50. Christopher Merritt, *A Short View of the Frauds and Abuses Committed by Apothecaries,* London, 1669, pp. 14–15. Cf. *Lex Talionis,* or a Short Reply to Dr. Merritt's Books, London, 1660, pp. 7 ff.; *A Discourse setting forth the Unhappy Condition of the Practice of Physic in London,* London, 1670, by Jonathan Goddard; Merritt, *Self-Conviction,* London, 1670, and *A Short Reply to the Postscript,* 1670; the anonymous *Medice cura Teipsum,* 1671; Robert Pitt, *The Frauds and Villanies of the Common Practice of Physick,* London, 1705.

51. *The Accomplisht Physician, the Honest Apothecary, and the Skilful Surgeon,* London, 1670, pp. 74–75.

52. *Op. cit.,* p. 17.

53. On the compounding of electuaries, see Arnoldus de Villa Nova, *Opera omnia,* Basileae, 1524, p. 463; Constantinus Africanus, *op. cit.,* pp. 202, 270–274; Haly filius Abbas, *op. cit.,* lib. X, caps. vii, viii.

54. The materal used in this chapter was published first in the *Philological Quarterly,* IV, pp. 1–24.

CHAPTER II

1. The materials in this chapter were first published in "The Malady of Chaucer's Summoner," *Modern Philology*, XIX, 395–404, and "The *Mormal* of Chaucer's Cook," *Modern Language Notes*, XXXVI, 274–276.

2. Lanfrank's *Science of Cirurgie*, EETS., 102, pp. 193 ff. (Cf. also *Cyrurgia parua Lanfranci*, Venetiis, 1499, f. 182). Guy de Chauliac seems to be impatient with the classification of skin diseases attempted by his fraternal enemy, *La Grande Chirvrgie*, ed. Nicaise, Paris, 1890, p. 413, or *Cyrvrgia Gvidonis de Cavliaco*, Venetiis, 1499, f. 51, r. 1. For further discussion of terminology among the Greeks, Arabians, Romans, and others, see *Seven Books of Paulus Aeginita*, trans. Francis Adams, II, 1–35 *passim*, and Commentaries to sections 1 and 2 of Book IV; J. H. Baas, *The History of Medicine*, pp. 313–15.

3. This is Constantinus Africanus of Carthage (1015–87), mentioned by Chaucer in his list of celebrated physicians (*C. T.*, A, 433) and also in connection with a work called *De coitu* (*C. T.*, E, 1807–11). The curious reader may verify Chaucer's reference to *De coitu* by consulting Constantinus's *Opera, conquisita undique magno studio jam primum typis evulgata*, Basileae, 1536, pp. 306 ff.

4. *Op. cit.*, Lib. VII, cap. xviii, p. 161.

5. Gilbertus Anglicus, *Compendium medicine*, Lugduni, 1510, f. clxx, v₁. For a discussion of Gilbert's life, see Handerson's *Gilbertus Anglicus, Medicine of the Thirteenth Century*.

6. *Batman vpon Bartholome*, London, 1582, pp. 114 ff. This is an English translation made in 1397 of Bartholomaeus de Glanvilla's *De proprietatibus rerum*, composed in 1366; see the Basil edition of 1475, p. 63, for the foregoing passage. On the author see Se Boyar's article in *Jour. Eng. Germc. Philol.*, XIX, 168 ff.

7. Bernardus de Gordon, *Practica dicta Lilium medicinae*, Lyons, 1491, sig. d₅, v₂. This is Chaucer's "Bernard" (*C. T.*, A, 434), concerning whom consult Hinckley's *Notes on Chaucer*, p. 35.

8. *Op. cit.*, p. 190.

9. Andrew Boorde's *Introduction and Dietary*, EETS. E. S., 10, p. 101.

10. Willan and T. Bateman, *A Practical Synopsis of Cutaneous Diseases*, Philadelphia, 1818, pp. 297–99. For further division of the " genus *gutta rosea*" into three species, see Erasmus Darwin's *Zoonomia*, Boston, 1809, Class ii, 1, 4, 6; iv, 1, 2, 13, 14.

11. Cf. Boorde, *op. cit.*, p. 101; *Batman vpon Bartholome*, p. 63; Bateman, *op. cit.*, p. 294, note; *Cyurgia Rogerii*, Venetiis, 1499, f. 225 — or any history of medicine.

12. See *Seven Books*, trans. Adams: Actuarius, II, 11; Avicenna, II, 12; Serapion (Chaucer's " Serapion," A, 432), II, 13, Cf. Haly filius Abbas, *Liber totius medicine*, Lyons, Lib. VIII, cap. xv.

13. *Op. cit.*, cap. xxii.

14. *Op. cit.*, p. 64.

15. Ioannes de Gadesden, *Rosa Anglica practica medicinae*, Pavia, 1492, car. 56, r_1. I quote from a translation of this passage found in Cholmeley's *John of Gaddesden and the Rosa medicinae*, pp. 45–46.

16. Baas, *op. cit.*, p. 231; Adams, *Seven Books*, II, 14.

17. *Batman vpon Bartholome*, p. 113. Cf. Arnoldus de Villanova, *Practica medicina*, Venezia, 1494, f. g_1, v_1.

18. *Op. cit.*, f. g_1, v_1.

19. *Op. cit.*, f. ccxl, v_1.

20. It is interesting to note that the physiognomists also associate this sign with leprosy: " Supercilia plane depilia, Luem Veneream Leprem, vel aliam sanguinis corruptionem indicant," Rudolphus Goclenius, *Physiognomica et Chiromantica Specialia*, Hamburgi, 1661, p. 60; cf. Samuelis Fvchsii Cvslino Pomerani *Metoposcopia & Ophthalmoscopia*, Argentenae, 1615, p. 91.

21. For example see Gaddesden's chapter " De infectione ex coitu leprosi," *op. cit.*, car. 61, r_2.

22. *Batman vpon Bartholome*, p. 113.

23. The *Isagoge*, by Joannitius (Arabic, Hunain), trans. Cholmeley, *op. cit.*, App. D, p. 145.

24. Adams, I, 117, 118.

25. *Op. cit.*, pp. 279, 351, 239. Cf. *The Babees Book*, ed. Furnivall, pp. 156, 214.

26. *Batman vpon Bartholome*, p. 330.

27. Adams, *op. cit.*, I, 172, 174.

28. *Op. cit.*, p. 190, and notes.

29. *Op. cit.*, p. 459.

30. *Ibid.*, pp. 631, 633. Cf. Lanfrank's "Of medicyns cauteratiuis & corrosiuis," *op. cit.*, pp. 349 ff. The chief ingredient of these ointments is arsenic.

31. Indeed it is so translated in Lanfrank, *op. cit.*, pp. 178, 293. See two descriptions of the "mormal," *Mod. Lang. Notes*, XXXIII, 379, *Trans. Conn. Acad. Arts and Sciences*, XXIII, 27.

32. *Chirvrgia edita et compilata ab excell. domino fratre Theodorico episcopo Ceruiensi*, Venetiis, 1499, Lib. III, cap. xlix.

33. *Op. cit.*, sig. d₇, v₁. Cf. also *Cyrvrgia Rogerii*, Venetiis, 1499, "De malo mortuo," f. 69, r₁; Gvy de Chavliac, *op. cit.*, "mal mort," pp. 8, 420, 551.

34. *Op. cit.*, f. 94, r₁.

35. *Op. cit.*, p. 191.

36. See my note, "The Bottom of Hell," *Mod. Lang. Notes*, XXXVIII, 253.

CHAPTER III

1. "Chaucer's Pardoner and the Pope's Pardoners," J. J. Jusserand, *Essays on Chaucer*, 2nd Ser. No. 2, p. 423. Cf. also the same author's *English Wayfaring Life in the Middle Ages*, p. 210.

2. "Chaucer and the Seven Deadly Sins," F. Tupper, *Pub. Mod. Lang. Assoc.*, XXIX, 115.

3. "The Pardoner's Tavern," F. Tupper, *Jour. Eng. Germc. Philol.*, XIII, 558. This theory was exploded by Lowes, *PMLA.*, XXX, 260 ff.

4. *Jour. Eng. Germc. Philol.*, XIII, 565.

5. G. L. Kittredge, *Chaucer and His Poetry*, pp. 212 ff., and a fuller discussion by the same author in the *Atlantic Monthly*, LXXII, 830 ff.

6. See my study, "The Secret of Chaucer's Pardoner," *Jour. Eng. Germc. Philol.*, XVIII, 593 ff.

7. Walter Clyde Curry, *The Middle English Ideal of Personal Beauty*, pp. 3, 51, 66, etc.

8. *Ibid.*, p. 48; J. Fürst, *Philologus*, LXI, 384; G. L. Hamilton, *Mod. Lang. Notes*, XX, 80; G. P. Krapp, *MLN.*, XIX, 235.

9. He was a famous rhetorician and historian who flourished under Trajan and Hadrian and who died about 144 A.D. For

a full discussion of his life and influence, see R. Foerster, *Scriptores physiognomici*, I, lxxiv ff.

10. Polemonis *Physiognomon*, in *Scriptores physiognomoniae veteres*, ed. I. G. F. Franzius, 1780, p. 209.

11. *Anonymi de Physiognomonia liber Latinus*, ed. Foerster, *op. cit.*, II, 121 ff.

12. *Secreta Secretorum*, ed. R. Steele, EETS. E. S., 74, p. 223/18, 231/8.

13. Foerster, *op. cit.*, II, 22. Rudolphus Goclenius agrees in substance (*Physiognomica et Chiromantica Specialia*, Hamburgi, 1661, p. 35), and adds regarding the color: " Valde vero flavi et albicantes rudelatem, magnitatem et rusticitatem notant," p. 37. He states further: " Sed valdi ruffi insipientiam, iracundiam et insidias; imprudentiam et animi malignitatem indicant," p. 38.

14. *Ibid.*, pp. 84, 82. (But for a contrary opinion see Admantius, in Franzius, *op. cit.*, pp. 259, 391).

15. Admantii Sophistae *Physiognomonicon*, trans. Franzius, *op. cit.*, p. 376.

16. Polemonis *Physiognomonicon*, trans. Franzius, p. 308.

17. Rasis (Mohammed Abou-Bekr ibn Zacaria), born at Rey (Ragès), and died 923, *Biographie Universelle*, Michaud.

18. Baptista Porta, referring to Polemon, has this to say about men without beard: " Imberbis viri mulieribus & spadonis similes existunt. Ait Polemon, spadones naturali nequitia pessimis esse moribus, ingenio immites, dolosus, facinorosos, aliisque sceleribus se immiscentes," *De humana physiognomonia*, Hanoviae, 1593, p. 261.

19. *Rasis Phisiognomoniae versio Latina a Gerardo Cremonensi facta*, in Foerster, II, 178.

20. Foerster, II, 58.

21. *Bartholomeus de Proprietatibus Rerum*, trans. Trevisa, 1495, Lib. V, cap. lxvi.

22. *Op. cit.*, De Voce, Lib. V, caps. xxiii, xlix. Cf. Porta's fuller explanation, *op. cit.*, p. 245.

23. *Op. cit.*, De Barba, Lib. V, cap. xv.

24. Foerster, II, 58.

25. Michaud, *op. cit.* Favorinus was still alive in the year 155 A.D., Foerster, I, lxxx ff.

26. Polemonis *de physiognomonia liber Arabice et Latine*, ed. G. Hoffman, in Foerster, I, pp. 160–4.

27. My theory, therefore, in no way vitiates the sound conclusions drawn by Jusserand in the article cited above.

28. For a discussion of Chaucer's probable purpose in this satire, see *The Pardoner's Prologue and Tale,* a critical edition, J. Koch, p. xxx.

29. *Chaucer and His Poetry,* pp. 211–212.

30. Cf. Steele's Introduction to *Secrees of Old Philisoffres,* EETS. E. S. 66.

31. *The Tale of Beryn,* ed. Furnivall and Stone, EETS. E. S. 105.

32. For a different interpretation of this interruption, cf. Ten Brink, *History of English Literature,* trans. Robinson, II, 161, and R. F. Jones's excellent study, "A Conjecture on the Wife of Bath's Prologue," *Jour. Eng. Germc. Philol.,* XXIV, p. 541.

CHAPTER IV

1. *Secreta Secretorum,* ed. R. Steele, EETS. E. S., LXXIV, p. 220. With this should be compared by Lydgate and Burgh, *Secrees of Old Philosoffres,* ed. Steele, EETS. E. S., LXVI, p. 104.

2. Richard Saunders, *Physiognomie, and Chiromancie, Metoposcopie, Dreams, and the Art of Memory,* London, 1671, p. 189.

3. Aristotle's *Physiognomonika,* ed. R. Foerster, *Scriptores Physiognomonici,* I, 55.

4. *Polemonis de physiognomonia liber Arabice et Latine,* ed. G. Hoffman, in Foerster, *op. cit.,* I, 204. This work is edited also in I. G. F. Franzius's *Scriptores physiognomoniae veteres,* 1780, pp. 209 ff.

5. *Anonymi de physiognomonia liber Latinus,* ed. Foerster, II, 133.

6. F. Tupper, "The Quarrels of the Canterbury Pilgrims," *Jour. Eng. Germc. Philol.,* XIV, 265.

7. *Ibid.,* p. 269.

8. *Op. cit.,* Foerster, I, pp. 29, 37.

9. *Op. cit.,* Foerster, I, p. 31.

10. *Rasis physiognomoniae versio Latina a Gerardo Cremonensi facta,* ed. Foerster, II, 176.

11. *Op. cit.,* Foerster, I, 35.

12. *Op. cit.,* Foerster, II, 173 f.

13. *Ibid.,* Foerster, II, 138. A like opinion may be found in

Physiognomica & Chiromantica specialia, à Rodolpho Goclenio, Marpurgi Cattorum, 1621, p. 29.

14. *Physiognomoniae secreti secretorum pseudaristotelici versiones Latinae*, ed. Foerster, II, 214.

15. *Op. cit.*, Foerster, II, 170.

16. *Op. cit.*, Foerster, I, 67.

17. *Ibid.*, I, 232.

18. *Ibid.*, II, 206.

19. Giraldus Cambrensis, *Opera*, Rolls Series, No. 21, ed. Brewer, IV, 240.

20. *Op. cit.*, Foerster, II, 32, 132.

21. *Op. cit.*, p. 182.

22. *Op. cit.*, p. 33.

23. *Op. cit.*, Foerster, II, 168, 205, 226 ff.

24. *Op. cit.*, p. 196.

25. *Op. cit.*, Foerster, I, 85, 103; II, 169, 209, 266.

26. *Op. cit.*, Foerster, I, 266.

27. *Op. cit.*, Foerster, I, 228; II, 203–4. Cf. Goclenius, *op. cit.*, p. 68.

28. *Op. cit.*, Foerster, II, 167.

29. T. R. Lounsbury, *Studies in Chaucer*, II, 394. Cf. also J. L. Lowes, *Modern Philology*, XI, 391 ff., and O. F. Emerson, *ibid.*, XVII, 287.

30. Saunders, *op. cit.*, p. 305.

31. *La Metoposcopie*, Paris, 1658. He appends to his treatise the original discussion of moles by Melampus (with a French translation). Cf. Baptista Porta, *Physiognomoniae coelestis libri sex*, Rothomagi, 1650, pp. 125–139.

32. *Op. cit.*, p. 287.

33. Translated in Cardan, *op. cit.*, p. 223. Melampus flourished in the time of Julius Caesar.

34. *Op. cit.*, p. 203.

35. *Op. cit.*, p. 203.

36. *Op. cit.*, p. 195.

37. *Op. cit.*, p. 334.

38. *Op. cit.*, p. 335. The materials in this chapter were first published in *PMLA.*, XXXV, 189–209.

CHAPTER V

1. G. L. Kittredge, *Chaucer and His Poetry*, p. 189.

2. Professor Skeat has already given sufficient explanation of the astrological terminology used by Chaucer: see "mansions," *op. cit.*, I, 497; III, 348; "term," V, 395; "face," V, 372, 395. For his discussion of the conjunction of Venus and Mars in Taurus see his notes on "The Compleynt of Mars," II, 468, III, 249. See also J. M. Manly, "On the Date and Interpretation of Chaucer's Complaint of Mars," Harvard *Studies and Notes in Philology and Literature*, V, 107 ff. The other mansion of Venus is Libra.

3. That Venus is the dominant star in this nativity is suggested by the power which she exerts over the native and by the fact that she is further referred to as "my dame." And that Venus is situated also in the ascendent sign Taurus — and is therefore in conjunction with Mars — seems certain, because the good Wife has the "prente of sëynt Venus seel" upon her person; Venus in any other than the ascendent sign would be powerless to leave a mark.

4. Chaucer's immense knowledge of astrology has been pointed out by many scholars: Skeat's notes to *The Astrolabe*; T. R. Lounsbury, *Studies in Chaucer*, II, 395 ff.; Florence M. Grimm, "Astrological Lore in Chaucer," *Univ. Neb. Stud. in Lang. and Lit.*, No. 2, 1919; A. E. Brae's Introduction to his edition of *The Astrolabe*, etc.

5. *Absolvtissimae Chyromantiae Libri Octo*, In quibus quicquid ad chyromantiae, physiognomiae, & naturalis astrologiae perfectionem spectat, continentur, Coloniae Agrippinae, 1563, p. 496. A figure may be found facing the same page. Taisnier is following closely Ioannes Indagine, *Introductiones apotelesmatice elegantes, in chyromantiam, physiognomiam, astrologiam naturalem*, Lugduni, 1556.

6. Philippi Finella, *De metroposcopia*, Antverpiae, 1648, p. 134. See my article in *PMLA.*, XXXVII, 34, for further quotations from this work.

7. Erra Pater (pseud.), *The Book of Knowledge*, Boston, p. 14.

8. Ioannes Baptista Porta, *Coelestis physiognomoniae libri sex*, Neapoli, 1603, p. 116.

9. *Op. cit.*, p. 61. To this imposing array of opinion may be added that of Finella, *op. cit.*, p. 27; Taisnier, *op. cit.*, p. 493; *Les Oevvres de M. Iean Belot*, Lyon, 1654, p. 235; Rosa Baughan, *The Influence of the Stars*, London, 1889, p. 26; William Lilly, *Christian Astrology, modestly Treated of in Three Books*, London, 1659, pp. 85, 265; Iean de Indagine, *Chiromance & Physiognomie* (trans. Antoine de Moulin Masconnois), Lyon, 1549, p. 279; Ioannes Fredericus Helvetius, *Amphitheatrum physiognomiae medicum*, Hydelbergi, 1660, p. 79, and the same author's *Microscopium physiognomiae medicum*, Amstelodami, 1676, pp. 87–91 — all of whom are in more or less amplified agreement with Porta and his authorities.

10. *Op. cit.*, pp. 64–65. Compare like accounts by Helvetius, *Amphitheatrum*, p. 79; Taisnier, *op. cit.*, p. 493; Finella, *op. cit.*, pp. 27, 36.

11. Helvetius, *Microscopium*, pp. 91–95.

12. Indagine, *op. cit.*, p. 279. It is a well-known astrological fact that Venus is found only in roots of nativities of phlegmatic natures, Belot, *op. cit.*, p. 235. The Wife of Bath's nature, therefore, is phlegmatic.

13. It may be of interest to observe how the above conclusions are strengthened by reference to the principles of geomancy. Skeat has already explained how fortunes may be determined by the use of the geomantic method (V, 82–83); it is necessary here only to point out that the figure which he calls Puella (p. 83) and to which he assigns — quite erroneously — the zodiacal sign Libra, is the geomantic " figure " of the Wife of Bath and corresponds to the sign Taurus. (The other figure of Venus is Amissa, corresponding to the sign Libra, her other mansion.) The following interpretation is given by M. Belot: " Alors qu'il se rencontre *Puella* ou Amissio, qui sont les deux maisons de Venus, l'vne representent Taurus & l'autre (Libra) au sort des points, ils nous represent l'homme ou la femme Venerienne; s'ils sont nés, s'il se rencontre Puella ou Taurus en leur ascendant, ils sont d'vne couleur pure, & le corps massif, nitide, beau, net & sans macule, les levres grosses, eminentes, particulierement la superieure; ils sont d'vne stature petite; ils ont la face belle, les cheveux longs, non crespus, blandides, les yeux grands," *op. cit.*, p. 249. For further description see Le Sievre de Pervchio, *La Chiromance, la Physionomie, et la Geomance*, Paris, 1657, p. 228.

14. *Op. cit.*, p. 279.

15. *Op. cit.*, p. 147. Cf. Albohazen Haly filius Abenragel, *Libri de ivdiciis astrorum*, Basileae, 1551, pp. 12, 170 (Mars), p. 165 (Venus); Firmicus Iulius Maternus, *De nativitatibus*, Venetiis, 1497, sigs. d₁, f₆.

16. *Op. cit.*, p. 615.

17. Indagine, *op. cit.*, p. 278. Cf. also the account of M. Belot (*op. cit.*, p. 233), which concludes with the remark that " cette nature est fort vicieuse."

18. Guido Bonatus, " Choice Aphorismes of Cardan's Seven Segments," in *Anima astrologiae, or a Guide for Astrologers*, (Trans. W. Lilly), London, 1683, pp. 9–33, *passim.*

19. *Christian Astrology*, p. 595.

20. Quoted from Porta, *op. cit.*, Rothomagi, 1560, p. 77.

21. *Ibid.*, p. 79.

22. This paragraph is a free translation of the exposition given by M. Belot (*op. cit.*, pp. 219–221) except that I have omitted his irrelevant illustration which takes up the Sun and certain other planets in conjunction in the sign Aries. For further discussion of natural marks and moles see Lilly, *op. cit.*, pp. 149, 155; Pervchio, *op. cit.*, p. 104; H. M. Cardan, *La Metoposcopie*, Paris, 1658, p. 220; Richard Saunders, *Physiognomie and Chiromancie, Metoposcopie, Dreams, and the Art of Memory*, London, 1671, Introduction to the section on Physiognomy; M. de Mirbel, *Le Palais du Prince dv Sommeil, ou est enseignée L'Oniromancie, Autrement L'Art de Devinir par les Songes*, Lyon, 1670.

23. Each sign of the zodiac is divided, for astrological purposes, into three equal parts: from one to ten degrees is called the first face, from ten to twenty the second face, from twenty to thirty the third face. Cf. Skeat, V, 395.

24. *Op. cit.*, p. 221.

25. *Op. cit.*, p. 110.

26. *Op. cit.*, p. 184.

27. *Op. cit.*, p. 107.

28. *Op. cit.*, p. 225.

29. *Op. cit.*, p. 223. Cf. Pervchio, *op. cit.*, p. 106.

30. The physiognomists agree on the significance of large hips, see Angellus Blondus, *De cognitione hominis per aspectum*, Romae, 1544, p. xv; Rudolphus Goclenius, *Physiognomica et chiromantica specialia*, Hamburgi, 1661, p. 93; Porta, *De*

humana physiognomia, Hanoviae, p. 249; Rasis and others in *Scriptores physiognomonici*, ed. R. Foerster, II, 172, 217, etc.

31. See Goclenius, *op. cit.*, p. 63; Indagine, *op. cit.*, p. 134; Saunders, *op. cit.*, p. 197.

32. On the significance of the Wife's voice, see *PMLA.*, XXXVII, p. 45, note 36.

33. For a full discussion of the Wife of Bath's teeth set far apart, see my study in *PMLA.*, XXXVII, p. 45, note 38.

34. For a discriminating appreciation of this story, see Lounsbury, *op. cit.*, III, 418.

35. Ten Brink, *The History of English Literature*, trans. Robinson, II, 163.

36. R. K. Root, *The Poetry of Chaucer* (First ed.), p. 239.

37. *Ibid.*, p. 231. Cf. Ten Brink, II, 126.

38. W. E. Mead, "The Prologue of the Wife of Bath's Tale," *Pub. Mod. Lang. Assoc.*, XVI, 388 ff.

39. "More About Chaucer's Wife of Bath," *Pub. Mod. Lang. Assoc.*, XXXVII, 51.

CHAPTER VI

1. See Cook, "The Historical Background of Chaucer's *Knight's Tale*," *Trans. Conn. Acad. Arts and Sciences*, XX; Lowes, "The Loveres Maladye of Hereos," *Mod. Philol.*, XI, 491 ff.; Cook, "The Arming of the Combatants in the *Knight's Tale*," *Jour. Eng. Germc. Philol.*, IV, 504 ff.; Robinson, "Elements of Realism in the *Knight's Tale*," *J. E. GPh.*, XIV, 226 ff.; Curry, "Chaucer's Tempest Again," *Mod. Lang. Notes*, XXXVI, 272; Ker, *Epic and Romance*, pp. 364 ff. Most of the materials of this chapter were published in *Anglia*, XLVII.

2. J. S. P. Tatlock, "Astrology and Magic in Chaucer's *Franklin's Tale*," *Kittredge Anniversary Papers*, pp. 339 ff.

3. All this passage, ll.2014–2040, is original with Chaucer except this line, which was suggested by *Teseide* VII, 37. In comparing the *Knight's Tale* with the *Teseide* I have used Mr. Henry Ward's side-notes to the Cambridge and Lansdowne Texts in the *Six-Text Print of Chaucer's Canterbury Tales*, ed. Furnivall.

4. Quoted from Skeat, V, 81.

5. Albohazen Haly filius Abenragel, *Libri de ivdiciis astrorum*, Basileae, 1531, p. 11. Cf. *Libellus Ysagogicvs* Ab-

dilazi . . . qui dicitur Alchabitivs, Venetiis, 1591, sig. bb₃v. This is the Arabian astrologer 'Abd al 'Azziz ibn 'Uthmán, al Kabísí.

6. William Lilly, *Christian Astrology* . . . in Four Books, London, 1647, p. 67.

7. For a discussion of geomancy and the geomantic figures, see Skeat, V, 82. He observes, rightly, that the other " figure " of Mars is Puer and not Puella, this last being one of the figures of Venus. I suspect that Chaucer's knowledge of geomancy was extremely limited, hence his confusion of these two figures. Cf. my study, "Fortuna maior," *MLN.*, XXXVIII, 95.

8. Quoted from Skeat, V, 86. See further on astrological hours, Alchabitius, *op. cit.*, sig. bb₆; *The Compost of Ptolemaeus*, London, 1535, cap. xl; Richard Saunders, *Palmistry*, London, 1664, pp. 517–548.

9. From Skeat, V, 86.

10. Albohazen Haly, *op. cit.*, p. 10.

11. Quoted from Guido Bonatus, *De astronomia tractatus* X, Basileae, 1850, col. 101.

12. *Compost of Ptolemaeus*, cap. xliii. Cf. Lilly, p. 57, who says that Saturn runs his course in " 29 years, 157 days, or thereabouts."

13. *Op. cit.*, sig. bb₂. Cf. Haly, *op. cit.*, p. 9; Bartholomaeus de Glanvilla, *De proprietatibus rerum*, Venetiis, 1483, lib. VIII, cap. xxiii.

14. *Op. cit.*, Pars IIII, cap. lxiii.

15. Albumasar, *De magnis coniunctionibus annorum reuolutionibus*, Venetiis, 1489, sig. h₃. This is the Arabian astrologer Ja 'Far ibn Múhammad (Abu Ma 'sar), Al-Bálkhí.

16. Lilly, *op. cit.*, p. 59. Cf. Richard Saunders, *The Astrological Judgment and Practice of Physic*, London, 1677, p. 19, for a still further list of Saturnalian diseases, and pp. 86 ff. for the cure of them. See also Joannes Baptista Porta, *Physiognomiae coelestis libri sex*, Rothomagi, 1650, p. 18, for diseases attributed by various authorities to Saturn.

17. Mr. Henry Ward supposes that certain lines in Chaucer's description of Lycurgus, only one of the many knights mentioned in the *Teseide*, are taken from Boccaccio's description of Agamemnon: 2129, *Tes.* VI, 14; 2130, *Tes.* VI, 21; 2135, *Tes.* 21; 2138–9, *Tes.*, VI, 21; 2141–2, *Tes.* VI, 22. Otherwise the passage seems to be original with Chaucer.

18. Mr. Ward grants the passage, ll.2156–2180, to be original except the following lines, which find some suggestion in the *Teseide:* 2162, *Tes.* VI, 17; 2163–4, VI, 16; 2175, VI, 41; 2158, VI, 29.

19. Claudius Ptolemaeus, *De iudiciis astrologicis,* in *Opera,* Basileae, 1541, p. 473.

20. *Op. cit.,* sig. bb₄.

21. *Op. cit.,* p. 165.

22. Porta, *op. cit.,* p. 30.

23. *Op. cit.,* p. 67.

24. *Ibid.,* p. 85.

25. Richard Saunders, *Physiognomie & Chiromancie,* London, 1653, p. 152.

26. *Op. cit.,* p. 473.

27. *Op. cit.,* p. 164.

28. Porta, *op. cit.,* pp. 15, 17, 20.

29. *Op. cit.,* p. 58.

30. *Ibid.,* p. 84.

31. Richard Saunders, *Physiognomie, Chiromancie, Metoposcopie,* p. 151.

32. *Ibid.,* p. 168.

33. Undoubtedly, I think, "kempe" means rugged, rough, unkempt; and the "heres on hise browes stoute" are eyebrows. But see Skeat's note to this line, V, 84.

34. *Mod. Lang. Notes,* XXIII, 54.

35. *Svmmi in omni philosophia viri Constantini Africani,* Basileae, 1539. My outline is taken from the following chapters: De virtutibus, p. 79; De uirtute naturali in epate, pp. 81–87; De uirtute spirituali dilantante et constringente, pp. 89–91; De uirtute animata, pp. 91 ff. A garbled account of Constantinus's medical theory may be found in Bartholomaeus de Glanvilla (Anglicus), *De proprietatibus rerum,* Lugduni, 1452, fol. b₃ff.; or in Batman's translation made in 1397, *Batman vpon Batholome,* London, 1582, fol. 16b ff.

36. Arnoldus de Villa Nova, *Opera omnia,* Basileae, 1524, p. 22; otherwise his classification is similar to that of Constantinus. See p. 23 for the editor's outline.

37. Constantinus, *op. cit.,* p. 88.

38. Gilbertus Anglicus, *Compendium medicine,* Lugduni, 1510, fol. clxxxiiii.

39. *Ibid.,* De virtute in genere, col. clxxxiiii, verso.

40. *Ibid.,* fol. clxxxv.

41. *Ibid.*, fol. clxxxvii, verso.

42. Richard Saunders, *The Astrological Judgment and Practice of Physic*, London, 1677, p. 81.

43. *Ibid.*, p. 193.

44. *Ibid.*, pp. 82, 102 ff.

45. *Ibid.*, p. 193.

46. *Ibid.*, p. 103.

47. For accounts of ancient usages in blood-letting, see Francis Adams, *The Seven Books of Paulus Aegenita*, II, 316–319, 324–328; Constantinus, *op. cit.*, pp. 326–331; Arnoldus, *op. cit.*, pp. 366 ff.

48. For digesters and purgers of choler and melancholy caused by Saturn in the various signs, see Saunders, *op. cit.*, pp. 87–93, 120–3; Arnoldus, *op. cit.*, p. 363.

49. See Cicero, *De natura deorum*, lib. II, cap. 1921; Augustine, *De Civitate Dei*, in *Opera*, Vercellis, 1809, lib. VII; Isidore, *Etymologiarum libri XX*, lib. III, cap. xi, xxiii; Fabius Planciades Fulgentius, *Mytologiarum*, lib. I, cap. ii, in *Auctores Mythohraphi Latini*, ed. Staveren, 1742; Caius Julius Hyginus, *Poeticon Astronomicon*, cap. xiii–xx, ed. Staveren, 1742.

50. Albericus, philosophus, *De deorum imaginibus libellus*, ed. Staveren, *op. cit.* For a detailed account of the sources used in this work, see Robertus Raschke, *De Alberico Mythologo*, in *Bresl. Phil. Abhandl.*, H. 45. He thinks that the primary sources are Fulgentius, Macrobius, and Martianus Capella, and the secondary sources Cicero, Hyginus, and Isidore.

51. Albericus describes the planets-gods in the following order: Saturn (cap. I), Jupiter (II), Mars (III), Sol (IV), Venus (V), Mercury (VI), Luna (VII). Skeat has reproduced in part the descriptions of Venus (V, 78), Mars (V, 82), and Diana (V, 82), but he has omitted as not being "material" the astronomical remarks of Albericus. If Chaucer drew from this source his descriptions of the gods — and that seems likely — I see no reason why he might not also have received from this same source the idea of treating them as planets.

52. *Allegoriae poeticae*, ceu de veritate ac expositione poeticarum fabularum libri quatuor Alberico Londonensi Authore, (Paris), 1520. Raschke does not seem to have known of this important work.

53. Bartholomaeus de Glanvilla, *op. cit.*, Lyons, 1482, sig. ik₅v.

54. *Ibid.*, sig. ik₆r.

55. *Ibid.*, sig. ik$_6$r.

56. *Ibid.*, sig. ik$_6$v.

57. *Ibid.*, sig. ik$_8$.

58. *Batman vppon Bartholome*, London, 1582. For myths with interpretations of Saturn, see lib. VIII, cap. xxiii; Mars, VIII, xxv; Venus, VIII, xxvi, etc.

59. Robert Greene, *Planetomachia*, London, 1585, p. 3.

60. *Ibid.*, p. 4.

61. *Ibid.*, sig. B$_2$–F$_2$.

62. *Ibid.*, sig. G$_1$–I$_3$.

63. See B. L. Jefferson, *Chaucer and the Consolation of Philosophy of Boethius*, p. 118.

64. Boethius, *De consolatione philosophie*, trans. Chaucer, ed. Skeat, Book IV, Prose VI, 45–100.

65. *Idem.*, 100–110.

66. On Fortune see Book II, Proses ii, vii, etc., and Jefferson, *op. cit.*, pp. 49 ff.

67. Bk. II, M. viii; III, M. ix; IV, M. vi. Jefferson, *op. cit.*, p. 65.

68. Bk. V, Pr. i. Jefferson, *op. cit.*, p. 62.

69. See Chapter V.

70. See Chapter VII.

71. These sentiments are attributed to Theseus in the *Teseide*, but by the skilful introduction of l.2838 Chaucer has transferred them to the old Egeus.

72. These passages were suggested by certain lines in the *Teseide*.

CHAPTER VII

1. Skeat, III, xl. Cf. also Bech, *Anglia*, V, 365–371. The materials of this chapter were first published under the title "O Mars, O Atazir," *J. E. G. Ph.*, XXII, 347 ff.

2. Ioannes Baptista Porta, *Coelestis physiognomiae libri sex*, Neapoli, 1603, p. 61. Cf. Albohazen Haly filius Abenragel, *Libri de ivdiciis astrorum*, Basileae, 1551, p. 171; Mā Shā'a Allāh Al Misri (Messahala, 754–813), *De ratione circuli & stellarum*, in *Astronomici scriptores*, Basileae, 1533, p. 119; Firmicus Maternus, *De nativitatibus*, Venetiis, 1497, sig. e$_1$; Claudii Ptolemaei Pelvensis Alexandrini *Omnia, que extant, opera*, Basileae, 1541, p. 481.

3. *Op. cit.*, p. 169.

4. *Idem.* Cf. also Porta, *op. cit.*, p. 107; Ptolemaeus, *op. cit.*, p. 482; Ja 'far ben Muhammad al-Balchi abu Ma' sar (Albumasar), *De magnis conjunctionibus annorum revolutionibus*, Augsburg, 1489, sig. E₄; Abou Bakr ibn Al Kasil, Al Kharaschi Abubather (Albubather), *Liber natiuitatum de Arabico in Latinum translatus*, Venetiis, 1501, fol. 7v.

5. See Albumasar, *op. cit.*, sig. G₂; Haly, *op. cit.*, pp. 9, 165 — or any other astrology mentioned in these notes.

6. *Op. cit.*, fol. 16r. Cf. Skeat, V, 65.

7. Skeat (V, 408) is inclined to think that the *Man of Law's Tale* was originally composed about 1380 and that, at the time of revision (probably about 1387), various independent passages were interpolated. On the relative dates of these stories see Tatlock, *Development and Chronology of Chaucer's Works*, ch. v, § 6; Hammond, *A Bibliographical Manual*, pp. 282–3.

8. For a full discussion of the popularity accorded the science of elections among ancient astrologers, see Wedel's *Mediaeval Attitude toward Astrology*, pp. 53–5, 65, 149. Anyone in Chaucer's time might have elected a fitting time for beginning a voyage or a journey. Haly, *op. cit.*, 327 ff., devotes forty folio pages to all kinds of elections, giving a whole section to the subject *De electione itineris*. Cf. Ptolemaeus, pp. 493 ff.

9. Ioannis ab Indagine, *Introductiones apotelesmaticae in physiognomiam*, Argentorati, 1622, pp. 125–6. Cf. Ioannis Taisnier, *Absolutissimae Chyromantiae Libri Octo*, Coloniae Agrippinae, 1563, p. 494.

10. *Op. cit.*, sig. E₁.

11. *Op. cit.*, p. 319.

12. *Op. cit.*, V, 150. Cf. Albumasar, sig. F₄; William Lilly, *An Introduction to Astrology*, p. 63.

13. *Op. cit.*, p. 106. Cf. Alchabitius, *Libellus ysagogicus*, Venetijs, 1482, sig. b₁.

14. *Op. cit.*, p. 156.

15. William Lilly, *The Astrologer's Guide*, Lon. 1886, p. 5.

16. *Op. cit.*, p. 303. Cf. further on the ten evil situations of the Moon, Lilly, *op. cit.*, p. 4; Ioannis Ganivetus, *Amicus medicorum*, Lvgduni, 1550, p. 170; Zaehl, Sahl ibn Bashr Hóbib ibn Hani (Abu-'uthman), *De electionibus*, Basileae, 1533, p. 114.

17. *Ibid.*, p. 66.

18. *Ibid.*, p. 373. The interested reader will find detailed discussions of the *good* aspects and positions of Luna, for elections, in Haly, pp. 65, 328.

19. *Ibid.*, p. 373.

20. *Ibid.*, p. 8.

21. *Op. cit.*, sig. I₇.

22. *Op. cit.*, p. 299.

23. *Ibid.*, p. 371.

24. *Ibid.*, p. 12.

25. *Ibid.*, p. 260.

26. *Op. cit.*, p. 394.

27. Goclenius, R., *Astrologae generalis*, Marpurgi, 1618, p. 134.

28. *Op. cit.*, p. 507.

29. Lilly, *An Introduction to Astrology*, London, 1886, pp. 240–44.

30. Haly, *op. cit.*, p. 65. Note the same author's discussion of planetary influences to be observed in elections of *good* marriages, p. 65. Cf. Zaehl, *op. cit.*, p. 109.

31. R. Dozy, *Glossaire des Mots Espagnols et Portugais dérivés de l'Arabe*, p. 207. Cf. the same author's *Commentaire Historique sur le Poeme d'Ibnabdoun*, p. 80. Skeat, V, 150.

32. *Op. cit.*, p. 147. Haly devotes two folio pages (148–149) to hyleg, in which he enumerates not only the five places prescribed by Ptolemy (*op. cit.*, pp. 569–572) but in addition something like a dozen other places apt *pro hylech*. Cf. on hyleg and alcocoden Omar, 'Umar ibn Farkhan ('Abu Halfs), *De nativitatibus*, in *Astronomici scriptores*, Basileae, 1533, pp. 120–121; Alchabitius, *op. cit.*, sig. c₆r.; Albubather, *op. cit.*, sig. B₂ ff.

33. See William Lilly, *An Introduction to Astrology*, p. 24 (aspects); pp. 27–34 (nature of the houses); pp. 57–67 (nature of the signs); p. 69 (dignities); pp. 391, 393, 413, 403 (hyleh); pp. 238–249 (explanation of technical terms).

34. Haly, *op. cit.*, p. 148. The suceeding eight folio pages, filled with technical matter regarding *alcocoden* and with greatly conflicting opinions of wise men, indicate how vexed a question this was in the time of Haly.

35. *Ibid.*, p. 147.

36. It will appear that Luna has just fallen out of quartile aspect with the third face of Cancer. It must be remembered,

however, that the orb of Luna is 12°, that is to say, she exerts a powerful immediate influence for six degrees in every direction. If she has not progressed farther than six degrees in Scorpio, therefore, she is still — so far as her influence is concerned — in quartile aspect with Cancer. See Plate VI.

37. *Op. cit.*, sig. B₁ v.

38. *Ibid.*, sig. A₂.

39. *Idem.*

40. *Idem.* Luna is also considered by some authorities to be the hyleg when situated in the eighth house of the figure, see Haly, *op. cit.*, p. 148; Albubather, *op. cit.*, sig. B₂.

41. *Ibid.*, sig. B₂.

42. Or perhaps he is too good a philosopher, as we have already seen in our discussion of the *Knight's Tale.* But in this story he seems to take the religious point of view rather than the philosophical. Wedel, however, finds that Chaucer seems to be an outspoken determinist in astrological matters (*op. cit.*, pp. 143–153), and the scholars to whom he refers in the foot-notes are, for the most part, in agreement. But since these opinions are usually based on astrological references taken *as isolated fragments*, I ask for an unbiased consideration of my point of view based on a treatment of these independent passages *as organic.*

43. See Wedel, *The Mediaeval Attitude toward Astrology,* pp. 7, 55, 115, 125–7, 145 ff.

44. J. L. Lowes, *Convention and Revolt in Poetry,* pp. 67–71.

45. *Cant. Tales,* E, 2218–2320.

CHAPTER VIII

1. The subject-matter of this and the succeeding chapter was published first in *Englische Studien,* LVIII, pp. 24–60.

2. It may be mentioned that Calkas arrives at his conclusions regarding the fall of Troy through divinations by "sort," by "augurie," and by "astronomye" (IV, 115–17), though he has no vision of any kind. For this kind of thing neither Criseyde nor Pandarus has any patience; Criseyde finds that through the "sort" the gods speak in "amphibologyes" and tell twenty lies (IV, 1404–6); and Pandarus is of the opinion that augury from "ravenes qualm, or shryking of thise oules" is the foul and false nonsense of old women (V, 378–82).

3. Ambrosii Theodosii Macrobii *Commentariorum in Som-mium Scipionis,* lib. I, cap. iii (Teubner).

4. Bernhard Ten Brink, *Chaucer Studien,* etc., p. 101.

5. On the virtues and their functions, see *Svmi in omni philosophia viri Constantini Africani,* Basileae, 1539, pp. 81–93; Bartholomaeus Anglicus, *De proprietatibus rerum,* Lugduni, 1482, fol. b₃ ff.; Arnoldus de Villa Nova, *Opera omnia,* Basileae, 1524, pp. 22 ff.; *Compendium medicinae Gilberti Anglici,* Lugduni, 1510, fol. 184.

6. Avicenna, *Libri Canonis quinque,* Venetiis, 1564, lib. III, fen i, tract. i, cap. 7. This is the Arabian physician, Hussain ibn 'Abd Allah (Abú Alí Al), called Ibn Síná, born in Bokhara in 978 A.D., died 1036, whom Chaucer calls "Avicen" (*C. T.,* A, 431) and whose "canon" and "fen" he mentions without apparently any too great acquaintance with them (*C. T.,* C, 888 ff.). See Lounsbury, *Studies in Chaucer,* II, 394; Antonius Gaizo, *De somno ac eius necessitate,* Basileae, 1539, cap. i. Ex Galeni Libris *De dignotione ex insomniis,* in *Opera,* Venetiis, 1609, IV, 213.

7. *Loc. cit.* For further discussion of sleep and waking, see Aristotle, *De somno et vigilia,* text and commentary in the *Opera omnia* of Thomas Aquinas, Venetiis, 1594, III, fol. 28–34; Vincent de Veauvais, *Speculum naturale,* lib. XXVI, cap. i; Averroes, *Colliget Averrois totam medicinam,* Venetiis, 1542, fol. 51. This last is Muhammad ibn Ahmad ibn Rushd (Abu Al Walid), an Arabian physician, born at Cordova in A.D. 1126 and called by Chaucer "Averrois" (*C. T.,* A, 433).

8. *Loc. cit.*

9. *Op. cit.,* IV, 213; cf. Gaizo, *op. cit.,* cap. x.

10. Gaizo, *op. cit.,* cap. vii. Cf. also Petri Aponensis *Liber Conciliator differentiarum philosophorum precipueque medicorum appelatus,* dif. CLVII, fol. 202.

11. *Op. cit.,* *lib.* XXVI, cap. 41. Cf. Turisanus, *Plus quam commentum in parvam Galeni artem,* Venetiis, 1557, p. 53.

12. Gaizo, *op. cit.,* cap. vii; Petrus Aponensis, *op. cit.,* dif. CLVII, fol. 202v.

13. *Op. cit.,* dif. CLVII, fol. 202. He is quoting largely from Avicenna, *Compendium de anima,* Venetiis, 1546, lib. IV. Cf. Aristotle, *De somniis,* in *op. cit.,* III, fol. 35.

14. Petrus Aponensis (de Abano), *op. cit.,* dif. CLVII, fol. 202.

15. Quoted from Petrus de Abano, *idem.* Cf. Thomas Bradwardine, *De Causa Dei*, ed. Savillius, London, 1618, p. 13.

16. This is St. Augustine's commentary upon the *phantasma* of Macrobius, *De spiritu et anima*, cap. xxv. Cf. also Augustine, *Liber de divinatione daemonum*, cap. v; Guido Bonatus, *De astronomia tractatus x*, Basileae, 1550, col. 646; Henry Cornelius Agrippa, *De occulta philosophia*, lib. III, cap. li; Haly filius Abenragel, *De iudiciis astrorum*, Basileae, 1551, Pars III, cap. xii.

17. *Op. cit.*, cap. xii, p. 114.

18. *Ibid.*, cap. xiii, p. 115. It must not be forgotten that all the illusions wrought in the *Franklin's Tale* by the Clerk of Orleins are the result of his control over occult powers in some way liberated by his manipulations of the "eighte and twenty manciouns that longen to the mone" (*C. T.*, F, 1130). See Tatlock, "Astrology and Magic in Chaucer's *Franklin's Tale*," *Kittredge Anniversary Papers*, p. 342.

19. Arnoldus de Villa Nova, *Expositiones visionum quae fiunt in somnia* (in *Opera omnia*, Basileae, 1524, pp. 625 ff.), Pars I, cap. i, ii.

20. *Op. cit.*, lib. XXVI, cap. 63.

21. *Op. cit.*, Pars I, cap. iv.

22. *Ibid.*, Pars II, cap. ii. See Plate V. Second House.

23. St. Augustine, *De spiritu et anima*, cap. 24, 25.

24. Augustine, *De Genesi ad literam, liber XII*, cap. vii.

25. *Op. cit.*, lib. XXVI, cap. 56.

26. *Ibid.*, cap. 61, 74–96. Cf. Augustine, *De spiritu et anima*, cap. 24.

27. *The Second Nun's Tale*, C. T., G, 200–250. This type of vision is, of course, exceedingly common in the lives of saints and in the writings of the Church Fathers.

28. Gregory shows at considerable length just how it was possible for Moses to receive his revelation of divine will without sensuous imagery or thought, *Expositionum*, lib. IV, cap. v, § 8; and Thomas Aquinas devotes one whole chapter to answering affirmatively the question, "Utrum Moyses fuerit excellentior aliis prophetis," Quaestio XII, art. xiii, *Opera*, VII, fol. 378.

29. Cornelius Agrippa, *op. cit.*, lib. III, cap. 51.

CHAPTER IX

1. *Op. cit.*, lib. III, fen i, tract. 4, cap. 18.

2. *Ibid.*, lib. I, fen 2, doc. 3, cap. 7.

3. *Op. cit.*, in *Opera*, Venetiis, 1609, VI, 213.

4. *Almansor* (or *Al-Mansuri*), cap. 204. The quotation is transcribed in Gaizo, *op. cit.*, cap. x. This Rhazes is Abu Bakr Muhammad ben Zakariya, who was born near the middle of the ninth century, studied in Baghdad, and who died A.D. 932. The *Almansor*, was dedicated to Al-Mansur, prince of Khorassan.

5. *Op. cit.*, Pars I, cap. iv.

6. *Op. cit.*, Pars III, cap. xii.

7. *Op. cit.*, dif. CLVII, fol. 202.

8. Avicenna, *op. cit.*, lib. I, fen 2, doc. 3, cap. 7.

9. Pedanii Dioscoridis Anazarbei *De materia medica libri quinque*, ed. Springel in *Opera quae extant*, I: *laurus*, lib. I, cap. 106; *centauria*, cap. 7; *fumaria*, cap. 108; *elleborus*, cap. 149; *euphorbium*, cap. 86; *rhamus*, cap. 119; *hedera helix*, cap. 210. For further quotations from Avicenna, see *Englische Studien*, LVIII, p. 49.

10. *Op. cit.*, lib. IV, fen 1, tract. 1, cap. i.

11. *Ibid.*, lib. IV, fen 1, tract. 2, cap. i.

12. *Ibid.*, lib. IV, fen 1, tract. 2, cap. 35.

13. *Ibid.*, lib. IV, fen 1, tract. 2, cap. 36.

14. *Ibid.*, lib. IV, fen 1, tract. 1, cap. 4.

15. *Op. cit.*, cap. vii. For the sources of the cock's illustrations, see Cicero, *De divinatione*, lib. I, cap. 27; Valerius Maximus, *Factorum et Dictorum memorabilium libri novem*, lib. 1, cap. vii. Cf. Lounsbury, II, 272.

16. Bradwardine, *op. cit.*, pp. 810–12; Augustine, *De Civitate Dei*, cap. 14; Boethius, *De consolatione philosophiae*, V, 6; C. F. Brown, " The Author of the *Pearl* Considered in the Light of his Theological Opinions," *PMLA.*, XIX, 265; H. R. Patch, " Troilus on Predestination," *JEGPh.*, XVII, 399 ff.; Wedel *The Mediaeval Attitude toward Astrology*, pp. 147–149; *Die Philosophischen Werke des Robert Grosseteste*, ed. Bauer, pp. 158–60.

17. *Op. cit.*, p. 811.

18. Sypherd, *Studies in Chaucer's House of Fame*, pp. 1–41.

19. Kittredge, *Chaucer and His Poetry*, p. 68.

20. *Sextum Consulatum Honorii Augusti Praefatio*, 3–10. Cf. Lounsbury, II, 257; Skeat, I, 509.

21. F. Tupper, "Chaucer's Lady of the Daisies," *JEGPh.*, XXI, pp. 297 ff.

22. *Op. cit.*, pp. 68–70.

23. *Ibid.*, p. 50.

24. *Op. cit.*, pp. 296–97. Professor Tupper's theory is correct, but I hold no brief for the "actual ideas, latent dream-material" which he maintains become "dream-content" in this instance.

CHAPTER X

1. G. L. Kittredge, *Chaucer and His Poetry*, pp. 112–117.

2. R. K. Root, *The Book of Troilus and Criseyde*, p. xlix. See the same author's *The Poetry of Chaucer*, rev. ed., pp. 117, 125 ff.

3. Boethius, *De consolatione philosophiæ*, trans. Chaucer, ed. Skeat, Book IV, Prose VI, 45–100. (See B. L. Jefferson, *Chaucer and the Consolation of Philosophy of Boethius*, p. 118.)

4. *Idem*, 100–110.

5. On Fortune see Book II, Proses ii, vii, etc., and Jefferson, *op. cit.*, p. 49. The interested reader should consult H. R. Patch's illuminating book, *The Goddess Fortuna in Mediaeval Literature*, pp. 18 ff.

6. Bk. II, M. viii; III, M. vi. Jefferson, *op. cit.*, p. 65.

7. Bk. V, Pr. i. Jefferson, *op. cit.*, p. 62.

8. See Chapter Six, pp. 119–149.

9. *The Oxford Chaucer*, ed. W. W. Skeat, *C. T.*, E., 1966–1976.

10. See Chapter Five, pp. 91–118.

11. See Chapter Seven, pp. 164–171.

12. *Ibid.*, pp. 171–194.

13. Meteorologica I. 2. Quoted from T. O. Wedel, *The Mediaeval Attitude toward Astrology*, p. 3.

14. *Introductorium in Astronomiam*, Augsburg, 1489, bk. 3, chap. i. I have quoted the excellent summary of Wedel, *op. cit.*, p. 57.

15. Though this conception is not necessary for our understanding of the destiny back of Chaucer's *Troilus*, I have given an

exposition of it because the relations between Nature and destiny (or fate) and fortune do not seem to be generally understood. See H. R. Patch, *op. cit.*, pp. 65, 75 ff., 78.

16. Lynn Thorndike, *A History of Magic and Experimental Science*, New York, 1923, I, 620.

17. See, for example, Chapters Six and Seven, pp. 119–194.

18. A. C. Bradley, *Shakespearean Tragedy*, New York, 1926, p. 45.

19. Cf. *Boethius*, 2, m. 8, and Root, *op. cit.*, pp. 415, 493.

20. Cf. *Boethius*, 2, m. 1; 2, pr. 2; Root, *Troilus*, p. 425; B. L. Jefferson, *op. cit.*, pp. 49–60.

21. 'Ali ibn Abí Al-Rajjál (Abú Hassan), *Liber in judicijs astrorum*, Ventiis, 1485, pp. 120–121 (Cf. Thorndike, *op. cit.*, I, 680–82).

22. *Ibid*, p. 125.

23. See Chapter Five, pp. 97–100.

24. On the seventh house, see Chapter Seven, p. 172, note, and p. 173, Plate V. Cf. also Root, *Troilus*, p. 446.

25. See *Libellus ysagogicvs* Abdilazi . . . qui dicitvr Alchabitivs, Venetiis, 1485, sig bb₃r, and the Commentary of John of Saxony, sig mm₇v.; Albohazen Haly, *op. cit.*, p. 117.

26. Root, *op. cit.*, p. 446.

27. Root, *Troilus*, p. 463.

28. *Idem.*

29. *Idem.*

30. Chaucer is astrologically correct in attributing this deluge of rain to the "great conjunction" of Luna, Saturn, and Jupiter in the "watery sign," Cancer. One early anonymous writer says that such a conjunction produces "submersio*nes et* diluuia *et* secundum quantitate*m* fortitudinem i*n* loco erit euentus," *Opusculum repertorii in mutationes aeris tam via astrologica tam metheorologica*, Venetiis, 1485, p. 18v. See also R. K. Root and H. N. Russell, "A Planetary Date for Chaucer's *Troilus*," *PMLA.*, XXXIX, 58 ff. Considering this conjunction astronomically, Professor Root in most admirable manner dates the poem not earlier than 1385, *ibid.*, p. 63. He holds, further, that Chaucer possibly intended this conjunction "should suggest to his readers the impending downfall of the kingdom of Troy," *ibid.*, p. 62. I should like to believe this, but it does not seem to me likely. However, for the influence of such a conjunction upon kings, kingdoms, and

peoples, see Albumasar, *De magis conjunctionibus, annorum, revolutionibus, ac eorum profectionibus*, Augsburg, 1489, sigs. B_1–B_3.

31. Albubather, *Liber nativitatum de Arabico in Latinum translatus*, Venetiis, 1501, B_4v.

32. *Ibid.*, "De natis multi coitus," cap. 76, "De natis pauci coitus," cap. 77, C_2v.

33. Quoted in Abraham ibn Ezra, *De nativitatibus*, Venetiis, 1484, sig b_7.

34. See Root, *Troilus*, p. 476. For the nature of Saturn, see Chapter Six, pp. 129–30.

35. *Op. cit.*, p. 120.

36. On the beneficence of Jupiter, see Chapter Seven, p. 167.

37. Root, *Troilus*, p. 476.

38. Cf. *Boethius*, 2, m 8, and Root, *Troilus*, p. 493 ff.

39. Root, *Troilus*, pp. 494, lxxi, and *The Textual Tradition of Chaucer's Troilus*, Chaucer Society, pp. 155–57.

40. *Op. cit.*, p. 120.

41. Root, *Troilus*, pp. lxxi, 517; *The Poetry of Chaucer*, rev. ed., p. 117; *The Textual Tradition of Chaucer's Troilus*, pp. 216–20.

42. T. R. Lounsbury, *Studies in Chaucer*, New York, 1892, III, 372.

43. A. W. Ward, Chaucer (*Eng. Men of Letters*, Morley), New York, p. 92.

44. *PMLA.*, XI, 311.

45. J. M. Manly, *Kittredge Anniversary Papers*, p. 77.

46. Root, *The Poetry of Chaucer*, rev. ed., p. 117.

47. G. L. Kittredge, *Chaucer and His Poetry*, p. 115.

48. T. R. Price, *PMLA.*, XI, 311.

49. Courthope, *History of English Poetry*, New York, 1895, I, 262.

50. Ten Brink, B.: *History of Early English Poetry*, trans. W. C. Robinson, New York, 1893, II, 92.

51. H. R. Patch, "Troilus on Predestination," *Jour. Eng. Germc. Philol.*, XVII, 3.

52. *Ibid.*, p. 23.

53. *Troilus*, p. xli.

54. *Ibid.*, p. lxiii.

55. He does indeed suggest as a general proposition that God disposes all things according to their merits (IV, 965), but

Troilus's merits or demerits in the sight of God do not seem to have anything to do with what comes upon him. That is to say, Troilus is not in any sense a criminal; at worst he is only blindly human.

56. Bk. V, pr. 3. See Root, *Troilus*, pp. 517–20; Patch, *op. cit.*, pp. 6–7.

57. Root, *Troilus*, p. 517; Boethius, Bk. V, pr. 4–6.

58. Patch, *op. cit.*, pp. 8–12.

59. *Ibid.*, pp. 11–12.

60. See Chapter Eight, p. 209.

61. See Root, *Troilus*, p. 553, note to 1. 1451.

62. *Ibid.*, pp. 553–56.

63. *Consolation of Philosophy*, Bk. IV, pr. VI, 1. 104 (Chaucer's translation).

64. *Ibid.*, II. 130–35.

65. *Summa Theologica*, I. I. 115.4. I quote from Wedel's translation, *The Mediaeval Attitude toward Astrology*, p. 68.

66. T. R. Price, "Troilus and Criseyde," *PMLA.*, XI, 314. Professor Price is so eager to show that the *Troilus* is modern in its dramatic quality (p. 310) and in the "inevitable deduction of human action from purely human motives" (p. 311) that he concludes: "There is the same scornful rejection of the supernatural element (p. 311) . . . He [Chaucer] holds back from all use of supernatural means to influence human action" (p. 313). It seems to me, however, that Chaucer has made human action more rational by referring it to those mysterious destinal forces—superhuman or supernormal—through which, along with the destiny inherent in human character, the plans of Providence are executed.

67. From "Epistle to Can Grande," tr. Barret H. Clark, *European Theories of the Drama*, Cincinnati, 1918, p. 47.

68. *Consolation of Philosophy*, Bk. II, pr. 2, 78–80.

69. For example, see Root, *Troilus*, pp. xlix, 409.

70. *Op. cit.*, p. 310.

71. See Professor Price's analysis, *op. cit.*, pp. 313–322. Was Chaucer acquainted with the five acts of Senecan tragedy?

72. I cannot agree with Professor Price that the action of the story grows only out of character. And one may question his making Criseyde the chief character of the drama (*op. cit.*, p. 308); her character is highly developed in order that it may serve,

among other things, as a powerful destinal force in the life of Troilus, the protagonist.

73. See Price, *op. cit.*, p. 319.

74. See my *Shakespeare's Philosophical Patterns*, Baton Rouge, 1937, reprint, 1959, Chapter IV, especially pp. 131–137.

75. Quoted from Barret H. Clark, *European Theories of the Drama*, p. 416.

76. I conclude, therefore, that, since Chaucer has created a tragedy which is artistically so far in advance of mediaeval theory and practice, he must be conscious of that fact and is probably satirizing not only the Monk but also the mediaeval conception of tragedy when he defines it in the prologue to the *Monk's Tale* and illustrates it with those monstrosities of rhetorical dullness called 'tragedies.' Or, if he could conceive no better *theory* than that of his contemporaries, at least his genius has enabled him to create a tragedy which successfully transcends the theory.

77. On the reasons for Chaucer's denial of the courtly love embodied in *Troilus*, see G. L. Kittredge, *Chaucer and His Poetry*, p. 143, and Karl Young, "Chaucer's Renunciation of Love," *Modern Language Notes*, XL, 270 ff.

78. On the paganism in the poem and Chaucer's renunciation of it in the Epilog, see J. S. P. Tatlock's study "The Epilog of Chaucer's *Troilus*," *Modern Philology*, XVIII, 625–59.

79. For a discussion of Ralph Strode, philosopher of Merton College, Oxford, and his relation to the Ralph Strode, who was elected Common Pleader of the City of London, see Root, *Troilus*, p. 564; Israel Gollancz, *Dict. Natl. Biog.*, under Strode; E. P. Kuhl, "Some Friends of Chaucer," *PMLA.*, XXIX, 272–75; Edith Rickert, London *Times Lit. Sup.*, Oct. 4, 1928, p. 707; H. W. Garrod, *ibid.*, Oct. 11, 1928, p. 736. For an indication of the philosophical Strode's probable adverse attitude toward an entirely deterministic philosophy see Wyclif's *Responsiones ad Raduphum Strodum*, National Library of Vienna, MS. 2603, now No. 62 of Rotographs of Manuscripts and Rare Printed Books, Library of Congress, Washington, D.C.

80. *Op. cit.*, p. 636.

81. See Root, *Troilus*, pp. lxxii, 559–60.

82. Chaucer gets the materials for the stanzas on Troilus's flight to heaven from the *Teseide* of Boccaccio, who in turn is dependent for the idea upon Cicero's *Somnium Scipionis*. It should

be observed, however, that Clement and Origen elaborated the same conception. See Origen, *De principiis*, II, cap. iii, tr. *The Ante-Nicene Fathers*, IV, 274.

83. Root, *Troilus*, p. 1.

84. *Ibid.*

85. The substance of this chapter appeared first in *PMLA.*, XLV, 129–168.

CHAPTER XI

1. See Chapter Six, pp. 140 ff.

2. Skeat, *The Oxford Chaucer*, C. T., A, 2794–2815.

3. The "vital strengthe" which Chaucer says left Arcite's arms refers no doubt to the spirits through which the soul gets its work done in the body. Robert Burton says: "Spirit is a most subtle vapor, which is expressed from the *blood*, and the instrument of the soul, to perform all his actions; and a common tie or *medium* betwixt the body and the soul, as some will have it. . . . Melanchthon holds the fountain of these spirits to be the heart; begotten there, and afterwards conveyed to the brain, they take another nature to them. Of these spirits there be three kinds, according to the three principal parts, *brain, heart, liver; natural, vital, animal*. The *natural* are begotten in the *liver*, and thence dispersed through the veins, to perform those natural actions. The *vital spirits* are made in the heart of the *natural*, which by the arteries are transported to all the other parts; if these *spirits* cease, then life ceaseth, as in a *syncope* or swooning. The *animal spirits* formed of the *vital*, brought up to the brain, and diffused by the nerves, give sense and motion to them all." *Anatomy of Melancholy*, Part. I. Sect. I. Mem. II. Subs. II. In our further discussion we are not concerned with these spirits.

4. See Tertullian, *De anima*, cap. xiv (Trans. *Ante-Nicene Fathers*.)

5. Aristotle, *De anima*, trans. G. Rodier, *Traité de L'Ame*, Paris, 1900, lib. II, cap. i (412b, 5). Cf. Burton, *op. cit.*, Part. I. Sect. I. Mem. II. Subs. V; Duns Scotus, *Quaestiones super libros Aristotlelis De anima*, Quaes. xiii, in *Opera omnia*, ed. R.P.F. Luca Waddingus Hibernus, Parisiis, 1891, III, annotations of Cavellus, p. 546.

6. *Ibid.*, lib. II, cap. i (413a, 1).
7. *Ibid.*, lib. II, cap. i, iv (412b, 20, 415b, 20).
8. *Ibid.*, lib. III, cap. iv, (429b, 5).
9. *Ibid.*, lib. II, cap. ii (41a, 27 ff.).
10. *Ibid.*, lib. II, cap. iv (415b, 10).
11. *Ibid.*, lib. II, cap. i (413a, 4).
12. *Ibid.*, lib. II, cap. ii (415a, 4).
13. *Ibid.*, lib. II, cap. iv (416a, 20 ff.; 415a, 28 ff.).
14. *Ibid.*, lib. II, cap. v (416b, 32 ff.).
15. *Ibid.*, lib. II, cap. iii (414b, 10 ff.).
16. *Ibid.*, lib. II, cap. iv (415b, 10 ff.).
17. *Ibid.*, lib. III, cap. iv (430a, 5).
18. *Ibid.*, lib. III, cap. v.
19. *Ibid.*, lib. III, cap. iii ff. (427b, 13-429a, 3).
20. *Ibid.*, lib. III, cap. vi (430b, 5).
21. *Ibid.*, lib. III, cap. viii (432a, 1 ff.).
22. *Ibid.*, lib. III, cap. v (430a, 22). See also *Metaphysica*, trans. Smith and Ross, lib. XII, cap. iii (70a, 26).
23. Alfred Weber, *History of Philosophy*, trans. Frank Thilly, pp. 97 ff.
24. *Idem.*
25. *Ibid.*, p. 99.
26. Wilhelm Windelband, *History of Philosophy*, trans. J. H. Tufts, p. 150.
27. See Chapter Six, pp. 140–149.
28. Windelband, *op. cit.*, pp. 328 ff.
29. Tertullian, *De anima* (trans. *Ante-Nicene Fathers*), cap. xxii.
30. *Idem.*
31. *Ibid.*, cap. xiv.
32. Lib. VII, cap. xvii, trans. J. G. Pilkington, *The Nicene and Post-Nicene Fathers*.
33. Augustine, *In Joannis Evangelium*, Migne, *Patr. Lat.*, 35; 1516.
34. *De anima*, Quaest. xiii, Resolutio, *Opera omina*, III, 546. See also Thomas Aquinas, *Summa Theologica*; part. I, quaest. 75, art. 5.
35. Duns Scotus, *De anima*, Quaest. xiii, Resolutio, III, 546.
36. See Cavellus's commentary on Duns Scotus, II, 548.
37. *Ibid.*, II, 546.

38. *Op. cit.*, Part. I. Sect. I. Mem. II. Subs. X.

39. For a digest of these opinions, see Tertullian, *op. cit.*, cap. xiv; Duns Scotus, *op. cit.*, III, 668; Burton, *op. cit.*, Part. I. Sect. I. Mem. II. Subs. IX.

40. *Opera quaedam hactenus inedita*, ed. J. S. Brewer, p. 185. Cf. Lynn Thorndike, *History of Magic and Experimental Science*, II, 631—633.

41. *Op. cit.*, III, 668.

42. Cf. *Troilus*, IV, 785, Myn herte and ek the woful goost therinne, etc.; *ibid.*, IV, 775, Till I my soule out of my breste unshethe, etc.; *ibid.*, IV, 305, 910, 1620, 1700.

43. Quoted from Duns Scotus, *op. cit.*, II, 668. See also Lactantius, *On the Workmanship of God*, cap. xvi, *The Ante-Nicene Fathers*, VII, 296.

44. *De anima*, cap. xiv. For the idea of this concept's being of Egyptian origin, see H. B. Hinckley, *Mod. Phil.*, XIV, 126. But see also the same author's *Notes on Chaucer*, p. 113, where he quotes Boccaccio's

> sol nello intelletto
> E nel cuore era ancora sostenuta
> La poca vital. *Teseide*, 10.111.

But Boccaccio's account is scarcely parallel to Chaucer's.

45. *Sermones*, Migne, *Patr. Lat.*, 38; 184.

46. *De proprietatibus rerum*, trans. John Trevisa *(On the proprytees of thynges)*, Wynkyn de Worde, London, 1495, fol. CVI verso.

47. For these opinions, see Duns Scotus, *op. cit.*, III, 668.

48. J. P. Pilkington, in *The Confessions of St. Augustine*, trans. *Nicene and Post-Nicene Fathers*, p. 111, note 1. Pilkington refers further to Delitzsch, *Biblical Psychology*, II. 4 ("The True and False Trichotomy"); Olhausen, *Opuscula Theologica*, IV ("De Trichotomia"); R. W. Evans, *Ministry of the Body*, cc. 2, 17 & 18.

49. *De anima*, lib. II, cap. ii, trans. Peter Holmes and R. E. Wallis, *Nicene and Post-Nicene Fathers*. See also Tertullian, *De anima*, cap. xi.

50. Windelband, *op. cit.*, p. 235.

51. *Ibid.*, p. 232 and note 3.

52. *Ibid.*, p. 233.

53. *Ibid.*, p. 234.

54. *De anima*, lib. II, cap. ii.

55. H. B. Hinckley, *Notes on Chaucer*, p. 113.

56. Origen, *De principiis*, lib. II, cap. ii, trans. *The Ante-Nicene Fathers*, IV, 274 ff.

57. *Letters of St. Augustine*, Letter CLVIII, trans. J. G. Cunningham, *Nicene and Post-Nicene Fathers*, I, 512.

58. "Chaucer and Wyclif," *Modern Philology*, XIV, 266.

59. *Somnium Scipionis*, with the commentary of Macrobius, (Teubner), cap. xii; see Chaucer's *Parl. Foules*, MP., V, 51–84.

60. *Ibid.*, cap. ix; MP., V, 70 ff.

61. See Origen, *De principiis*, lib. II, cap. iii, trans. *The Ante-Nicene Fathers*, IV, 273, where he says: "But now I do not understand by what proofs they can maintain their position, who assert that worlds come into existence which are not dissimilar to each other, but in all respects equal. . . . For souls are not driven on in a cycle which returns after many ages to the same round. So therefore it seems to me impossible for a world to be restored for the second time, with the same order and with the same amount of births, deaths, and actions." See also Augustine's refutation of this heresy, *De Civitate Dei*, lib. XII, cap. xx, trans. Marcus Dods, *Nicene and Post-Nicene Fathers*, II, 239 ff.

62. Tatlock, *MLN.*, 29, 140–4.

63. J. L. Lowes, "Chaucer and Dante," *Modern Philology*, XIV, 705–735; Curry, *MLN.*, 38, 253; Mabel Stanford, "The Sumner's Tale and St. Patrick's Purgatory," *JEGPh.*, 19, 377–81; Theodore Spencer, "Chaucer's Hell," *Speculum*, II, 177–200, etc.

64. Tertullian, *De anima*, cap. xxvii, xxxi, xxxiii.

65. Quoted by Thorndike, *op. cit.*, I, 207 as the opinion of Plutarch. See Burton, *op. cit.*, Part I, Sect. II, Mem. II, Subs. II.

66. But see Hinckley: "I am not sure how we should understand Chaucer's *the servyce of my goost*. It may mean 'the memory of me' or 'the pious office of praying for my soul' . . .; or it may mean 'the continued devotion of my soul after death.' " *Notes on Chaucer*, p. 111.

67. Professor Tatlock remarks: "Neither the pagan nor the Christian otherworld would have fitted the tone of the *Knight's Tale*." *Modern Philology*, XIV, note 3.

68. See Chapter Six, pp. 119–163.

69. *The Consolation of Philosophy*, Bk. II, M, vi. I have used Chaucer's translation and that of I.T. (1609) revised by H. F. Stewart (Loeb).

70. The substance of this chapter appeared first in *Journal of English and Germanic Philology*, XXIX, 83–99.

SELECTED BIBLIOGRAPHY

AIKEN, PAULINE. "Vincent of Beauvais and Chaucer's Knowledge of Alchemy." *SP*, XLI(1944), 371–89.

————"Arcite's Illness and Vincent of Beauvais." *PMLA*, LI(1936), 361–369.

————"The Summoner's Malady." *SP*, XXXIII(1936), 40–44.

————"Vincent of Beauvais and the 'Houres' of Chaucer's Physician." *SP*, LIII(1956), 22–24.

————"Vincent of Beauvais and Dame Pertelote's Knowledge of Medicine." *Speculum*, X(1935), 281–287.

American Bibliography. Ed. yearly by Albert C. Baugh and others for the Modern Language Association of America. *PMLA*, 1922–

Annual Bibliography of the English Language and Literature. Ed. for the Modern Humanities Research Association. New York: Cambridge University Press, 1920–

BALDWIN, CHARLES SEARS. *Medieval Rhetoric and Poetic (to 1400). Interpreted from Representative Works*. New York: Macmillan, 1928. Reprint, Peter Smith, 1959.

————"Cicero on Parnassus." *PMLA*, XLII(1927), 106–12.

BASHFORD, H. H. "Chaucer's Physician and His Forebears." *Nineteenth Century*, CIV(1928), 237–248.

BAUM, PAULL F. *Chaucer, A Critical Appreciation*. Durham: Duke University Press, 1958.

BEICHNER, PAUL E. "Chaucer's Man of Law and *Disparitas Cultus*." *Speculum*, XXIII(1948), 70–75.

BIRNEY, EARLE. "The Beginnings of Chaucer's Irony." *PMLA*, LIV(1939), 637–655.

————"Is Chaucer's Irony a Modern Discovery?" *JEGP*, XLI(1942), 303–319.

BLOCK, EDWARD A. "Originality, Controlling Purpose, and Craftsmanship in Chaucer's *Man of Law's Tale*." *PMLA*, LXVIII(1953), 572–616.

————"Chaucer's Millers and their Bagpipes." *Speculum*, XXIX(1954), 239–243.

BLOOMFIELD, MORTON W. "Distance and Predestination in *Troilus and Criseyde*." *PMLA*, LXXII(1957), 14–26.

BOLDAUN, NILS W. "Chaucer and Matters Medical." *New England Journal of Medicine*, CCVIII(1933), 1365–1368.

BOUGHNER, DANIEL C. "Elements of Epic Grandeur in the *Troilus*." *ELH*, VI(1939), 200–210.

BOWDEN, MURIEL. *A Commentary on the General Prologue to the "Canterbury Tales*." New York: Macmillan, 1948.

BRADDY, HALDEEN. "The Cook's Mormal and its Cure." *MLQ*, VII(1946), 265–67.

BROOKS, CLEANTH. "Chaucer: Saturn's Daughter." *MLN*, XLIX(1934), 459–61.

BROWNE, WILLIAM H. "Notes on Chaucer's Astrology." *MLN*, XXIII(1908), 53–54.

BRYAN, WILLIAM FRANK, AND DEMPSTER, GERMAINE. Eds. *Sources and Analogues of Chaucer's Canterbury Tales*. Chicago: University of Chicago Press, 1941. Reprint, Humanities Press, 1959.

BUSHNELL, NELSON SHERWIN. "The Wandering Jew and *The Pardoner's Tale*." *SP*, XXVIII(1931), 450–60.

CAMPBELL, DONALD. *Arabian Medicine and its Influence on the Middle Ages*. New York: Dutton, 1926.

CHAPMAN, COOLIDGE OTIS. "*The Pardoner's Tale*: A Mediaeval Sermon." *MLN*, XLI(1926), 506–9.

CHUTE, MARCHETTE. *Geoffrey Chaucer of England*. New
York: Dutton, 1946.

CLARK, THOMAS BLAKE. "The Forehead of Chaucer's Prioress." *PQ*, IX(1930), 312–314.

COFFMAN, GEORGE R. "Chaucer and Courtly Love Once
More—'The Wife of Bath's Tale'." *Speculum*, XX(1945),
43–50.

COGHILL, NEVILL. *The Poet Chaucer*. New York: Oxford
University Press, 1949.

COOK, ALBERT S. *The Historical Background of Chaucer's
Knight*. New Haven: Yale University Press, 1916.

CUMMINGS, H. M. *The Indebtedness of Chaucer's Works to
the Italian Works of Boccaccio*. Univ. of Cincinnati Studies, X(1916).

CURTISS, JOSEPH T. "The Horoscope in Chaucer's *Man of
Law's Tale*." *JEGP*, XXVI(1927), 24–32.

DAMON, S. FOSTER. "Chaucer and Alchemy." *PMLA*,
XXXIX(1924), 782–8.

DEMPSTER, GERMAINE. "The Merchant's Tale." *Sources and
Analogues*, 333–56.

DODD, WILLIAM G. *Courtly Love in Chaucer and Gower*.
Harvard Studies in English, I(1913). Reprint, Peter Smith,
1959.

DONALDSON, E. TALBOT. "Chaucer the Pilgrim." *PMLA*,
LXIX(1954), 928–936.

DUFFEY, BERNARD I. "The Intention and the Art of *The
Man of Law's Tale*." *ELH*, XIV(1947), 181–93.

DUINO, RUSSELL. "The Tortured Pardoner." *Eng. Jour.*,
XLVI(1957), 320–325.

DUNCAN, EDGAR HILL. "The Yeoman's Canon's 'Silver Citrinacioun'." *MP*, XXXVII(1940), 241–262.

———"Chaucer and 'Arnold of the Newe Toun'." *MLN*, LVII(1942), 31–33.

———"Narrator's Point of View in the Portrait-Sketches, Prologue to the *Canterbury Tales*." *Essays in Honor of Walter Clyde Curry*. Nashville: Vanderbilt University Press, 1954, 77–101.

DUSTOOR, P. E. "Chaucer's Astrology in 'The Knight's Tale'." *TLS*, May 5, 1927, 318.

EMERSON, OLIVER F. "Chaucer's 'Opie of Thebes Fyn'." *MP*, XVII(1919), 287–291.

The Equatorie of the Planetis. Ed. from Peterhouse MS. 75. I. by Derek J. Price. Cambridge, England: At the University Press, 1955.

FAIRCHILD, HOXIE NEALE. "Active Arcite, Contemplative Palamon." *JEGP*, XXVI(1927), 285–293.

FARNHAM, WILLARD E. "The Dayes of the Mone." *SP*, XX(1923), 70–82.

FOREHAND, BROOKS. "Old Age and Chaucer's Reeve." *PMLA*, LXIX(1954), 984–989.

FRENCH, R. D. *A Chaucer Handbook*. 2nd ed., New York: Appleton, 1947.

FRENCH, W. H. "The Lovers in the *Knight's Tale*." *JEGP*, XLVIII(1949), 320–328.

FRIEND, ALBERT C. "Analogues in Cheriton to the Pardoner and His Sermon." *JEGP*, LIII(1954), 382–388.

———"The Dangerous Theme of the Pardoner." *MLQ*, XVIII(1957), 305–308.

FROST, WILLIAM. "An Interpretation of Chaucer's *Knight's Tale*." *RES*, XXV(1949), 298–304.

GEROULD, GORDON H. *Chaucerian Essays.* Princeton: Princeton University Press, 1952.

GRIFFITH, DUDLEY DAVID. *Bibliography of Chaucer, 1908–1953.* Seattle: University of Washington Press, 1955.

GRIMM, FLORENCE MARIE. "Astronomical Lore in Chaucer." *Univ. Nebraska Studies in Language, Literature, and Criticism,* 1919.

HAGOPIAN, JOHN. "Chaucer as Psychologist in *Troilus and Criseyde.*" *Lit. and Psych.*, V(1955), 5–11.

HAMILTON, MARIE P. "Death and Old Age in *The Pardoner's Tale.*" *SP*, XXXVI(1939), 571–576.

————"The Credentials of Chaucer's Pardoner." *JEGP*, XL(1941), 48–72.

————"The Clerical Status of Chaucer's Alchemist." *Speculum*, XVI(1941), 103–108.

HARDER, KELSIE B. "Chaucer's Use of the Mystery Plays in the *Miller's Tale.*" *MLQ*, XVII(1956), 193–198.

HARRIS, ELIZABETH. *The Mural as a Decorative Device in Mediaeval Literature.* Nashville: Vanderbilt University Press, 1935.

HARRISON, BENJAMIN S. "Medieval Rhetoric in the *Book of the Duchesse.*" *PMLA*, XLIX(1934), 428–442.

————"Rhetorical Inconsistency of Chaucer's Franklin." *SP*, XXXII(1935), 55–61.

HASKINS, CHARLES HOMER. *Studies in the History of Mediaeval Science.* Cambridge: Harvard University Press, 1924. 2nd ed., 1927.

HERDAN, G. "Chaucer's Authorship of *The Equatorie of the Planetis*: The Use of Romance Vocabulary as Evidence." *Language*, XXXII(1956), 254–59.

HILL, MARY H. "Rhetorical Balance in Chaucer's Poetry." *PMLA*, XLII(1927), 845–861.

HITCHINS, H. L. Ed. *Canterbury Tales: Chaucer for Present-Day Readers*. London: John Murray, 1956.

HOLMAN, C. HUGH. "Courtly Love in the Merchant's and Franklin's Tale." *ELH*, XVIII(1951), 241–52.

HOTSON, J. LESLIE. "Colfax versus Chantecler." *PMLA*, XXXIX(1924), 762–81.

HOUSEMAN, PERCY A. "Science in Chaucer." *Scientific Monthly*, XXXVIII(1934), 561–4.

HULBERT, J. R. "What Was Chaucer's Aim in the *Knight's Tale?*" *SP*, XXVI(1929), 375–85.

————"*The Canterbury Tales* and their Narrators." *SP*, XLV(1948), 565–577.

HUTSON, ARTHUR E. "Troilus' Confession." *MLN*, LXIX (1954), 468–470.

JEFFERSON, BERNARD L. *Chaucer and the Consolation of Philosophy of Boethius*. Princeton: Princeton University Press, 1917.

JONES, GEORGE F. "Chaucer and the Medieval Miller." *MLQ*, XVI(1955), 3–15.

JONES, RICHARD F. "A Conjecture on the Wife of Bath's Prologue." *JEGP*, XXIV(1925), 512–47.

JORDAN, ROBERT M. "The Narrator in Chaucer's *Troilus*." *ELH*, XXV(1958), 235–257.

KELLOGG, ALFRED L. "An Augustinian Interpretation of Chaucer's Pardoner." *Speculum*, XXVI(1951), 465–81.

KELLOGG, A. L., AND HESELMAYER, L. A. "Chaucer's Satire of the Pardoner." *PMLA*, LXVI(1951), 251–77.

KELLY, AMY. *Eleanor of Aquitaine and the Four Kings*. Cambridge: Harvard University Press, 1950.

KIMPEL, BEN. "The Narrator of the *Canterbury Tales.*" *ELH*, XX(1953), 77–86.

KIRBY, THOMAS A. *Chaucer's "Troilus": A Study in Courtly Love.* Baton Rouge: Louisiana State University Press, 1940.

KITTREDGE, GEORGE LYMAN. *Chaucer and His Poetry.* Cambridge: Harvard University Press, 1915.

KLEINSTÜCK, JOHANNES WALTER. "Chaucer's 'Troilus' und die Höfische Liebe." *Archiv*, CXCIII(1956), 1–14.

————*Chaucers Stellung in der Mittelalterlichen Literatur.* Hamburg: Cram, de Gruyter & Co., 1956.

KÖKERITZ, HELGE. "Rhetorical Word-play in Chaucer." *PMLA*, LXIX(1954), 937–952.

LAWRENCE, W. W. *Chaucer and the Canterbury Tales.* New York: Columbia University Press, 1950.

LEWIS, CLIVE S. *The Allegory of Love: A Study in Medieval Tradition.* Oxford: Clarendon Press, 1936. Reprint, 1948, 1959.

LOWES, JOHN LIVINGSTON. "The Loveres Maladye of Hereos." *MP*, XI(1914), 491–546.

————*Geoffrey Chaucer and the Development of his Genius.* New York: Houghton Mifflin, 1934.

LUMIANSKY, R. M. "A Conjecture Concerning Chaucer's Pardoner." *Tulane Studies in English*, I(1949), 1–29.

————"The Function of the Proverbial Monitory Elements in Chaucer's *Troilus and Criseyde.*" *Tulane Studies in English*, II(1950), 5–48.

————"Benoit's Portraits and Chaucer's General Prologue." *JEGP*, LV(1956), 431–438.

————"Chaucer's Philosophical Knight." *Tulane Studies in English*, III(1952), 47–68.

————"Calchas in the Early Versions of the Troilus Story." *Tulane Studies in English*, IV(1954), 5–20.

————"The Story of Troilus and Briseida according to Benoit and Guido." *Speculum*, XXIX(1954), 727–733.

LYONS, CLIFFORD P. "The Marriage Debate in the *Canterbury Tales*." *ELH*, II(1935), 252–262.

MCGALLIARD, JOHN C. "Chaucerian Comedy." *PQ*, XXV (1946), 343–370.

MALONE, KEMP. "Style and Structure in the Prologue to the *Canterbury Tales*." *ELH*, XIII(1946),38–45.

————"A Poet at Work: Chaucer Revising His Verses." *Proceedings of the Amer. Philosophical Soc.*, XCIV(1950), 317–321.

————*Chapters on Chaucer*. Baltimore: The Johns Hopkins Press, 1951.

MANLY, JOHN MATTHEWS. *Canterbury Tales by Geoffrey Chaucer*. New York: Holt, 1928.

————*Some New Light on Chaucer*. New York, 1926.

MANLY, JOHN MATTHEWS, AND RICKERT, EDITH. *The Text of the "Canterbury Tales."* Chicago: University of Chicago Press. 1940.

MARCKWARDT, ALBERT H. "Characterization in Chaucer's *Knight's Tale*." *Contributions to Modern Philology*, No. 5. Ann Arbor: University of Michigan Press, 1947, pp. 1 ff.

MARTIN, WILLARD E. JR. *A Chaucer Bibliography, 1925–1933*. Durham: Duke University Press, 1935.

MAYO, ROBERT D. "The Trojan Background of the *Troilus*." *ELH*, IX(1942), 245–56.

MILLER, AMANDA. "Chaucer's 'Secte Saturnyn'." *MLN*, XLVII(1932), 99–102.

MILLER, MILTON. "Definition by Comparison: Chaucer, Lawrence, and Joyce." *Essays in Criticism*, III(1953), 369–381.

MILLER, ROBERT P. "Chaucer's Pardoner, the Scriptural Eunuch, and the Pardoner's Tale." *Speculum*, XXX(1955), 180–199.

MITCHELL, EDWARD R. "The Two Mayings in Chaucer's 'Knight's Tale'." *MLN*, LXXI(1956), 560–564.

MIZENER, ARTHUR. "Character and Action in the Case of Criseyde." *PMLA*, LIV(1939), 65–81.

MOFFETT, H. Y. "Oswald the Reeve." *PQ*, IV(1925), 208–23.

MOORE, ARTHUR K. "Chaucer's Lost Songs." *JEGP*, XLVIII (1949), 196–208.

————"Chaucer's Use of Lyric as an Ornament of Style." *Comparative Literature*, III(1951), 32–46.

————"The Pardoner's Interruption of the *Wife of Bath's Prologue*." *MLQ*, X(1949), 49–57.

MUSCATINE, CHARLES. "Form, Texture, and Meaning in Chaucer's *Knight's Tale*." *PMLA*, LXV(1950), 911–929.

————*Chaucer and the French Tradition: A Study in Style and Meaning*. Berkeley: University of California Press, 1957.

NICHOLLS, ALBERT G. "Medicine in Chaucer's Day." *Dalhousie Review*, XII(1932), 218–30.

NORRIS, DOROTHY M. "Chaucer's *Pardoner's Tale* and Flanders." *PMLA*, XLVIII(1933), 636–641.

O'CONNOR, JOHN J. "The Astrological Background of the *Miller's Tale*." *Speculum*, XXXI(1956), 120–125.

————"The Astronomical Dating of Chaucer's *Troilus*." *JEGP*, LV(1956), 556–562.

OLSON, CLAIR C. "Chaucer and the Music of the Fourteenth Century." *Speculum*, XVI(1941), 64–91.

OWEN, CHARLES A., JR. "The Significance of Chaucer's Revisions of *Troilus and Criseyde*." *MP*, LV(1957), 1–5.

———"The Crucial Passages in Five of the *Canterbury Tales*: A Study in Irony and Symbol." *JEGP*, LII(1953), 294–311.

———"Chaucer's *Canterbury Tales*: Aesthetic Design in Stories of the First Day." *Eng. Studies*, XXXV(1954), 49–56.

PAFFARD, M. K. "Pertelote's Prescription." *N&Q*, IV(1957), 370.

PARKER, ROSCOE E. " 'Pilates Voys'." *Speculum*, XXV(1950), 237–244.

PARR, JOHNSTONE. "The Date and Revision of Chaucer's *Knight's Tale*." *PMLA*, LX(1945), 307–324.

PARRY, JOHN J. tr. *The Art of Courtly Love of Andreas Capellanus, with Introduction, Translation, and Notes*. New York: Columbia University Press, 1941.

PATCH, HOWARD ROLLIN. *The Tradition of Boethius*. New York: Oxford University Press, 1935.

———"Necessity in Boethius and the Neoplatonists." *Speculum*, X(1935), 393–404.

———*On Rereading Chaucer*. Cambridge: Harvard University Press, 1939. Reprint, 1949.

———*The Goddess Fortuna in Mediaeval Literature*. Cambridge: Harvard University Press, 1927.

PRATT, ROBERT A. "Chaucer's Use of the *Teseida*." *PMLA*, LXII(1947), 598–621.

———"Was Robin the Miller's Youth Misspent?" *MLN*, LIX(1944), 47–49.

————"Was Chaucer's Knight's Tale Extensively Revised after 1390?" *PMLA*, LXIII(1948), 726–736.

————"The Knight's Tale." *Sources and Analogues*, 82–105.

PRICE, DEREK J. "Chaucer's Astronomy." *Nature*, CLXX (1952), 474–475.

PURDY, ROB ROY. "Chaucer Scholarship in England and America: A Review of Recent Trends." *Anglia*, LXX (1951–52), 344–381.

READ, JOHN. *Prelude to Chemistry: An Outline of Alchemy, its Literature and Relationships.* New York: Macmillan, 1937.

ROBERTSON, STUART. "Elements of Realism in the Knight's Tale." *JEGP*, XIV(1915), 226–255.

ROBINSON, F. N. *The Complete Works of Geoffrey Chaucer.* Boston: Houghton Mifflin, 1933. Second Edition, *The Works of Geoffrey Chaucer.* Boston, 1947.

ROOT, ROBERT KILBURN. *The Poetry of Chaucer.* New York: Houghton Mifflin, 1906. Rev. ed., 1922.

————Ed. *The Book of Troilus and Criseyde.* Edited from all the known MSS. Princeton: Princeton University Press, 1926.

ROOT, R. K., AND RUSSELL, HENRY N. "A Planetary Date for Chaucer's *Troilus.*" *PMLA*, XXXIX(1924), 48–63.

RUSKA, JULIUS. "Chaucer und das Buch Senior." *Anglia*, LXI (1937), 136–137.

SALTER, F. M. "The Tragic Figure of the Wyf of Bath." *Proc. & Trans. Royal Soc. of Canada*, 3 ser., XLVIII (1954), Sec. II, 1–14.

SAMS, HENRY W. "The Dual Time-Scheme in Chaucer's *Troilus.*" *MLN*, LVI(1941), 94–100.

SARTON, GEORGE. *Introduction to the History of Science.* Vol. III, Part 2. Baltimore: Carnegie Institution of Washington, 1948.

SCHAAR, CLAES. *The Golden Mirror: Studies in Chaucer's Descriptive Technique and Its Literary Background.* Lund: C. W. K. Gleerup, 1955.

SCHLAUCH, MARGARET. *Chaucer's Constance and Accused Queens.* New York State Library, 1927.

——————"The Man of Law's Tale." *Sources and Analogues,* 155–206.

——————"The Marital Dilemma in the 'Wife of Bath's Tale'." *PMLA,* LXI(1946), 416–430.

SCOTT, FORREST S. "The Seventh Sphere: A Note on *Troilus and Criseyde.*" *MLR,* LI(1956), 2–5.

SEDGEWICK, G. G. "The Progress of Chaucer's Pardoner, 1880–1940." *MLQ,* I(1940), 431–458.

——————"The Structure of the *Merchant's Tale.*" *Univ. of Toronto Quarterly,* XVII(1948), 337–345.

SEDGWICK, H. D. *Dan Chaucer.* New York, 1934.

SEVERS, J. BURKE. "Chaucer's Originality in the *Nun's Priest's Tale.*" *SP,* XLIII(1946), 22–41.

SHANLEY, JAMES L. "The *Troilus* and Christian Love." *ELH,* VI(1939), 271–281.

SHANNON, E. F. *Chaucer and the Roman Poets.* Cambridge: Harvard University Press, 1929.

SHELLY, PERCY VAN DYKE. *The Living Chaucer.* Philadelphia: University of Pennsylvania Press, 1940.

SINGER, CHARLES. *Early English Magic and Medicine.* British *Acad. Proc.,* 1919–20. Milford, 1924.

SINGER, DOROTHY WALEY. *Catalogue of Latin and Vernacular Alchemical Manuscripts in Great Britain and Ireland.* Brussels: Lamortin, 1930. 2 vols.

SKEAT, WALTER W. *The Complete Works of Geoffrey Chaucer:* ed. from Numerous Manuscripts. 6 vols. Oxford: Clarendon Press, 1894–1900.

SLAUGHTER, EUGENE EDWARD. *Virtue According to Love—in Chaucer.* New York: Bookman Associates, 1957.

————"Love and Grace in Chaucer's *Troilus.*" *Essays in Honor of Walter Clyde Curry.* Nashville: Vanderbilt University Press, 1954, 61–75.

————"Chaucer's Pandarus: Virtuous Uncle and Friend." *JEGP*, XLVIII(1949), 186–195.

SMITH, ROLAND M. "Chaucer's *Man of Law's Tale* and Constance of Castile." *JEGP*, XLVII(1948), 343–51.

SMYSER, H. M. "The Domestic Background of *Troilus and Criseyde.*" *Speculum*, XXXI(1956), 297–315.

SOUTHWORTH, JAMES G. *Verses of Cadence: An Introduction to the Prosody of Chaucer and his Followers.* New York: Oxford University Press, 1954.

SPARGO, JOHN WEBSTER. "The Canon's Yeoman's Prologue and Tale." *Sources and Analogues*, 685–698.

SPEIRS, JOHN. *Chaucer the Maker.* London: Faber and Faber, (1951).

STAUFFER, DONALD A. *The Nature of Poetry.* New York: Norton, 1946.

STEADMAN, JOHN M. "The Age of Troilus." *MLN*, LXXII (1957), 89–90.

SULLIVAN, WILLIAM L. "Chaucer's Man of Law as a Literary Critic." *MLN*, LXVIII(1953), 1–8.

TATLOCK, J. S. P. AND KENNEDY, ARTHUR G. *A Concordance to the Complete Works of Geoffrey Chaucer*. Baltimore: Carnegie Institute of Washington, 1927.

TATLOCK, J. S. P. "Astrology and Magic in Chaucer's *Franklin's Tale*." *Anniversary Papers by Colleagues and Pupils of George Lyman Kittredge*. Boston: Ginn and Co., 1913, 339–350.

———"The Epilog of Chaucer's *Troilus*." *MP*, XVIII (1921), 625–659.

———*The Mind and Art of Chaucer*. Syracuse: Syracuse University Press, 1950.

———"The People in Chaucer's *Troilus*." *PMLA*, LVI (1941), 85–104.

TEAGER, FLORENCE E. "Chaucer's Eagle and the Rhetorical Colors." *PMLA*, XLVII(1932), 410–418.

THORNDIKE, LYNN. *A History of Magic and Experimental Science during the First Thirteen Centuries of our Era*. New York: Columbia University Press, 1923–1958. 8 vols.

TILLYARD, E. M. W. *Poetry Direct and Oblique*. New York: Macmillan, 1948.

TUPPER, FREDERICK, AND OGLE, MARBURY, B., *Master Walter Map's Book: De Nugis Curialium (Courtier's Trifles)*. Chatto and Windus, 1924.

UTLEY, FRANCIS LEE. *The Crooked Rib: An Analytical Index to the Argument about Women in English and Scots Literature to the End of the Year 1568*. Columbus: Ohio State University Press, 1944.

VAN DOREN, MARK. *The Noble Voice: A Study of Ten Great Poems*. New York: Henry Holt, 1946.

WAITE, ARTHUR EDWARD. *The Secret Tradition in Alchemy:*

Its Development and Records. New York: Alfred Knopf, 1927.

WALKER, CURTIS HOWE. *Eleanor of Aquitaine.* Chapel Hill: University of North Carolina Press, 1950.

WEBB, HENRY J. "A Reinterpretation of Chaucer's Theseus." *RES*, XXIII(1947), 289–296.

WEDEL, T. O. *The Mediaeval Attitude toward Astrology.* New Haven: Yale University Press, 1920.

WEESE, WALTER E. "Vengeance and Pleyn Correccioun." *MLN*, LXIII(1948), 331–333.

WELLEK, RENÊ, AND WARREN, AUSTIN. *Theory of Literature.* New York: Harcourt, 1948.

WELLS, JOHN EDWIN. *A Manual of Writings in Middle English, 1050–1400.* New Haven: Yale University Press, 1916. Eight Supplements to 1941. Ninth Supplement to 1945.

WHITING, B. J. *Chaucer's Use of Proverbs. Harvard Studies in Comparative Philology and Lit.*, XI(1934).

WILLIAMS, ARNOLD. "Chaucer and the Friars." *Speculum*, XXVIII(1953), 499–513.

WILSON, H. S. "The *Knight's Tale* and the *Teseida* Again." Toronto: *University of Toronto Quarterly*, XVIII(1949), 131–146.

WILSON, W. J., "Catalogue of Latin and Vernacular Alchemical Manuscripts in the United States and Canada." *Osiris*, VI(1939).

Year's Work in English Studies. Issued Yearly by the English Association. New York: Oxford University Press, 1920–

YOUNG, KARL. "Chaucer's 'Troilus and Criseyde' as Romance." *PMLA*, LIII(1938), 38–63.

———"The 'Secree of Secrees' of Chaucer's Canon's Yeoman." *MLN*, LVIII(1943), 98–105.